FROM HELL TO FIRE

COMPTON FIRE
DEPARTMENT

BOOK 1
SEX AND POLITICS

ALLISON BROOKS

Acknowledgments

To the Fellas…There are entirely too many of you to mention by name, so here we go. R.I.P. to my uncles Lieutenant, William, John and Bernard. To my uncle Eric, A.K.A. Silky, get well and stay strong. To my cousin Cedric, thanks for talking me into keeping the juice in this book, and for helping me to appreciate the timing of it. Thanks again to my cousin Marqueb, for not allowing me to put this project off another twenty years. To my little brothers Walter, Celester, A.K.A. Doc Sizzle, Michael and Maurice, you guys have always kept things interesting and comical. To my father Walter, love you dad. To the pride and joy of my life, my two wonderful and handsome sons, Asa and Isaac… thanks to the two of you, I now know how to love unconditionally. I love you boys with every ounce of my being. And finally, thanks again to my husband and friend Alex, for giving me enough space to be me.

To all the women in my life…I love you all. R.I.P. to my grandmother Will E. Brooks, from whom I get my strength. A Helen…Tennessee toddy over nobody's body. To Tonie, Linda, Brenda and my stepmother Danette, stay strong. To my sister Delana, get your paper, the struggle is real. Jeanette, stop cheating and behave. To my cousin Javone, A.K.A Boogie, I don't think anybody's listening but keep preaching. Allison, A.K.A. big Allison, continue showing us how to live peaceably, we'll get there, eventually. To my aunt Mary Ellen, keep the Norwood, Pierce, and Williams sides of the family glued together, we appreciate you. To Crystal, you're a wonderful mother. Erica, keep singing kid, you got something. Hi Kamala.

To my aunts Cecelia, A.K.A. Big Momma, Shauna, A.K.A. Shaunerrr, and Elizabeth, A.K.A. Liz. The three of you are uniquely wonderful women. I don't know how I would have gotten through my late teens and early twenties without the three of you…love always. To my little cousins Angel, Shaunte, Charron, Paulette, Carmale, Terica and Marlecia. You girls are and always will be my A squad. I'm proud of the women you've become. I love each and everyone of you, Rock On! Shaunte, the two of us will always have a special bond. After all, even though I fell to sleep, I was there the night you were born.

To two of the baddest women I know. Lakesia M. Oats and Sheila I. Hopper. Monique, the two of us were more like sisters over the years. There were very few secrets between us, I love you girl. Sheila, I don't know where to start, so I'll just start. Thank you. Thanks for looking into the eyes of a 17-year old kid and knowing she was different from all the other girls you attempted to help. Thanks for expecting more when I thought I was at my best. Thank you for being an example not only for women in the fire service, but for girls and women of all careers and industries. Without you, there would be no three-part book. It would be more like a three-page pamphlet.

And finally, a special thanks to my mother, Delores Brooks. Thank you for teaching me to dream big. But more importantly, how to fight for those dreams. You are and always will be my favorite girl…Just not gone let you kill me. LOL

Chapters

FROM HELL TO FIRE

BOOK 1
SEX AND POLITICS

Prologue

The night I resigned…

We responded to a GSW (gunshot wound), there were three victims. All three victims were between 18 and 20 years of age. Two of them had apparently been shot with large caliber weapons. Two of the patients were females. One of the girls was laying in the middle of the street faced down with half of her head blown off and brain matter next to her on the pavement! When we turned her over, she had a butcher knife in her hand. The other girl was two houses down laying in the drive way. When we turned her over, not only was most of her chest cavity missing, she didn't have a pulse and wasn't breathing. About ten feet away from her was our only male patient. He was on the ground in a sitting position against the driver side of a car. He had obviously been shot with a smaller weapon than the girls, because he had a small entrance wound in his center right chest. The first girl with half of her head missing, was making very slow movements but would be dead by the time we got her to the trauma center. The other girl was dead, so I went with the best and smartest triage choice, the young man. Although he was struggling to breath, he was still breathing and had a very strong, lively pulse. As I was finishing his vitals, I was abruptly interrupted and told to come assist with one of the female victims. "Allison! Get over here; we need to get this girl going!" Yelled a senior medic. It was the girl laying in the drive way not far from the young man. They had already transported the girl with half of her head missing and brain matter showing.

Once we were done with her work-up, I hurried back to our male patient to resume his work-up. That was not only the logical thing to do, it was the right thing to do. Not that night! These miserable mutha fuckas decided to let this young man drown in his own blood! He could and should have been taken to the hospital that night just as the other two patients were transported. After all, he was the only one with a real chance to survive! To me this was beyond making a bad decision or a simple lapse of judgement. This was playing God! And I had seen enough!

"What the fuck was that? So we just leavin brothas to die now!" I exclaimed. "Yeah, it didn't look good to leave old boy behind like that." Said a medic. "You didn't just leave him behind! You let him die! You guys might as well have shot him your damn selves!" "Whoa, whoa, wait a fuckin minute. You betta watch yo fuckin tone girl!" As the senior officers and medics began to express how they felt. "Every last one of us out rank yo ass! Who the fuck you think you talkin to. You need to watch yo damn step girl!" "Watch my step! Watch my fuckin step! Oh you mean the way I watched it during the Clarence Thomas and Anita Hill hearings? When I listened to you guys tear sistas a new asshole! Or watch it the way I did during that ridiculous OJ Simpson trial! Go ahead and tell me which way to watch it! Cause I refuse to watch brothas pick up where whitey left off! You guys so use to being fucked over and bullshitted you doin it to yo damn selves now! And I refuse to watch! Shid I'm done watchin! You guys can go fuck yourselves!"

The city of Compton had more than its share of mayhem and most of our guys were plain burned the fuck out! Lots of changes were born due to the L.A. riots. Some good, some not so good. For instance, before the riots (April 29th, 1992) when we got a call to a GSW, we just went and did our thing. During the riots, a firefighter from a nearby department was shot. So shortly after the riots, a mandate was put in place that required all firefighters in L.A. County and neighboring cities to wear a bullet proof vest when responding to GSW's. Not only did we have to wear a vest, we also had to wait until P.D. (Police Department) cleared the scene of active shooters before going in. This of course worked to our advantage. Being able to work on a patient without worrying about becoming victims ourselves.

There were also the not so good changes that came along with the riots. Like the fact that paramedics in Compton and surrounding areas now had pronouncement rights. (The ability to declare someone dead at the scene of an incident.) As the protocols to pronounce someone dead were cut and dry, most of the times they got it right. Then there were nights like the above, when you knew without a shadow of a doubt, they made the wrong damn call! Bottom line!

Let's talk!

Chapter 1

HEARD ANYTHING?

I showed up that day as I did any other day. Uniform neatly pressed, jig line straight, hair slicked back into a perfect ponytail. American eagle boots professionally polished. Reserve Firefighter extraordinaire at your service! As I finished my equipment check, and begin to help the on-duty engineer mop the engine room floors, "Hey kid, did you get your letter yet?" "What letter?" "Most of the guys have gotten their interview results from the city. Was just wondering if you heard anything yet?" "No, not yet." I'm glad he said something. Had no idea we were getting our results so soon. Of course, not soon enough for me. My situation was completely different from most *reserve* firefighters. I had no car, which meant I had to catch the bus everywhere, which included: to my full-time job as a security guard, to the gym to work-out after work, and to the fire department to volunteer as a reserve firefighter on my days off work. Not to mention, I was still living with my mother and two brothers in her two-bedroom, one bathroom apartment. Between us, we didn't have a pot to piss in.

Most reserve firefighters, *even* if they did still live at home, came for money. Not to imply that they or their parents were rich, but they had more than life's necessities. Most of their parents had big beautiful homes, in nicely manicured communities. Me, I was born and raised in Compton. One of the most gang and drug infested cities on earth. Hopefully, things were about to change for the better.

When we were done mopping, I went *over* to the fire prevention bureau, the hazmat department. "Loretta, Loretta, where are you?" She was at her desk, on the phone. As I excitedly walked over to her desk, she told the person on the phone, "I'll call you back." She hung up the phone and asked me, "Have you heard anything?" "No, I haven't gotten anything yet." "Be patient, you will." "Can't believe they're moving this fast." "Well, that's what happens when you procrastinate as long as they have. A bunch of pure mess ups! Well, they're getting it together now. At least that's what everyone says." Just then we heard someone calling her from the front office. "Officer Loretta, Officer Loretta." As she looked at me, "Don't *move*. Look up front and tell me who it is." "I don't know, some Indian dude." "This moron again. Hold on; I got a *favor* to ask." She said as she walked to the front office. I was *very* excited. If everyone was receiving their letters, it was only a matter of time before I got mine.

"Officer Chandler, pick up line one. Officer Chandler pick up line one." She came back to her desk and picked up the phone. "Compton fire department, Officer Chandler speaking. Oh, hi Chief, sure, I'll be right there." As she looked at me, "You have a seat, don't move." "What if we get a run?" "Then let them know that I told you to stay put." "Ok." One of our office administrators walked in. "Hi Allison. Get your letter yet?" "No, not yet." "You'll get it soon. I don't know why you haven't gotten it by now. You live right here in the city so you will get it soon. It might be in your mailbox now." Oh my goodness. I hadn't thought about that. She's probably right. It could be sitting in the mailbox. Oh no, now I'm really excited! "Yeah, you're right. I'll check as soon as I get home." Loretta came back in to the office. "Get your gear off the engine and let's roll." She said. "Cool, where are we going?" I asked. "I'll explain it to you on the way." I hurried to the engine room to get my gear. As I was taking my gear off the engine, I noticed the other on duty reserve watching me. "Where are you going?" "Don't know yet." "When are you coming back?" "Don't know that either." "Well, have fun." "We usually do." As I was heading to the parking lot, I could hear the engineer, "Reserve, get your gear off the squad and put it on the engine. You're going to be on the engine until Brooks gets back." Loretta and I got in a company car and drove off.

Loretta Chandler was Compton Fire Department's first female firefighter. She is one of the most beautiful, smart, strong, and charismatic women I've ever met. It didn't take long to figure out how fortunate I was to have her in Compton not only as a mentor, but as a friend.

"Alright, so where the hell are we going?" I asked. "Oh no, what way is that to talk to someone who just got your ass out of sitting in the hot sun for hours on a chemical spill?" "No way! Seriously. What happened?" "All I know is, county hazmat is on the way to drug alley to rope off what appears to be PCP. They will then dispatch Compton, who will then dispatch my black ass. But I have a meeting with El Segundo fire department's hazmat team. By the time they call me, I will be about 50 miles away with an ETA of 2 to 3 hours. So those jackasses on 41's will have to babysit a hole in the ground until I get there. Which is why I brought you with me, so you wouldn't have to sit in the scorching heat with them. Besides, we need to get you home, so you can get your damn letter out of the mailbox."

That's what I call handling your business; I like the way this woman's mind works. "Open that folder and look over those stat sheets. You're going to give our opening presentation." "No problem. Anything for someone who could get me out of hours of sitting in the heat." "Let them take that scrawny white boy so he can get a closer look at his career in Compton. Checkmate motha fuckas." As we laughed. "What if that so-called spill turns out to be somebody's stash?" "Well if it is, those bloods down the street, will have to work it out with those Crips around the corner. And that will make for one hell of a story for that white boy to take home to his family, assuming they don't kick his ass."

Welcome to the city of El Segundo. "Before we get out, what's the deal with these guys?" I asked. "They're about to put a hazmat team together. They will use the same format we're using to get things going." "What's the ETA for their program?" "They're planning to have it running no later than January." "This January?" "That's what they said."

Hazmat is one of those areas of a firefighter's job description no firefighter in his or her right mind wants to be bothered with. There's little to no action involved and its painfully boring work. Standing around for hours at a time in a spacesuit identifying chemicals; oh yeah, sign me up!

As we walked into the lobby, the receptionist knew exactly who we were. "Officer Chandler, from Compton fire, right this way please." When we walked into the conference room, there was about 10 to 12 nerds along with other administrators, eager to hear what we had to say. I thought to myself, "This department shouldn't have any problems keeping their hazmat team assembled. They'll do just fine."

Once we were done, "So what did you think about that group?" Asked Loretta. "Those guys? They'll be just fine." The average firefighter is very athletic, type-A personality, with a 3.0 GPA. Not a bookworm, but hardly a dumb jock. It's as if someone went down to Comic-Con in San Diego and recruited the group we just left.

"Where are we going?" I asked. "I'm taking you home. Then I'll head to that ridiculous incident." "You know I don't mind rolling with you." After all, I was learning quite a bit. Hazmat "101 without all the boring books. "I know. But let's get you home so you can get your test results." The closer we got to my place, the faster my heart started beating. I know I did well on my interview, but was it good enough? What number did I place? On and on my mind wondered.

We finally pulled up to my apartment. I heard my brothers playing music from outside. "Alright Allison, call me and let me know your results either way. I have no doubts you did exceptionally well." "Thanks Loretta, I will."

Walking to the mailbox, I knew my mother and I had the only keys. So, if it's not with today's mail, it should be here tomorrow. What in the world, it's still not here! Anticipation is a two way bitch. And she was eating me alive with something this important on the line. Oh well. I sat the mail we did get on the coffee table and proceeded to put my gear on the side of the sofa. Since I didn't have a bedroom and was merely sharing space in my brother's room, I had to take advantage of my mother's room when she wasn't home. As I went to my mother's room to slip into something comfortable, I noticed a white envelope on the speaker. The city of Compton, this is it! I went to the middle of the living room floor and said a brief prayer, then opened my letter. There were only two things on that entire letter that I was interested in. My interview score, and the number I placed on the list. When I opened the letter, there it was. Score 96.4 and number 4 on the hiring list. I started jumping up and down and screaming as if I had hit the lottery. My brothers came running from every direction. "What's going on?" Asked Walt. "I did it; I'm finally going to become a firefighter!" We all hi-fived as they congratulated me. "Congratulations, you worked hard, and it's finally paying off." Said Walt. I could hardly collect my thoughts. Any reserve or other volunteer firefighters can relate to the excitement of the day, when they can finally call themselves a firefighter period. No reserve, or pay per call, in the title. You've spent years, working hard as a volunteer, hoping to someday be picked up as a professional firefighter.

"This is really happening. Oh shoot, I need to call Loretta." I said. As I picked up the phone, I could hear my brother Doc on the other phone. I'm sure he's talking to some rat. I hung up the phone and went to my mother's room where he was, and asked, "Are you going to be off the phone soon?" He didn't say anything. Just then Walt came out of the room and said, "Get off the phone man, Allison needs to make a couple of calls." Seconds later Doc said, "She can wait. We all need to use the phone!" "Man get yo punk ass off the phone. You always on the damn thing. Ain't like yo broke ass pay no bills around here!"

As they were arguing, I went to the kitchen, got the cordless phone, took it to my mother's room, then shut the door and locked it behind me. "Compton fire department, how may I help you?" "Is Loretta there?" "Hi Allison, she just cleared the hazmat incident. She should be back to the station shortly. Would you like me to have her call you?" "No. I'll just try back in about 30 minutes, thanks."

By the time I hung up the phone, Walt and Doc were in an all-out war. "Just get in your bucket and get the fuck on!" Said Walt. "At least I got a bucket to get in!" Doc said as he slammed the door and left. We didn't know where he was going, nor did we care. We just needed some peace for once. As Walt and I sat in the living room, "Thanks man." "You ain't gotta thank me. I'm sick of his ass. He always got his ass on the phone with a bunch of rats."

The phone rang while we were talking. "Hello." "Hey there. The girls told me you called." It was Loretta. "Yeah, I told them I would call you back. Didn't know if you would get through." "So, let's hear it. How did you do?" "Got a 96.4 and placed 4th on the hiring list." She was happy. "Congratulations Allison, I knew you would score high. Just goes to show, hard work does pay." "Thanks. Do me a favor and let the girls know." "Done." "And Loretta, thanks. Thank you for everything, this would have been a much harder road without you." "Don't do that. I'm glad to be of help."

Well, I better take a nap while I can. I'm sure Doc will be back by the time DD, our mother, gets home. Just in time to lie about his side of things. "Well Walt, its lights out for me. We can walk to BoBos later and get something to eat. "When DD get home, we can use her car and go." "Alright, sounds good."

Chapter 2

THE DAY AFTER

The Day After the Letter

I got up at 4 AM as I usually do to catch the bus to work. When I was getting ready for work, I could see my mother's bedroom light shining from underneath her door. She came out of her room, and said, "Walt told me about your test results. That's good; I'm happy for you. What all is left for you to do now?" "The only thing we have left at this point is our Chiefs' interviews." "Oh, is that a whole different set of interviews like you did before, or is it just the head Fire Chief?" "Yes, the Fire Chief." "Hopefully he will choose you for one of the positions". "Hopefully". "Then you can finally buy you a car and get off these dangerous buses". "Yeah. All right, I'll see you later. I need to get going before I miss my bus". I hauled ass to the bus stop.

As usual, I got to work at about ten minutes till six. Except this morning, I was overjoyed. My coworkers could tell I was excited about something. I proceeded with normal business, "Welcome to Union station. Have a good day". Talk about being excited; there were so many new possibilities open to me. All I could do for the moment was take it in. At 8:15 am, like clockwork, I was relieved for my morning break. I went outside to talk with one of my coworkers we call Rocky. Rocky was hell-bent on becoming a police officer, specifically, LAPD. She had been through their Academy twice and washed out both times. I couldn't wait to give her my news. "LAPD." "Hey CFD." "Speaking of CFD, guess what?" "What?" "I'm number four on the list dawg". "Get the fuck out of here!" "I plan to. As soon as I get hired." "Bring it in." She said as we hugged. "We need to celebrate. What are you doing after work?" Said Rocky. "Today?" "No next week! Of course, today." "I'm going to the gym." "You mean that sweatshop over off Crenshaw. Not today, I'm taking you to a baseball game. My girlfriend has an extra ticket, so you're coming with us to see the Dodgers tonight." Like this? I don't have a change of clothes." "Who cares? Normally you're Miss spontaneous. Suddenly you need a two-week notice to see the Dodgers. Give me a freaking break. Stop making excuses Brooks; you're coming." "What time does the game start?" "I believe it starts at six. Meet me at my car at 4 o'clock. I'll take you home after the game. Don't worry about it, see you at four".

After work, I went up to the cafeteria to grab a bite to eat. I talked and played around with a couple of people. At 3:30 I went down to meet Rocky at her car. She appeared to be very upset. "So, my girlfriends' boss gives her three fucking tickets to go see the Dodgers. Now the prick won't let her off work in time to go to the fucking game. What kind of next level bullshit is he pulling?" "Are you going to be OK?" "Yeah... I called another buddy of mine's, Valentino. She said she would go. That just pisses me off!"

We met up with Valentino about 10 minutes away from the stadium. We pulled up to the side of her car. As rocky road down the driver side window, "what, no hookers to kick out of the car?" "Fuck you Rocky! Suck my dick!" "Well of course. Right after I kiss your fat ass!" We all laughed as they hugged. Rocky told her who I was; she explained that I was the one she was telling, who was going to be a firefighter soon. She congratulated me and told me not to pull a dime out of my pocket. She said that beers and dodger dogs were on her.

We had a really good time. We also had good seats. We sat on the first level (yellow section), between 3rd base and home plate, only about four rows back from the field. We left after the seventh inning, being that we all had to work the next morning. Rocky had Valentino give me a ride home since she lived in Long Beach, which is right next door to Compton. During the car ride home, she explained what it was like to be an officer for LAPD. She educated me on a lot of the politics going on with their female officers. She told me that if I ever got hired, become familiar with the city's policies, the department policies, and my union M.0.A. She also gave me her best wishes. As we pulled up to the front of my mother's apartment, I could hear her arguing from outside. I thanked Valentino not only for the ride home, but also for her professional advice. As I got out of the car, she said, "Hurry and get inside. It sounds dangerous around here." As embarrassing as it was, thankfully she didn't know it was coming from our apartment. Sounds like I'm in for a long night.

When I got inside the house, I went straight for the cordless phone, picked it up, and went outside to the back porch. As she usually did, I knew the moment my mother saw me she would pick a fight with me. So, I called one of my friends and asked him to pick me up. He said he would be here in 30 minutes. Right on schedule. "Where the hell you been? You guys ain't worth a damn around here! Doc got his ass in jail!" Said my mom. "So you cain't take it out on everybody else!" Said Walt. "The only reason he's sitting in there is because you guys got into it yesterday and he ran out of here mad!" "No, he got his ass in there because he had a warrant out for his arrest!" "Because he ran out of here mad because you guys got into it first!" "You act like I said; yeah man take yo ass to jail! Man, Doc is a pure mess up." Walt went into his room and closed the door. She followed him and continued to argue with him through the door. I took that opportunity to go to the bathroom and change out of my uniform. My ride will be here any minute. Once she saw Walt wasn't going to come out of the room to continue arguing with her, she turned her anger towards me. I sat there cool, calm and collected. Any other night, I might have reacted to her. But not tonight. Not only was I tired, I was also still on a bit of a high from my exciting news. So, I quietly sat there. Finally, she went outside to turn off the power to the apartment. She did that when everyone ignored her. Once she was outside, I told Walt that I was leaving, grabbed my backpack, and went out to the front of the building.

A couple of minutes later, my friend Tyson pulled up. When I got into his car, he asked, "What's going on?" "The same old drama." "Your mom is at it again huh?" "Always. Before she could get mad enough to kick me out, I called you, so I could just leave." "You should look into getting a place. It's not safe for you to be walking the streets at all times of night because she's mad." "Yeah, I'm in a terrible position right now, it takes money to do everything, and I just don't have it." "Well, we need to figure out something. Because this is not going to work." "Hopefully the odds will be going in my favor soon. That's also why I wanted you to pick me up." "What?" "I got my test results back from the city of Compton. I came in number four overall on the list to be hired." "That's fantastic news! Congratulations." "Thanks."

"So what's left now?" "We still have our chiefs' interviews." "You should do fine with that interview too. Especially since you've been volunteering with them how long now?" "It's going on five years now, it will be five years this September."

It was late, and I was tired. I wanted him to take me to a hotel. Nothing extravagant, just somewhere clean, with no hookers in front. "No that's not right, we're going back to my place. I won't bother you. I know you're tired." We pulled up to his place. It was a small studio apartment, but it was clean. True to his word, other than one of his famous massages, he allowed me to rest.

The first ride along
after my test results

"Tailboard meeting in five minutes, tailboard meeting in five minutes". I was already in the engine room finishing my equipment check. The guys started coming in one by one to have our morning meeting, also known as the tailboard meeting. "Well fellas, said Captain Harvey, "looks like over-time will be coming to an end soon. The city is about to hire. Looks like we're going to pick up 10 new firefighters. So, for those of you who have gotten used to life in the fast lane, and you know what I'm talking about, you had better learn to readjust quickly". Laughter. "Oh, there will always be overtime. Won't be as much as we're used to now. But overtime is not going anywhere." Said a firefighter. Captain Harvey then pivoted toward me and asked, "by the way Brooks, where did you place on the list?" There is no way he can't know by now where I placed on that hiring list. But since he's giving me the honors of telling everyone, "I placed number four on the list". They all congratulated me. "And this is number four out of 150 candidates interviewed." Said Captain Harvey. Then one of the guys asked, "What was your score?" "96.4". They all started to talk about who was in the

FROM HELL TO FIRE

top 20. They also talked about the various options the Fire Chief had for choosing firefighters. It made for an exciting conversation, especially being that I would be directly affected.

At lunchtime, the guys were talking about how a lot of reserves have completely stopped showing up to do their scheduled ride along. The last time the city of Compton hired, I was one of the ones left behind. So, I completely get feelings of discouragement. But one thing I did not do was give up. Firefighting is not something someone does simply for a paycheck. Don't get me wrong, the money is the icing on the cake. But this is something that's either inside of you, or it's not. It's in the bones.

Think about it; we are running into buildings that everyone else is running out of. You can't put a price on that.

"Reserve firefighter Brooks, report to the fire marshal's office please, reserve firefighter Brooks report to the fire marshal's office." When I got there, one of our office's administrators, along with Officer Chandler, and Fire Marshal Colton were all standing there. "Have a seat; you're not in any trouble. Well, at least not yet." Said Fire Marshal Colton. Laughter. As the office administrator walked out, "I need you to do us a huge favor. Remember that warehouse over off Willowbrook?" "The ones with the water pressure problem, turned fire sprinkler problems. Yes, what about them?" "They finally replaced a few valves to get their water pressure up. But now they have sprinkler head issues. We are suspecting that they're trying to pull a fast one to get this place reopen faster than scheduled. So, the three of us will go out there and run a triangle offense on those bozos." We all laughed. "Let's get going; I'll give you ladies the plans along the way".

Believe me when I say I've seen it all. I watch multimillion dollar corporations try to cut corners all the time. Especially those who are not used to America's laws and ordinances. People are so hard up for money, they don't care who they maim or kill along the way.

When we arrived, I oversaw making sure no one turned the water off leading to the building. Chandler was told to walk through the establishment with the owner checking for various leaks and other water related issues. Fire marshal Colton had the best job of all: writing the report on our findings to submit to the Fire Chief and the mayor's office. Like clockwork, just as we expected, they were prepared to shut their water off the very second the fire marshal walked in to do the inspection. Except, there I was, standing there making sure they couldn't. The guy who was planning to shut it off walked over and asked, "How long are you planning to leave the water on?" "Until I'm told to shut it off." "Do you have any idea on when that will be?" "No. But I'm sure it will be within the next 30 minutes to an hour." I said. The nerve of this guy. He was very agitated. What are we supposed to do? We hold these guys hands every step of the way to help them pass these inspections before they open for business. And we tell them exactly what to do to maintain safety. These or not mom and pop businesses were talking about. These are multimillion dollar factories. 50 employees and more. Do they listen? Big fat resounding no!

About five minutes into the water test, water started to leak in a couple of spots. 10 minutes in, a couple of sprinkler heads popped off. Officer Chandler ran outside and signaled for me to turn off the water. On the way back to the station, Colton said, "a couple more minutes of that and we would've had to swim out of there!"

"Heard anything about your Chiefs' interview Brooks." Said Colton. "No, not yet." "Well let me give you something, and I want you to keep this under your hat. You guys orientations, for those of you who get hired, is in September. They haven't worked out a definite date, but they're looking at the middle of September." "That's what my sources are telling me," Said Loretta. That's great news! September is only a couple of months away. If we're expected to show for orientation in the middle of September, this means the Chief's interviews must literally come at any time now. "That's exciting news, thanks."

When we got back to the station, right on time was the business owner complaining about the unfair inspection we just finished conducting. It never fails. These guys go out of the way to cut corners, then want to cry foul when things don't go their way. He was in the lobby with the assistant Fire Chief. As he got louder and louder, the assistant Fire Chief asked him to come in to his private office and have a seat. While the two of them were in the assistant chief's office, Fire Marshal Colton told Loretta and I to come into his office. He continued, "This is why in this industry we do a little something called CYA. Here's months of inspection logs on this guy's business. Here's all our communication both verbal and written. Now all we have to do is wait for chief to come get us."

As we sat waiting, the assistant Fire Chief finally walked in. "Fire Marshal Colton, I have a very dissatisfied business owner sitting in my office." "I'm aware Sir." "He said that you treated him in a very unfair and undignified manner." "I'm sure he did." "Care to fill me in on the details." "Most certainly." He thanked Loretta and I for our assistance, then asked the two of us to leave his office and told us to shut the door on the way out. "Oh, I didn't realize the two of you were with Fire Marshal Colton. Please, have a seat." We both sat back down, as the assistant fire chief and fire marshal begun discussing the details. The assistant fire chief explained that the owner was most unhappy with the way we conducted ourselves. He also said he had no idea it was the three of us. "Now that I know the players involved, this guy is nuts! Fire marshal Colton, as we know, people complain about you from time to time, mostly because they're upset about their business being shut down. But that comes with the territory. The two of you, to my knowledge, have never had any complaints filed against you. Fire Marshal Colton, the business owner in question is still in my office. Will you please bring your logs and any other documentation you have regarding your dealings with this business and follow me."

When the two of them left the fire marshal's office, the two of us girls had a good laugh. "Now I think I know why Colton wanted us to come to this particular inspection." "You know you gone have to fill me in." "Every guy in this bureau has had several complaints from different businesses this year. Some have been written up as a result. Eventually, this guy will make his way across the street. And when he does, chances are the mayor will see our names attached to this last shut down and order the fire marshal to keep his establishment closed until further notice." The one good thing about being girls is that people usually trusted you. At least in the fire and law-enforcement industries. In most cases, you can't pay us enough to get our hands dirty. Not that any of us are saints. It's just that we understood these guys could and would, turn on us at the drop of a hat. So, when they do, our hands are clean; not to mention that neither Loretta nor myself had any problems with public relations. Although few they are, being a girl has its moments.

Fire Marshal Colton came back in to his office, closed the door behind him and said, "This guy got so upset he started foaming at the mouth. When that happened chief asked me to leave. I gladly got the hell out of there. Again, thank you girls for coming with me. It's just that I understand the gravity of this situation. I've been sending my guys out there for months trying to help this guy pass this inspection. The Three of us have a couple of things in common. None of us have any business complaints against us this year. And none of us have been written up this year. And to my knowledge Allison, you have never been written up for anything in any year." Got that right. "No sir, I haven't."

As Loretta and I walked out of the fire marshal's office, she whispered, "What did I tell you."

I thought about the fire marshal's strategy. What he did was bulletproof. CYA on steroids in this case. Very wise move on his part.

Get your safety in place! I watch business owners walk around dollars, to pick up dimes and nickels. As a good business person, one should always know when to fix something, versus when to replace it. You should also know when to buy used versus when to buy new. It's OK to pick up dimes and nickels, if you also pick up the dollars.

Later that night, at approximately 9 PM, "Engine 41, 441, 42, 442, GSW multiple victims, GSW multiple victims, multiple calls." This is going to be bad. Usually when we get a GSW with multiple victims, we have to arrive and discover that there are multiple victims for ourselves. Whenever dispatch tells us we have multiple victims with multiple calls to 911, it's always bad.

When we arrived, two helicopters were flying over the scene. PD's helicopter and one from a media outlet. There were several PD cars on scene. They told us to stage around the corner from where the victims were. "This is going to be unusually bad." Said the Captain. "You guys might as well get your minds set for what we're about to see. If these guys got us sitting here just until they get the crowd under control," as he took a deep breath, "just be ready."

It only took them about a minute after we got there to control the crowd and clear the scene of any shooters. Once we got an all-clear from PD, we slowly rolled in. It was just as we imagined. We had five victims, ranging from ages 17 to 22 years of age. One was sitting in a car, the passenger seat, with a hole the size of a baseball in his head, brain matter was all over the driver seat. The obvious driver to the car was laying 3 feet away from the vehicle, with the driver side door open and half his head blown off. There was another victim lying face down in someone's driveway. He took two shots to the back. When we turned him over, his entire chest cavity was missing. About two houses down from this carnage were two other victims. One was a young lady who was shot in the chest. And another young man shot three times; once in the arm, once in the side, and one to his lower thigh. These two were apparently shot with much smaller bullets than the first three victims. Their entrance and exit wounds were a lot smaller and much cleaner. The plainclothes officers cuffed the guy with the three gunshot wounds to our gurney, two of them rolled inside the paramedic unit with him on the way to General Hospital.

We took our only female patient to MLK hospital. "Where are you guys taking her?" Asked one of the officers. "To MLK," answered one of our medics. MLK has a bad reputation, but it's the best hospital in Southern California for gunshot victims. The best trauma center in the country if you could talk to professionals in this industry.

Now comes the nasty grievous task of covering those other three victims. Their families and all other onlookers know for sure at this point there's no way they're alive. The horrific screams coming from mothers, grandmothers, sisters, and other closely related family and friends is what sears your brain for weeks to come. Little did I know that night, covering victims would be the part of the job that I would soon come to hate! It's that feeling of hopelessness that it leaves you with. Knowing that you've done all you could, and it just plain old wasn't good enough. These are situations we must leave entirely to God.

A good firefighter would say, to save a life takes a trifecta of your excellent skills, the drugs you're pushing up an IV, and God. Only a real jackass would say that they were the ones who saved someone's life. And by the way, say what you want about God, but I've never met a dying atheist.

The next morning, as I was tidying up, Loretta came up to the kitchen where I was. "Are you alright kid?" "Yeah, I'm alright." "Come sit for a minute, just want to make sure you're OK. I know that wasn't your first GSW, not by a mile. But I also know it was pretty damn bad out there last night." "Yeah, it was the worst GSW I've been on."

We both sat there quietly. "Get your gear and all of your things together; I want to give you a ride home this morning." We had a very good conversation on the way home. She was mostly feeling me out, trying to make sure that I was going to be all right. Of course I would, what choice did I have?

As we pulled to the front of the building, we could hear arguing. "What the fuck are these people arguing about at nine in the morning? You are going to have to figure out where you're going to live shortly. There is no way you are going to survive as a probationary firefighter in this environment." She was right. I had to do something about my situation, and fast. Here I was at the doorsteps of one of the most important opportunities of my life. And as much as I wanted to stick around to try and help, it was not going to work.

Firefighting is the second most stressful job in the nation. Only second to being the president of the United States of America. There was no way I was going to leave a job that demanded so much, to come home to just as stressful an environment to recuperate.

Chapter 3

CHIEFS INTERVIEW

Chiefs Interview

Finally got my letter from the city of Compton for my Chiefs' interview. August 20, that's only about two weeks from now. Whenever it was going to be held, I was ready. I had prepared for this day ever since I was a snot nosed 17year old fire explorer.

Here it is. Today's the day. There I was. Hair whipped, navy blue skirt suit, navy blue pumps, small silver hoop earrings, silver charm holder with a 1 CT cubic zirconia, silver watch on my left wrist. Deep cut business attire. As I sat in the lobby of headquarters waiting patiently with two other guys, I had never felt more like an outsider until then. I was either going to walk up there, do exceptionally well on my interview, and be given a job offer. Or told, you will hear from us in a couple of weeks.

We could hear someone walking down the stairs. "Reserve Firefighter Brooks, the fire chief will see you now." It was Battalion Chief Hemet. "Right this way please." My heart was racing as the two of us walked up the stairs. As Chief Hemet opened the door, the fire chief was standing in his office behind his desk. "Come in Brooks. Have a seat." I walked over to his desk, shook his hand, and had a seat as I was instructed.

"When I came aboard as the head chief of this department a couple of years ago. I was under the impression that you were one of our full-time firefighters. You have shown indiscriminate loyalty, and commitment to this department. I've heard nothing but outstanding things about you. So you are to be commended for that. But I will ask you as I have the other candidates. Why should I hire you as one of our full-time firefighters for the city of Compton?" I took a deep breath, thought about it for a couple of seconds, then I exploded. As I began to speak, he picked up his pen and began to write.

"As a citizen of the city of Compton for 22 years, I was educated in its schools. I shop in its local plazas. I have used and am currently using its transportation systems. As a child, I played in its parks and backyards. As a volunteer firefighter of just under five years for the city of Compton. When I proudly put on my uniform and get on the equipment I'm assigned for that shift, I'm not simply serving the citizens of Compton. I'm keeping close watch over my family, friends, and neighbors. Both my paternal and maternal grandmothers are still alive and well in this city." As I pause for a few seconds, he stopped writing. He stared at me as I continued. "During the 1992 civil unrest. There was a firefighter on a nearby department who was shot! Because of this, no other department would come near Compton to assist us. We were on our own for the next 48 hours. We were also told to pace ourselves and prepare to eventually stand down. That wasn't going to happen. Standing by, while doing nothing was not optional. About 30% of our firefighters now serving in this department were raised in this city. And like myself, they too have family, friends, and neighbors still living here. We understood the challenges in front of us. We also understood fatigue would eventually get the upper hand. There was an unspoken communication amongst us that day; to not sit, and simply let our city burn to the ground.

I'm not just another candidate here to get experience until something better comes along. I plan to retire here if given the opportunity." I paused again for just a few seconds. He had completely stopped writing. "Chief, sir... I know your question was, why hire me? My answer sir, with all due respect, is why not me?" He continued to stare at me, then gave a very wide smile, followed by a laugh. "One of the captains who did your initial interview warned me that you could sell tires to a man with no car. Welcome to the Compton fire department. Congratulations. The only thing I'd like to see you do is to start getting some formal education under your belt. I need you to start taking management classes immediately. You are a very eloquent speaker, not to mention you clean up well. We are going to need you for multiple public appearances. In fact, as you were speaking, I could picture you in uniform giving public addresses and statements to city council members along with their constituents. I expect you to hit the ground running. I have high expectations of you. But I have no doubts in your abilities.

After all, if I didn't think you could do it, I wouldn't ask of you. Again, welcome aboard. Do you have any questions at this time?" "When is orientation?" Dope! Speaking of panicking. "It's good to see you're motivated to get to work." Ok, so then it wasn't the worst question to ask. "Rumor has it, and again this is only talks amongst city employees, that they want to get you guys going by the middle of September. Is there anything else?" "No, sir. Thank you for the opportunity. I will strive to go above and beyond your expectations." With those words, I stood up, gave him a very firm handshake, and walked out of his office.

The wait is finally over. It's official. I am now a full-time paid firefighter! I don't remember the last time I felt this good. I went straight down to the bureau, walked right over to Loretta's desk, and we looked at each other with a very gleeful smile. "What now?" "I don't know; I just want to soak this moment completely up, take it all in." I said. Fire Marshal Colton walked in. "From looking at the two of you, I don't have to ask how things went upstairs." We all laughed. If I had to credit someone for helping me get to this moment, other than myself, Loretta, and God, it would be Fire Marshal Colton. He was always watching to make sure those knuckleheads, as he called them, didn't pull anything fast and slick. In fact, it was Fire Marshal Colton who suggested that I ride alone after 8 PM only when Lauretta was on duty, just until I got the hang of things. That turned out to be until she went into hazmat. "Congratulations. If anybody deserves to be here, it's definitely you." "Thank you sir."

Later that day, Loretta offered me a ride home. She said she didn't want me to get on the bus looking like 1 million dollars. Of course, I jumped on that offer. My brother Doc had given me a ride there, but there was no telling where his ship had landed by now.

We talked on the way home. She pulled past the building where I lived and took me to the park around the corner. "What's up?" "Get out; we need to talk." "Wasn't that what we were doing before we got to the park?" "Oh hush girl and get your ass out of the car!" We went over to a nice shaded area and sat on a bench under a tree. What was this about? Usually, when she had something to say, she just came out and said it. We had a very open and honest line of communication. "Listen kid; I know this may seem a little out there to you because when we have something to say to each other, we just talk." "Exactly, so what's up?" "Listen, you are no longer a volunteer firefighter. Things are not going to be the same for you." "What do you mean?" "These guys have been cool with you for the most part. Now they will see you as a threat. You will soon be added to the city of Compton's payroll. You will make the same money, if not more than our other guys. They will never see you as an equal. Only as a threat!" I sat patiently hearing her out. She has never misinformed me before, so why would she start now?

She continued, "up until now, no matter how good you were at something, they knew in the backs of their minds you weren't being paid. So they still saw you as an underdog. But now kid, this shits about to get thick! Just to reiterate a few basics, be seen but never heard. Never sit in the same room with you and only one other firefighter, not until you pass probation. As usual, never go anywhere with any one of them. In fact, don't go anywhere with any group of them. We both know how men can be. They will usually lie and say they've had sex with you. You and I both know, nothing coming out of their mouths has to be true. All it takes is a couple of rumors to wreak havoc on your career. Never have a firefighter for a boyfriend, no matter what department he works for. If you see someone you're interested in, at least be smart enough to wait until you pass probation before going out with him." Up until that point, I had never even exchanged numbers with a guy I met while I was in uniform. You can never know what someone's expectations of you are, especially when you're a firefighter. Hell, that goes for guys and girls. She went on talking like that for the next 10 minutes.

"Allison, I know this is a lot to take in." It was a lot. But I also knew she only had my best interest at heart. "I want you to understand; when we put on that uniform, we don't get to just be good at our jobs. We don't get to simply blend in. And we damn sure don't have the luxury of representing ourselves. Unfortunately, when we put on our uniforms, we must represent not only ourselves, but every woman coming through those doors behind us. You will work two and three times harder than your male counterparts to receive the same accolades. They will also take any problematic, female related issues in their lives, out on you. Got into a fight with their wives or girl-friends, come to work and take it out on Allison. Couldn't get any pussy from some random ho, they will take it out on you. And by the way, good luck attempting to stand up for yourself. It's never you against him. It's always you against them; you against the entire department!"

Wow, talk about a lot to take on. It wasn't as if I was hearing most of this for the first time. But I will admit, it did feel different. I guess it was the real-ness of knowing that I was no longer a volunteer. Little did I know, every-thing she said that day would come to pass...plus some. "I know that what I'm saying must sound completely unfair. And it is! No one said this was going to be easy. There is only a hand full of female firefighters nationwide. So understandingly, we're close. A sisterhood. You are one of us, if you are never one of them." "A sisterhood hey. Sista's in suppression". We started laughing and hugging. "Come on crazy girl. Let's get you home".

About two weeks went by after my Chiefs interview. When I got home, I checked the mail. Not that I was expecting anything significant. When I got the mail out of the box, to my surprise there was a letter from the city of Compton. There is no way this could be information regarding orien-tation and hire dates this soon, so I thought. When I opened the letter, there it was: "Welcome to the city of Compton fire department. We are pleased to inform you of your official orientation and hire date of Sunday, September 18, 1994. You are to report to the training facilities, station #3, on Rosecrans, Compton California at 0800. We would also like to take this opportunity to thank you for your participation in the testing process, and to congratulate you for becoming one of our newest members."

Talk about being overjoyed. Wow, Sunday, September 18. That's only 12 days from now. As usual, I grabbed the phone to call Loretta. "That's won-derful Allison." She said. As I agreed and said, "It really is. It's all finally happening. I was kind of wondering why is orientation on a Sunday?" Not that I had a problem with that. Just thought that was an odd day to start the work week. "It's not only the first day of the week, but it's also the first pay-day in that pay cycle. They're probably going to load books and paperwork on you guys. Then on Monday, start the measuring for your turnouts and other gear. Who knows, it's been a while since I've done orientation." I was over the moon with excitement just thinking about it all. What shift would I be assigned? What station would I work out of first? And the money, oh my God the money! Going from earning about $14,000 a year before taxes. To making $65,000 a year after taxes base salary, starting pay. The insurance, health and dental, the retirement package, on and on. What a wonderful and exciting blessing. The more I thought about my new career, and all it would provide, the more I thought about things like, where I was going to live? What kind of car would I buy? These questions would be answered sooner than later. I had been patiently poor up until now. No sense in being overly anxious at this point.

Chief's interview, check. Orientation and hire date, check. Now I need to set up a date. No sense in showing up for my first day of work so sexually depraved, that all that's on my mind is gettin laid, instead of gettin paid.

That night I called Darren. "Long time to hear from you." He said. "I know, what have you been up to." "Same old, how about you?" I caught him up on my situation with my being hired full time by the fire department. "Damn girl, just like that." "Yeah, hell I worked hard enough!" "Calm down girl; I know you did. I was out there running with you on that dry, hot ass sand." "You came with me a couple of times." "Try several times." "Whatever." "Forget that, How we gone celebrate?" "That's why I was calling you." We made plans to get together that weekend. I would talk a good game. But my sexual stamina wasn't worth a dime; and if anybody knew that, it was Darren. "You better get something, so you can hang with me girl." "Don't worry about me, just do your part." "Oh, don't talk, you know I'm gone wear that ass out." He was a very patient lover. Slow and low, just like I like it, with even slower hands.

That weekend, I packed my duffel bag in anticipation of being away for a few days. I planned to catch the bus over to Darren's after work. But of course, things didn't go according to plan. As it turned out, the guy who was supposed to relieve me that evening was running late. By the time he got to work it was 7 o'clock. I was hotter than a firecracker by then. I was supposed to get off at 2 o'clock. A good buddy of mine's convinced me to hang around until she got off at 8 o'clock. "We'll hit up this new sports bar I heard about. It's supposed to have good food and decent prices. It'll be on me, kind of a celebration for your last day of being in this hole." She said. "Yeah, well I already have plans for this weekend. Besides, the last thing I want to do is hang out at some smoke infested bar with a bunch of drunken sailors." I said. "That's where you're wrong. This place is for women only. No smoking allowed." She said. "What? Do they even have those? I've never heard of a women's only bar." I said in disbelief. "Yeah, well that concept is starting to gain momentum. As you said, most women don't want to hang out in some smoke infested places with a bunch of, how did you put it, drunken sailors." No harm, no foul. Besides, it was getting late.

I called Darren and told him about my new plans. He was not happy to hear about my not coming over that evening. He offered to come pick me up from work. "No that's all right. I'll be there tomorrow at about 4 o'clock at the latest. How does that sound?" I asked. "Sounds like I don't have a choice but to wait." He said disappointingly. "This was supposed to be our last solid weekend before you go into training." He said. "And it will be. It's only being pushed back until tomorrow. Don't forget today was my last day working here. We got all the time in the world… well until next Saturday." He agreed to pick me up tomorrow from my mother's place. Besides, the last thing I wanted to do was show up to his place tired.

My coworker and I took off at 8 o'clock on the nose. That's the thing I liked about her post. It was outside at the rear parking lot. The parking lot closed at 8 o'clock, and all she had to do was get in her car and leave. "Jennings wanted to hang with us. Hope that's OK?" She said as we were leaving. "Jennings, as in Captain Jennings? Hell yeah, that's ok. She's cool as a fan.

I've been meaning to have a drink with her before I left. Where are we picking her up from?" I said. "She's right up the street. Turns out she had to cover for some dude who quit today." She said.

Jennings was very put together. She wasn't given any choice but to be successful in life. Both of her parents went to historically black colleges, and they both were retired from the military. Jennings was the youngest of five. She had three older brothers and an older sister. By her being the youngest, her parents allowed her to make a few choices on her own. For instance, she didn't have to go into law or practicing medicine as her older siblings did. She got to pick her own University and made her own career choices. She has a four-year degree from Stanford. She is 24 years old, stands at about 5'11 and weighs about 180 pounds. Very attractive, athletic girl. People said I was disciplined; this bitch gave the word a whole new meaning. She was working on getting hired with the L.A. County sheriff's department. As it turned out, she got hired that following spring.

As we pulled up to where she was standing, we could see steam coming from the top of her head. "Bullshit...this was complete and utter bullshit!" As she got in the car. "Where's the company car?" Asked Dell. "Lieutenant Humphrey dropped me off. He was supposed to cover this post. But he doesn't have his CPR and first aid certifications. We just found out that his Certs expired a couple of months ago." She said. "Isn't it a requirement that all lieutenants, captains, and higher-ranking officers have their certifications on them at all times?" I asked. "That's the way it's supposed to be. Now try asking me how it is that these white boys seem to always get away with not having their shit!" She said, as Dell and I laughed. "He was supposed to come pick me up at 8 o'clock tonight. I told him don't bother. And I will be calling in sick until Monday. He's gone to be one overtime working motha fucka until I get back. And since he doesn't have his Certs, he's going to have to work all the worst post, in all the worst areas. But enough about that. What's up for tonight?" She asked. "As I said earlier, we are going to check out this new spot. It's supposed to be a cool little hangout." Said Dell.

From the outside, the place looked packed. As we went in, we could see that there was about 75 to maybe 100 girls there. Not bad at all for a Friday night. It was a nice place. They had three pool tables, several video games, a couple of dart boards and TVs everywhere. We sat at a regular table tucked away in a cute little corner. We ordered a platter of Buffalo wings, and a pitcher of Coors light beer. "You don't get to hang out much. What brings you out tonight?" I said to Captain Jennings. She looked over at me and said, "I don't get to hang out much, you don't do too bad in that area yourself." She said as we all laughed. "You got me there." I said. "Truth be told, I wasn't supposed to be here now." "Yeah, I heard about that wrench being thrown in your plans. Where are you supposed to be?" She asked. "Somewhere gettin some TLC." "Yeah, I understand that. You damn sure need to get broke off before you start that stressful shit. Why didn't you just have him come pick you up?" She asked. "He wanted to. But it's gettin late. I'm more tired than I am rested. And I don't have sex when I'm tired." I said. Dell chimed in, "I don't know about that, I don't think there's ever a wrong time to have sex." "Oh yes the hell it is! Guys will give your coochie all kinds of black eyes when you're tired." Said Jennings. "Exactly. That's why I'll wait until tomorrow when I'm rested. Much more fun that way." I said. We ate our wings, drank our beer, talked plenty of mess, and shot several rounds of pool. Dell and I played each other twice. I won both games. Captain Jennings and I played four times, and she beat me three out of four games. Never met a girl who was more hell-bent on winning than me. We had a good time.

The next morning, I got up at about 11:30. Needed to take care of a few things before Darren came to pick me up. At 2:45 the phone rang, "Hello." It was Darren. He was over in this area and wanted to pick me up a little early. "Might as well. My bag is still packed from yesterday." I said.

He was happy to see me, and I was just as excited to see him. "So next Sunday is your big day." He said. "Yes, it is." I answered. "So, we gone make this weekend count." He said. "Those are my intentions. Being that I'm gone have to be on my best behavior for a while." "It's not like you really get into much." He said. That was true, I didn't get into much. And the sex I was having wasn't regular. Just a bunch of hit and runs. "You got the good, and I miss it girl." He said as he looked over in my direction.

Once we were in his apartment, we didn't waste any time. He came right at me. He pulled my pants and panties down to my ankles and ate me like I was his last meal. And like I usually do, a couple of minutes later I came. He got up and got a tube of something. It was a pinkish colored gel substance. He put it on two of his fingertips and worked his fingers inside of me. He took his fingers out, I put his condom on for him, and in he went. All eight thick inches of him. We had very passionate sex; off and on all weekend long.

Orientation

Sunday, September 18, 1994. Here it is, Orientation day! As we arrived at station three that morning, we were escorted to the classroom. Once in the class, we noticed 11 neatly stacked, groups of books and papers. As we stood around the tables, Chief Donley finally made his way to the classroom and introduced himself. "Welcome to the Compton fire department, I'm Chief Donley, I will be your training chief for the following year. Go ahead and have a seat at one of the stacks of books. I need to get a few more things together, then we'll get started." He said as he walked back into the library. We sat rather quietly for about the first five minutes. Finally, someone said, "Who's the 11th person? I thought there were only ten available positions." Then a guy, whose name turned out to be Talley, responded, "I don't know how many positions are available, I just know I'm not going home." As we all began to laugh. "I'm the 11th person. I was hired to be your new fire prevention officer." We all looked around the room shaking our heads in agreement. "Like I said before, I don't care what's what, I just know I'm not going home." Firefighter Talley said again, as we all laughed again.

We all took that opportunity to get to know each other. We took turns going around the room giving names, along with a brief description of our experience. We worked our way back to our new prevention officer. "Oh, you again." Said firefighter Talley. As it turned out, our new prevention officer went to long beach Poly. He played football a couple of years with Calvin Broadus Jr. a.k.a. Snoop Dogg. That was interesting.

In walked Chief Donley. He explained every book and booklet that was stacked in front of us, as well as how to use them. He explained in full detail what was going to happen every day that week. He also took the opportunity to give us each, two small shift calendars, along with our shift assignments. "You'll notice that three of you are assigned to each shift, except the A-shift. The A-Shift Will receive four new firefighters. I will give you your station assignments tomorrow. Are there any questions?" He asked. As it happened, I was assigned to the A-shift.

We were given measuring tapes and size sheets and instructed to measure each other for turnouts. "The turnouts you measure for today will be your primary turnouts. But those, must be ordered. Once we're done, we will drive over to station one, to get what will become your back up turnouts. I will need your full cooperation in selecting the best sizes we have on hand. Do your best. Try to get as close to your original size as possible." He said. After we were done measuring each other, it was 12:30 noon. He dismissed us for lunch until 2 o'clock. "Don't forget we will meet at station one, at 2 o'clock to get your new gear." He said.

The very next morning, we started to arrive at 7:30 AM. We were pumped, and ready to go. We could feel the excitement in the room. At 8 AM on the nose, Chief Donley walked in. He gave us our station assignments right away. I was assigned to station one, headquarters, directly across the street from city hall. "Listen up. You will not be sworn in until Thursday between noon and 4:00 PM. Therefore, your assignments will not begin until Friday. Your official hire date was Sunday, September 18, which was yesterday. You officially started getting paid as of yesterday." We all cheered. With that news came some confusion. "Sir. My next shift won't start until Monday?

Correct?" Said, one firefighter. "What shift are you on?" Asked chief. "I'm on the A- shift sir. The last day for them this week will be Wednesday." He said. "Then that's correct. You will show up no later than 8:00 AM on Monday ready to work." Said Chief. My ears puckered right away. I'm on the A-Shift. And like he said, we were going to start our official shift on a four day. That's what I'm talking about.

Chief Donley gave us all uniform sheets and instructed us to write our names on them. Then he gave us all ten fire department patches each. "Listen up. You will always receive your fire department patches, fire department belt buckles and of course fire department badges, from the fire department itself. Anything else such as uniforms, belts, boots, nameplates, and the like, you will purchase at Long Beach uniforms or any other uniform outlet. In the future, you will be given a uniform allowance. As for your current uniforms, we will leave here at 10 AM to meet at Long Beach uniforms by 10:30." He said as we all cheered. "Listen up. This is very important. You will receive five shirts, five pants, one pair of boots of your choosing. Either Chippewa or American eagle for this department. One nameplate, and one smooth black leather belt. All compliments of the city of Compton. Now here's where you come in. Do not sign off on anything you haven't received. The City of Compton is responsible for this tab, whether you have your uniforms and other gear or not. Any questions? If not, see you in Long Beach at 10:30." We all high-fived and started to walk towards the engine room. "Oh, wait a minute." Said chief. "As for your badges, the Fire Chief will pin those on you personally before the start of your first shift."

When we arrived at Long Beach uniform, we all had our own assistants. "Do we have any females in this group? Any females?" Said one of the ladies. "We got one." Said chief Donley. "Here I am." I said as I raised my hand. "Right this way please." She said. She opened the door to a 10x10' dressing room with wall to wall mirrors. "Here's what I need you to do. You're going to have to strip down to your underwear, which is why you get a big room with a locked door." I took off my T shirt and sweatpants. I had on a sports bra and biker shorts underneath. "Oh, that's perfect." She said as she began taking my measurements.

"What size bra do you wear? I need to measure your chest." She explained. "Now I will need to measure your waist and your hips." She explained that my hip size would be my pants size, and that they would obviously need to take my pants in around the waist. "Now spread your legs one last time." She said, as she measured for my inseam. I had never been measured for clothing or uniforms in my life. This is what personal tailoring is all about. She took all those numbers and gave them to a second lady, as the two of us stood there. About five minutes later, in walks a lady with my shirts, pants and belt. "Go ahead and put on one of the uniforms." She said. "Entirely too bunchy in the waist like I figured. You are a very shapely girl. Good for you, bad for men's clothing." She said. "We have to take her in about 6 inches around the waist." Said the other lady. The two of them began pulling and tugging on the pants I was wearing. As one of them began writing numbers, "You can put your clothes back on." Said the other.

About two hours into this process, I gave them my uniform patches. They gave me a receipt slip and told me to pick up my uniforms any time after 2 PM tomorrow. I thanked her for her help. She walked me over to the man who was responsible for our nameplates. "See you tomorrow." She said. "Here you go. One Firefighter Brooks." He said as he gave me my nameplate. Another lady walked over and handed me a box of boots, along with a bag of other stuff. "Here you go: A pair of Chippewa boots, one smooth black leather belt, and your nameplate." She said as she gave me my things and smiled. Talk about service. Don't get me wrong. For all the money that was laid out, I should have expected nothing less. That was going to take some getting used to. We were all in and out of there by 1:30 PM.

Thursday, September 22, 1994
"The day we were sworn in."

We arrived at City Hall's personnel department at 0800 as instructed. We finally got a chance to see each other in full uniform. Everything was brand-new, from head to toe. The only thing missing, were our badges. Once we had all arrived, we were taken into a large conference room. We all sat down at yet another stack of papers for us to sign. "Don't touch anything until given further instructions." Said the administrator. When she left the room, "well don't we look good in uniform?" Said one of the guys as we all laughed. When she came back into the room, we got started on what seemed to be tons of paperwork. We had to choose everything from our health insurance, dental insurance, to our retirement packages and everything in the middle. What facilities would we like to be airlifted to in the event of being severely burned? How would we like to be buried in the event of a death? Things that I had never given any thought. We went on and on like that for hours.

Finally, at about 4 o'clock, we were all told to stand. "You are about to be officially sworn in to the city of Compton's fire department. What will happen is; there will be a judge, a minister, and a couple of other personnel officials. Once you are officially sworn in, you will have a quick bite to eat, followed by your public swearing ceremony. She said as she walked out of the room. "Damn, I'm tired as hell, and all we did was fill out a bunch of papers." Said one of the guys. "I don't think it was so much of having to fill out so many papers. It was the gravity of the paperwork with these kinds of questions that was so eye-opening for me. That along with the fact that we haven't eaten anything." Said another guy. "That was probably the point. To get us so tired and hungry that we wouldn't put up a fight when it came time to sign our lives away." Said firefighter Talley as we all laughed.

We stood there talking as the door opened. Just as the administrator stated, in walks a judge, a minister, and two other people from the personnel department. It took all of about five minutes to swear us in. And just like that, they all left the conference room. The administrator instructed us to follow her. When she opened the door, it was another conference room. This conference room was three times the size of the one we had just left. Except, there was plenty of food and drinks on the tables. "You guys and girl, go ahead and eat everything your heart's desire. I will be back in about 30 to 45 minutes." Said the administrator. As she walked out, "Lord God Jesus Mother Joseph. I'm so hungry I could eat half of this by myself." Said one of our guys as the rest of us laughed. We all got a plate and went straight for the turkey sandwiches on wheat. We ate and drank until our hearts were content.

At a quarter after five, in walks the administrator with a couple of other city officials. "You are about to walk outside to the private council chambers where you will meet the mayor and other councilmembers. Once you have met all Council members, you will be escorted to the public Council room. Once there, you will be escorted to the platform or the stage. You will be told what to do from there. Are there any questions?" Asked the administrator. "This entire process should only take about 10 minutes. After this, you will be free to leave." She said.

Everything went exactly as she said it would. Once we walked out to the city chambers, we stood on the council platform. There were about 150 people there. There were lots of press, media person's, plenty of photographers, and several 8mm cameras. Now here's the swearing we were accustomed to seeing. This swearing was for the public and for show, being that we had been officially sworn in over an hour ago. We did what was asked of us. Once we were done, the matter of taking questions from the press and media was solely up to us. We had been briefed earlier that day on how to handle the press and the media. In true fashion, they rushed the stage when we were done taking our oath. About half of them swarmed around me, probably because I was the only female in the group. Two police officers, and a security guard walked over to where I was and asked if I intended to take any questions. "No, I'm exhausted." I said. Once it was clear that I wasn't going to take any questions, or do any interviews, the officers escorted me back to the private chambers. After all, we had a long day. And like all the other firefighters, I was ready to go home for some much needed rest.

When I got home that night; all I could think of was how fortunate I was to start my actual work week on a Monday. My four day had technically started today. As I lay there on the sofa, I could hear my mother's bedroom door opening. Was hoping she wouldn't start anything. I was dog tired and needed some rest. If she wanted to talk about anything, it could wait till tomorrow morning I'm sure. "So when do you have to go in for your first day of work?" She asked. "Monday morning." I answered. "We haven't talked about how much money you are going to give me now that you are working as a full-time firefighter." She said. "Yeah, I've been thinking about that. But can we talk about it in the morning? I'm exhausted." I said. "Don't be selfish! We need to talk about this now! I've been intending to talk to you about this for the last few days. But you haven't been here. So let's talk about it right now!" She demanded. Excuse me for being busy playing foot-sie with my little fire friends. She said that as if I haven't been working all week. "Mama, I don't even have a bedroom. I'm on the sofa. The first thing I wish we could discuss is the possibility of me getting that room. Walt and Doc could and should sleep on the sofa and the recliner. They're both men. I'm a woman and need a little privacy." I said. "You are not taking their room. That room belongs to them. And it's selfish of you to even bring it up!" She continued to scream and yell as I fell to sleep. I had to hear about how nasty and selfish I was the next day.

Chapter 4

THE FIRST DAY

The First Day

Monday, September 26, 1994. I'm on the bus, on the way to station one to report for my first official shift as a firefighter. I had a bunch of equipment, the bus was crowded, so I had to stand. But you better believe I was happy as hell. Just the thought of that possibly being my last bus ride, was all I could think about at that moment.

When I arrived, I went in through the back door as usual. Once In the lobby, all the office administrators came out and started saying different things. "Oh, look at her." Said one of them. "I told you we should nickname her firefighter booby." Said another one, as the three of them laughed. Now, wait just a damn minute! I had suffered my share of nicknames over the years of being there. They went from calling me Junior, to the kid, and from the kid, to fire mama. As bad as fire mama sounded at the time, I'll take it over firefighter booby. "Yeah, you ladies are going to have to work on that." I said as they started laughing again.

When I got to the engine room, I noticed one of our new hires standing there. "I suppose you're my relief." He said. "I Suppose so." I said. He started to brief me on what was going on with the equipment. While we were talking, "Firefighter Brooks, report to the Chief's office. Firefighter Brooks, report to the Chief's office." He explained that the Chief probably wanted to give me my badge. That's right. I had completely forgotten about that.

When I got to the Chief's office and knocked, "Come on in." Said the Fire Chief. Once I was inside, there along with him was hazmat officer Loretta Chandler and Fire Marshal Colton. "They both wanted the honor of putting your badge on your chest. So, I made the two of them arm wrestle for it. And of course, Loretta won." Chief said as we started laughing. "Badge number 38. That was the number of your first badge." I said as I looked at Loretta. "That's why I insisted on being the one to pin it on you." She said. "Wow, talk about a fortunate coincidence." I said. "You make me cry in front of these men, and I'll kick your ass later." She whispered as she pinned on my badge. We looked at each other and smiled. Once she was done, we hugged. "Congratulations again kid. We are going to miss you down in prevention for a little while." Said Fire Marshal Colton. The fire chief shook my hand and said welcome aboard. I thanked everyone and immediately left his office.

Returning to the engine room as quickly as I could to complete my equipment check, "tailboard meeting in the captain's office, tailboard meeting in the captain's office." Didn't get a chance to put my gear on the engine yet. Oh well, I'll handle it after the tailboard meeting. My first tailboard meeting as a firefighter. Everything was going to be my first everything as a professional firefighter for a while. How exciting, and familiar, but new.

We started our tailboard meeting with being updated about issues that had taken place over the weekend. The first topic was the lawns. One of our senior firefighter/ paramedics wanted to know why they hadn't been cut this past Saturday. "Our lawn mower is still under repair." Said the station captain. "Are we down to one lawn mower for the entire city now? Every station doesn't have its own lawn equipment? Know what, fuck it. We'll just start bringing our own lawn equipment from home, maybe that will work." Said the firefighter. "We are working on that situation as we speak." Said the captain. "On second thought, give me those scissors on your desk. Why don't you go ahead and take us out of service for the rest of the shift, I'll take firefighter Brooks and get started on the lawns." He said as we all laughed. "That's enough, on to other business." Said the captain.

One thing that was going to happen sooner than later, was burn out. It is every firefighter's responsibility to make sure they got enough rest, playtime, and whatever else within the parameters of the law, to keep them from being burned out, or over worked. This firefighter's star shined extremely bright. But he was a 10year veteran. And 10 years of being a firefighter/ paramedic in the city of Compton was enough to drive anyone mad. We got a lot of action, which meant we saw a lot, and dealt with even more.

"It's official, let's welcome our newest firefighter Allison Brooks. Welcome aboard." Said the captain, as they all clapped. "Thank you. I look forward to working with you all in a professional capacity." I said. Now that the morning meeting was finally over, I could finish my equipment check and put my gear on the engine. I needed to make sure to stay focused, being that things tended to go from 0 to 100 quite often around here. One minute you're checking equipment and making small repairs on something. The next minute you're responding to a traffic collision, gunshot wound, or a third alarm fire. Either way, I was glad to be of service and get paid for once. "You're going to have to drag those things through the mud or something to get them dirty." Said the engineer. "That's right, we don't like brand-new turnouts. We usually end up getting third alarm fires whenever there are new turnouts on the engine." Said the captain. They believed exactly what they were saying. Different firefighters had different superstitions. And enough of them believe that until you get your new turnouts dirty, you are destined to get a third alarm or higher fire. "Yeah, that's right. I'll think of something." I said. Deep down inside, I couldn't give a rat's ass about their superstitions. At the same time, I didn't want them to think I was starting off on the wrong foot by disrespecting what they had to say. From my experience, we had a much higher chance of getting a GSW from having brand-new turnouts on the engine, than we did a fire.

"Engine 41, squad 441, GSW in the Compton courthouse parking structure." Said dispatch. It's not even noon. Who the hell is shooting each other this early?

When we got on scene, there was a man shot dead by his ex-wife's boyfriend. A case of a custody hearing gone in the wrong direction. At least from his ex-wife's point of view. It's too bad to see parents often using their children as pawns against one another in their own selfish game of chess.

The rest of my first shift was pretty much business as usual. At least Business as usual for the city of Compton. The only thing suspect to me was a TC in which the passenger of the vehicle, female, approximately 18 years of age, was partially decapitated. I found that situation very disturbing, even if she wasn't wearing a seatbelt as the driver had suggested. According to him, he didn't notice he was driving on the wrong side of the street until just before impact. It seems to me that he would have something wrong with him other than a few scratches. He wasn't intoxicated, nor under any other influences from what we could tell. Nevertheless, we did call an ambulance to transport him to be checked out and further observed. She was dead on arrival. If she was DOA, and he only had a few scratches...it just doesn't pass the smell test. Not my smell test.

At about 2:30 AM, "Engine 41, sheared hydrant, on the corner of Long Beach Blvd. and Alondra." Of course, I wasn't going to get off that easy for my first shift. This intersection was a doozy. Slanted downward because of the freeway off-ramp heading west. I'm sure water was filling it like a swimming pool. When we got there, oh my goodness, water was shooting about 30 feet in the air! The intersection was a lot worse than I had imagined. Water was everywhere. The engineer had to park the engine about 200 feet from where the hydrant was, to keep the hose bed from flooding with water. "Strip down rookie. You know what to do." Shouted my captain. Strip down was precisely right. I took off as much as I could, put on my turnout boots, and went for a swim. The closer I got to the hydrant, the deeper the water got. At its deepest point, it had to be at least 2 feet deep, with a 20 to 30-foot overreach. In short, I was screwed. There I was, in the middle of the street, looking for an 8-inch in diameter metal covering, supposedly painted yellow. A flashlight, a pry bar, and a prayer were what I had to get the job done.

After only about a minute in, I found the hole cover. The problem was, due to the water pressure, it was nearly impossible to get the cover off. So, I recommended to my captain that I go ahead and shut the street valve off. We generally didn't like to do that, because the residents wouldn't have water until we were done. Being that it was 3 o'clock in the morning, I didn't think that would be an issue. We would have the water back on before anyone would miss it. When I was done, of course, I was drenched. Just another day on the job.

Two Months In

A couple of months into being a firefighter, some things had changed, while others remain the same. Of course, I was still living with my mother. I was still sleeping on the sofa. And like always, she was verbally, and mentally abusive. When she wasn't arguing with one of my brothers, she was picking an argument with me. Either way, it was a horrible environment, especially for a probationary firefighter.

Loretta couldn't have put enough emphasis on what I could expect now that I was making money like the rest of the guys. It was open season on my ass. The heat was on, and the politics were insurmountable.

In all the years of my volunteering there, I was led to believe they didn't want women around because most women were physically inferior to men, which made for incompetent firefighters. But I soon came to learn that they didn't want us here for entirely different reasons. Mostly sex and politics. What most people don't know is that there are three sides to every station on most fire departments. Monday through Friday from 8 AM until 6 PM, when most business is conducted. Monday through Friday from 8 PM until 6 AM when most structure fires, GSW's, and other tragic events occur. Then there are the weekends after 10 PM, where anything goes! Friday and Saturday nights after 10, there's usually wall to wall hos! Half-dressed women everywhere. They would have girls on the roof, girls in their dorms, but mostly in the parking lots in their cars. And the married firefighters were the worst! They would sometimes come to the station in their uniforms, change into very dressy outfits, hang around for a while, and then ride off with a completely different woman. If their wives called, you were supposed to simply say to them, "he's out on a run right now. Would you like to leave a message?" It was a bulletproof alibi. Think about it. Firefighting had a 10 day a month, 24 hours, ¾ work schedule, for the most part, which meant you work three days every other day, followed by four consecutive days off. Some departments work 48 hours consecutively, followed by 96 consecutive hours off. In either case, these schedules are used to control stress levels, along with managing fatigue; physical, mental, and psychological. If the 3/4 or 48/96 schedules wasn't confusing enough, add to it an ever- changing schedule due to over time because of brushfires and other catastrophic emergencies. It all adds up to perfect conditions for cheaters and hoes!

My stress level was slowly starting to rise, and I needed to do something quickly. There I was, on the phone calling up the old gang from my security post. First on the docket was Dell. Next up was Rocky. Then I had to call Sam, aka Captain Jennings. They all agreed to meet me Friday night at 8:30 sharp at that nice little spot in LA - the women's only sports bar. When I got there, it was about 8:15. Wanted to get there a little early to save us a table. As I was walking around, "hold it right there! Freeze, put your hands up." It was Rocky. We gave each other a big hug. "Guess who wanted to come hang out with us?" As I saw Daphne, our sergeant from my old post. "Hey, you! Why did you sneak off without saying goodbye?" She said as we hugged each other. We went over to the table that Rocky and Daphne had already gotten for us. We sat there for a little while, catching up on things. Then finally, in walks Dell and Sam. "What's up? Look at you, looks like you lost weight." Said Sam, as we started to hug. "No, if anything I lost hair". I said as they laughed, and I hugged Dell. "Damn I miss you. Your little ass is a lot harder to replace than we thought." Said Dell. There was nothing little about my entire ass. Usually, when people call someone younger than them little, they're talking about age. Someone five or more years younger than them. "Yeah, I know I miss you." Said Rocky. "And it does look like you've lost weight. Stand up." Said Daphne. "If anything, and this is a very slight chance, I might have taken off about 10 pounds. But that's only because of all the training and drills that they put us rookies through." I admitted. "That's about right. People usually take off about 10 to 15 pounds during their rookie year. If not from all the drills, then the stress will definitely get you." Said Sam. "Yeah, I hate to admit it, but you look like you got yourself a little rookie chisel going." Said Rocky.

We all talked and laughed the night away. They told me about some new girl who filled in for my old position. They said that no one seemed to be getting along with her. "What's wrong with her?" I asked. "She's a bitch!" Said Daphne. "Come on, that's an obvious answer. I mean more specifically, what's up with her?" I asked. They all got very quiet for the first time that evening. "Well damn, don't all speak at once, is she fuckin the boss?" I said. "That's a strong possibility." Said Dell as the other girls laughed. "Here's the issue, I'm going to try to sum it up, so bear with me." Said Sam. As she continued, "she's an OK looking girl, but doesn't look as good as she thinks she looks. She's ghetto as hell but tries to come off as Miss high society. She's always running late, which leaves people having to cover for her. She calls in sick all the time. And when she is there she don't do shit. And those are only the things I'm at liberty to speak about. How did I do?"

And that was coming from Sam. She could be a bit of a hard ass. But that was usually reserved for supervisors directly under her. Or those of us trying to climb into the professional world, such as myself and Rocky. But with what she termed everyday security guards, she didn't give a damn! She usually just patted them on the head and gave them the standard job well done. With Rocky or myself, we could have arrested every felon within 5 miles of our post, and she would have found 10 ways we could have done a better job. One day, I asked her why the difference. She said, "You and Rocky are good at what you do. But I don't want you to get cocky, so I ride your asses like a couple of stallions. I want you to stay polished without becoming arrogant. Besides, you can't teach motivation. So I don't waste my time with those other guards. You and Rocky, you girls are a different breed from most of these guys. Especially you. Your ass is a completely different species standing next to most the women I know."

As they all began to get quiet again, Daphne chimed in and said, "Sam might not be at liberty to say it, but I am. She got busted trying to sell food stamps on the premises." As she said that, I laughed so hard I had to turn my head the other way. The beer I was drinking shot right back out of my mouth. "You guys are stroking me, right? I know damn well you're just playing!" I said as I looked at the other girls' expressions. Daphne continued, "We all know that's a triple felony. So that caused a lot of problems for some of us. Just that, we didn't know exactly how to handle the situation. So I called Lieutenant Humphrey, who called Sam. When Sam got there, she called the account manager." "As I was supposed to do. We all did what we should have done that day. But as it turns out, the bitch is still there." Said Sam. "So now, as you can imagine, people say she must be screwing somebody in management at the facility. Because if she was only messing around with one of our higher ups, she would have at least been reassigned to a different post or something like that. Which is why we think she's messing around with a facility manager." Said Dell. "You guys are right. Trying to sell food stamps, I don't know which laws were broken, but I'm sure she broke a law or two." I said as we all laughed hysterically.

I filled them in on some of the stuff I was going through at the department. I told them about the revolving door of women. And of course, about my recent found stress. "No, your situation has been messed up for quite some time. It's just starting to wreak havoc on you because your full time now. When was the last time you've been with a man?" Said Sam, as the girls started to laugh. "Samantha, really?" Said Daphne. "So, is that what Sam is short for, Samantha?" Said Dell, as Rocky chimed in, "No, it's short for Sammy Davis Junior. What the fuck! Who the hell doesn't know her name is Samantha?" We all laughed. "I know you guys think I'm being off cuff, but seriously. You need to make sure you're being broken off on the regular." Said Sam. "Hell, sex on the regular could cause you to have less energy and more stress in some situations." Said Daphne. "Not quite, at least not for everybody. Sex is a stress reliever for some of us." Said Dell. "Exactly. Myself and Allison or those girls who need it on the regular. Workouts, running 5 miles a morning, doesn't matter. We're Scorpios. And for us, trying to go too long without sex, is like a fish trying to live without water. That shit ain't gone happen!" Said Sam. She continued, "You don't need no marathon man for this situation. Just get you one of those two-minute brothas who knows the art of eatin pussy. Give him some body oil, let him give you a good 20-minute massage, then let him eat you until you come.

Once he goes inside of you, you won't have anything to worry about; his ass is coming in a minute or two anyway. See, that way you both win. I bet you bitches ain't laughing no more." Mic drop. She was right as usual. And I knew just who to call.

Suddenly, the girls started asking Sam questions as if she was Dr. Ruth. All, except Rocky. She was a bonafide lesbian. And wasn't a damn thing gone change tonight. "You girls have to get your little black books in order. Not every man has to be a 20, to 30-minute stud. The way I see it is all of them have areas of strengths and weaknesses. Categorize them accordingly, but never push them to the side." Said Sam. What the girls may or may not have known is, Samantha practiced exactly what she preached when it came to men. There were times she would call me to cover a post for her when someone called off or plain didn't show up. And since she knew I was on the bus, she would come and pick me up in the company car. The two of us spent several nights at a post talking about life, men, and plenty of sex. Samantha was a bad ass girl. She had men just about everywhere she frequented. "Don't try to lie or be slick with anybody. Let them know that they're not the only ones you're messing around with.

Another thing you're going to have to learn to do is keep your own damn condoms. If you're going to have different partners, you are going to have to be responsible about it. Something else you always want to do, is protect yourself. What I mean by that is, if you know a dude is hung like a horse, don't let him stretch your shit out. Not unless you intend to marry his ass. Ain't no sense in letting him wreck your shit. You'll mess around and not be able to feel anybody else." Sam continued like that for a while. She was giving some good advice. The problem was, the two of us were the youngest two at the table. I had just turned 23, and she was a whopping two years older than me at just 25. Rocky was next in line coming in at 26 years old. Dell, she was in her late 30s, while Daphne was in her early 40s. If these women didn't already know about what Sam was saying, chances were, their shit was already wrecked. But since that train had not only left the station, but was plowing down the tracks, I wasn't going to be dumb enough to jump in front of it! At that moment, we were true testimonies for what too much alcohol would do for you. We all hugged it out and left at about 1:30 the next morning.

Chapter 5

WHERE THE BOYS AT?

"Where the Boys At"

When it came to little black books, hell men in general, Sam had her thing together. She went to Stanford, where she majored in something to do with criminal justice and management. So of course, Sam had men in California that she either met at school or somewhere close to campus. Her parents were from Virginia, so she had men in Virginia. Her grandmother lived in South Carolina. And since Sam spent every summer since her 13th birthday in South Carolina with her grandmother, you guessed it; she had plenty of male friends in South Carolina. In the south, she was known as what they called a Holy Trinity. Someone who had nice sized breast, a nice big well-rounded butt, and big legs. Those southern boys couldn't get enough of her. The company we worked for had post in the Beverly Hills mall. And from the looks of things, there were lots of women who couldn't take their eyes off of her either.

Well, I didn't do too bad myself. I got nowhere near the attention she got but didn't do too bad. Just that, 80% of what tried to talk to me was black men. I had a few Hispanics, a few whites, even a few women try to get my number. I've dated a couple of white guys, a couple of guys from India, never any Hispanic men, or women. Rocky once told me, "If women find you attractive, you know you got your shit together. Especially California women. They are some of the best looking women in the world. A lot of people think, that when they see two girls together, they couldn't find a man. That's plain bullshit! For whatever the reasons are, they usually don't want a man. Some of the finest women I've ever met were lesbians. So if you find yourself being hit on by a lesbian, consider it a compliment. Most of them are very picky. Much more picky than any three men when it comes to women." When I discussed that information with Sam, she agreed. She said from her experience, a lot of the guys who try to talk to her are handsome, some not. Some had money, some didn't. But every woman who's ever hit on her was fine as hell, and usually smelled of money. From what I've seen, it was true.

The problem for me as I saw it, is I didn't have my own place, and I was still borrowing my mother's car. I had a little money put away because I was planning to buy a car as soon as possible. Then I was planning to find an apartment, preferably somewhere in Long Beach. But for now, I needed a man. I got on the phone and called one of my male companions. "Hi Tyson, how are you?" I said. "Good as hell whenever you call. How about yourself, how's the department treating you?" He asked. Tyson's a brotha I met about a year ago. His family lived in Georgia until he was about 9, then they came to California. He lives with his mother and aunt in Inglewood. "Things could be better. But I'm a first-year boot. And they take every opportunity to remind me of it. How about you? How are things coming on your end?" I asked. "Finally got my car running and fixed the way I wanted it. Sounds and all. So I'm excited about that." He said. We stayed on the phone talking for a while. We made plans to go out later tonight. Tyson was exactly the kind of brother Sam describe last night, he came in all of two minutes. But you better believe, what he lacked in size and stamina, he more than made up for in oral sex. He was good with his hands too. So I planned to pick up a bottle of baby oil for tonight.

Tyson had never seen me dressed up before. In fact, hardly anyone I knew had seen me in makeup. Just wasn't my thing. I very seldom wore it. But I wanted to do something a little different. So I decided to treat myself. I bought a new outfit, these nice leather boots with 4-inch heels I've had my eyes on, and I went and got my hair done.

When I went to the beauty salon, that was a trip all its own. People always say, if you want to know what's going on in your community, or in life in general, go to the beauty salon or the barbershop. These women were brutal! For anybody who thinks men are bad, or so-called hard on the opposite sex, you need to be a fly on the wall of a beauty salon for a day, these women will straighten you right out.

The first topic on the docket, men with little dicks. "Tall, big feet, big hands, big ears, doesn't matter, you can't tell a man's size by any of these." Said one beautician. According to her, all of that was plain bullshit. "I've met some short men with normal sized feet and hands and got him home, thinking I was going to be let down and got my ass taken for a loop. Honey, dropped his pants, and whipped out 10 thick inches on my ass!" Said another beautician. "So that goes to show, you don't know what you're working with until you're working with it." Said another girl, as everyone else laughed. "That's what we call a papoose, little guys with big packages." Said another girl. "Yeah, but those are rare. That only happens with little guys, one out of 10 times." As everyone else agreed.

"Sometimes you can tell what they got by who they're with. Especially with brotha's. What they don't get, is when they're with Hispanic women or Asian women, that's a-tell sign that he's only working with a few inches." Said one beautician, as she looked over to one of their shampoo girls, who happened to be Hispanic. At that moment, everyone got uncomfortably quiet. "She's right. I've been with a few black guys. And all of them were little. I guess they must have thought I wouldn't know any better. You know, that I would just buy into that stereotype about black men. But who the hell doesn't know the difference between 3 and 4 inches, versus 8 and 10 inches, come on. Where Latinas, not blind!" As everyone laughed.

Next on the docket, men with big dicks who couldn't fuck! They went on and on like that for what seemed to be forever. I couldn't give a rat's ass about what any of them had to say. Most of them were bitter washed up hags. And like most of the fellas who ran their mouths, they were running their mouths out of sexual frustration. When it came to men, I was on the Samantha Jennings plan. Different men had different strengths and weaknesses. Just categorize them in your little black books accordingly. As long as they had a job, a car, and no issues you didn't want to deal with; whatever they didn't know, as long as they were willing to learn, they were good to go. But never sideline any of them. Just put them in the game at different times. If that philosophy could work for a bad ass bitch like Sam and was working for me, even though these were some gargoyle looking heifas, I'm sure it could work for them. Hell, it wasn't like any of them were looking for husbands. Most of them had been married at least once. So you figure they would keep quiet long enough to learn how to get a booty call. Not in a million years! Finally, the mailman walked in. Thank goodness. I had never seen some of them with their mouths closed before.

I had a nice navy-blue silk blouse, my leather boots, and a pair of tight-fitting jeans. My hair was whipped, and I was wearing more makeup than a cheap hooker. Had to borrow a little perfume from my mother. It's funny how she never had any money, but she always had a variety of expensive perfumes.

At 6:05 PM I could hear Tysons' car pulling up. I grabbed my clutch bag and made sure I had my driver's license, ATM card, keys, and anything else I thought I would need for the weekend. When he walked up to the door, his eyes got wide, and I could see his tongue hit the ground. "Damn girl, you look hella good. I don't think I've ever seen you with a purse before." He said. "You haven't. I don't usually carry one. I bought this one for interviews. Fire and police department interviews specifically." I said. We walked to his car; he opened my door as he usually does. When he got in the car, he was very quiet. "Don't leave this hanging out, wouldn't want you to step on that while you're driving." I said referring to his tongue, as we both laughed. I thought that would have broken the ice. But now he appeared to be even more nervous. "What's wrong?" I asked. "You've always kept it real with me; now I want to be completely honest with you. I've always felt like you were out of my league. After seeing you tonight, I know for sure you are. Shit, I feel like you should be stepping out of a much nicer car than this looking the way you're dressed." He said as I interrupted. "Wait a minute Tyson. I can't help the way you feel. But this is me, Allison. The same girl you met on the train a year ago. The same girl you talk to on the phone a couple of times a week. The same girl you took out about three months ago. And the same girl who intends to spend the weekend with you. If it's too much, I understand. Let me get out, and go call someone with a much nicer car. I'm sure he would love to spend the weekend helping me sweat this makeup off, and undoing my hair." I said. "To hell with him! I'm not stupid! You called me, so I'm the one taking you out!" He exclaimed. "Now that I've gotten your undivided attention can we please get going?" I said.

On one hand, I completely got where Tyson was coming from. I didn't dress up often. And the few times that I did, he wasn't around to see it. There were times I would dress up and get my hair done but didn't put on any makeup. To put the entire package together, clothes, shoes, hair, makeup, purse, it was usually for an interview. And you better believe me, 60 thousand and better a year was on the line. But dressing up just for the sake of dressing up, I only did it occasionally. Usually to treat myself.

On the other hand, I never picked guys based on what they were driving. The first thing I looked for was physical attraction. If I wasn't attracted to him, it didn't matter if he drove a clunker or a Bentley. If I wanted to ride around in a particular kind of car, then I felt I needed to buy it my damn self. Again, not to use any of these guys, but I made it clear to them from day one what I wanted. I wasn't looking for a steady relationship, and I damn sure wasn't looking for a husband. After all, I had just started the whole dating thing. It was all still very new to me. Not to mention I was usually busier than a one leg man in an ass kicking contest. For now, I needed to focus on my career and giving myself a decent financial foundation. There will be plenty of time for relationships.

He continued to be very quiet; which was making me uncomfortable. We usually talked, laughed, and had lots of fun headed to wherever our destination was. "You know what, just take me back home. I'd rather sit and argue with my mother than to do whatever the hell this is." I said. He continued to drive. We pulled into a parking lot of a park across from the beach. "Baby listen, I'm sorry. Can we talk?" He asked. "Whatever." I responded." Listen, I'm just gone put myself out there. I'm starting to really get into you. It's been happening for months now. I've been trying to lay low on it because I know this is not what you really want. And then the fact that I don't really have anything ain't helping either. Look, I'm not trying to excuse my behavior, but at least now, hopefully, you'll understand why I've been acting salty all night." He said. "Thanks for being honest. The thought of a relationship with not just you, but anybody hasn't even crossed my mind. I've been so wrapped up in my own bullshit...it's just a lot for me to think about. Not saying that it's a bad idea. Just give me a while to think about it." I said. "Well, it's not a no, so thanks." He said. "Please don't thank me for thinking, it's kind of what I do." I said as we laughed. He leaned in, and we started kissing. "Now can you please put on some music? I've been dying to hear this new system of yours." I said. "Well, you should've said something." He said as we laughed. He started the car and put on "right now" by Al B Sure.

We arrived at the restaurant, at 7:35. I had reservations, but by the time we got there, we were 35 minutes late. And there was no way they would hold a table that long on a Saturday night. As it turned out, one of the hostesses working remembered that I was a frequent customer, and I had a reputation for tipping well. So she was kind enough to give us a couple of seats in the sports bar area. The Lakers were playing tonight, so I didn't mind. We sat at the bar where there were several TVs. The restaurant was very nice, and although I was a bit overdressed for the bar area, I didn't care, because I was in my element.

The waitress gave us our menus and explained; we could order anything from the regular menu, plus sports bar specials. I ordered the Cesar salad with chicken. Tyson was unsure, so he took a little time to look at the list. While he was looking over the menu, I ordered a Coors light from the bartender. By the time Tyson ordered his food, I was knee-deep into the Lakers game. As I started yelling at Eddie Jones for not giving up the ball. A guy sitting a few seats down asked, "Do you think the Lakers are going to do anything this year?" "Hell no! The Lakers need to rebuild their team." I said as Tyson, and the other guy started laughing. "If you could, what would you have Jerry West do differently?" He asked. "First of all, they need to hire Magic to help run their front office. Second, start rebuilding the team around Eddie Jones, Nick Van Exel and Elden Campbell. They can start there." I said. "What about James Worthy and Vlade Divac?" He asked. "What about them?" I answer. "Well, they're still decent players." He said. "Exactly; decent. But not good enough to keep on a new roster. James Worthy was and still is one of the best players the NBA has ever seen. But I would talk to him about retiring while he's still on a high. Vlade, I think we've seen the best of him. We need to trade him before he starts spiraling downward." I said.

When I kept quiet long enough to pay attention, I noticed a couple of other guys standing around us. I almost forgot I was on a date. It felt like I was at home in front of my mother's TV talking to my brother Walt. "She's a keeper man. A good looking girl who's into sports like that. Don't let her get away." He said looking at Tyson. "Thanks man. I don't intend to." Said Tyson. "I'm sorry about that. I got so into this game, I almost forgot I was on a date." I said. "Don't be. You know what the hell you're talking about, and I like seeing that side of you." He said. "Only because that's the side of me you're most familiar with. The tomboy." I said.

We ate our food and took a walk along the pier. "Tonight shaped up pretty good after all." Said Tyson. "Yes, it did thanks to my not allowing you to mess it up." I said as we laughed. "Yeah, I have to admit, I came pretty damn close." He said. We started holding hands as I walked over to where the boats were docked. As I started to daydream, a nice wooden sailboat got my attention. That girl had to be at least 50 feet long, it was beautiful. "Penny for your thoughts." "Listen. I don't want you to ever feel insecure around me. If I didn't believe you to be good enough, I wouldn't go out with you. You're a nice guy. I like you. And none of that changed because I'm a firefighter. Even when I'm at my worst, I know who I am. And I have enough sense to choose accordingly." I said. "You're right...I Get it." He said. He put his arms around my waist, as I put my hands on his shoulders. We started kissing very passionately. He whispered, "Let's go."

When we got to our room, we could hardly get in the door. He started biting on my nipples through the blouse I was wearing. As we laid on the bed, he unbuttoned my blouse, and started kissing me all over. He unzipped my pants and pulled them down to my boots. He pushed my legs up and open my thighs. He took two fingers and started working his magic like he usually does. Except this time, when he started eating me, he didn't bother taking his fingers out. Damn! I was good as through. He made it apparent that he wanted the job full time. And if he kept this up, it was going to be his to have. After I had an orgasm, he got the baby oil out of my backpack. He helped me turn on to my stomach, and gave me a massage. Couldn't tell you what happened after that, because I fell to sleep.

Escondido here I come

A couple of weeks, along with Thanksgiving had come and gone since I last saw Tyson. We were in the first week of December, with Christmas well on the horizon. What I had not realized in all my years of being a reserve firefighter, was how stressful this time of the year was. Not only on our guys but on the average citizens. Murder-suicides were always a part of our routine, but they were alarmingly high around Thanksgiving and Christmas. I had somehow escaped having to work Thanksgiving, which was I'm sure by pure coincidence with my being a rookie firefighter and all. But I'm sure I wouldn't be fortunate enough to be off for Christmas.

With all the mandatory overtime going on, I had finally saved a sizable down payment for a car. Tyson and I both were looking in the recyclers and the penny savers, for good running used cars. We both set up a few appointments to go see some in person. We had looked at cars off and on for about five days. Nothing. I was pretty much giving up on the whole concept of a used car. What's wrong with buying a new car, I thought to myself. My uncle Silky had always taught me, if I could afford to, always go with a new car. "When you buy a used car, you're only buying someone else's headache." He told me that a car could cause you to lose a job. "If you're not careful, you'll be busy breaking down, which will cause you to get to work late, and eventually miss work altogether. You're better off on the bus than fooling around with a used car." He said. And the way it was looking, I might just have to take his advice. After all, I could definitely afford a new car.

With Christmas just a couple of weeks away, stress levels were up, and tensions were very high. And right on schedule, every weekend, were the women. For those who didn't have any visitors at the station, they were out chasing and looking for them. Chores and equipment maintenance was falling way behind schedule. I was doing all I could to make sure that any repairs needed on any of the equipment I was assigned to was being maintained. If I could fix it, I fixed it. If I could clean it, I cleaned it. "Firefighter Brooks, report to the captain's office. Firefighter Brooks, report to the captain's office." What fresh hell could this be? When I went to the captain's office, he ordered me to wash all the dirty backboards in the back of the station. "Sir, cleaning backboards is the paramedic's responsibility." I said. "Well, today I'm making it your responsibility!" He exclaimed. "With those two out chasing women all week, I haven't only had to do my chores, but I've also had to do their chores. Which leaves me with more than my share of responsibilities. It's downright unfair." I said. "Stop everything you're doing, and go scrub down those backboards, and that's an order." He said. "Sir, yes sir." I replied.

Cleaning dirty backboards was a paramedic's responsibility. What generally happens is, being that we get lots of calls in the city of Compton. When we get to the hospital, and there's a patient on our backboard, we usually have to leave it at the hospital, so that we won't have to go out of service waiting around for our used backboard. Usually, by the end of the week, we will drive up to MLK to retrieve all of our dirty backboards, up to 7 or more at a time. Most of the times I would help the guys with this chore. And gladly so. It wasn't that big of a deal. Just that I knew these medics, I knew their character and that they didn't give a rat's ass about me or anyone else. One of them went out of his way to make my life a living hell. Now here it was the captain wanted me to do more of their chores, while they were out on a ho hunt. Being that I was a rookie firefighter, I had no choice. I had never been written up before, and I wasn't about to start now.

Not as a probationary firefighter. No other rookie, and there were 10 of us, was being treated nowhere near as badly as I was being treated. When I did have the chance to sit and talk with them, they were being treated like all the other guys. Which made them feel like part of a brotherhood. Me, of course not. It was worse than Loretta said. And I had two choices. Walk out, leaving an auspicious career behind, and them gleefully happy. Or, shut up and deal with it. Giving me more than my share of pain and misery.

The next morning, "Firefighter Brooks, report to the captain's office. Firefighter Brooks, report to the captain's office." When I got to the captain's office, "you've got mandatory overtime on engine 43. Get your stuff off of the engine. Your ride is waiting in the back to take you over to station three." Said the Captain. When I got in the department pick-up truck, there was an older veteran engineer I had worked with on a few occasions in the driver's seat. "Hey girl. It's good to see you. How are things going?" He asked. "As good as can be expected." I answered. "That doesn't sound very promising." He said. "How are you still around? Aren't all of you veterans on vacation by now?" I asked. "Oh don't worry. I'm leaving next week. And I won't see you guys again until about January 10th. By then these assholes would have burned all of the Christmas trees they plan to burn for the year." He said as I laughed. "Yeah, hopefully so." I said. "Let me give you some advice to make things a little easier for you since you're going to be working a lot of overtime." He said. The way our department overtime worked, was by sign-ups. If more than one person signed up for overtime, it went to the person with the most seniority. Unless someone who signed up had the least amount of overtimes worked that year. In that case, it will be given to the person who worked the least amount. But if no one signed up for overtime, then they had to mandatory the person with the least amount of seniority. Which was usually going to be a rookie firefighter. If there were no rookies, then the person with the least amount of seniority, would get the mandatory overtime. "Around this time of year, there are a few guys who might sign up, but the overwhelming majority want to be home with their families. So there's going to be a lot of mandatories." He said. He also explained that if I signed up, I would be allowed to choose where I wanted to work. Being that I never worked overtime, not only would I be the first one hired. I would also be the first one to choose the station and the equipment that I wanted to work on. Which in the long run, could make things a little easier. Where the hell was this information all this time?

When I got to station three, "Tailboard meeting in five minutes, tailboard meeting in five minutes." Said the station captain. I put my gear on the engine and gave it a brief once over. Being that the Tailboard meeting is in a couple of minutes, I was going to have to do a more thorough check after the meeting. We discussed issues from the prior shift as we usually do. Being that the guys didn't get to the lawns yesterday, we were going to have to play catch-up and cut them today. Translation, I was going to be the one struggling to get everything done. We were busy, so that meant we had to juggle between calls. Once I finally got outside to get started on the lawns, the edger had run out of twine. So my captain instructed me to do the best I could with what I had. I started at the very front of the station, being that it was what the public was going to see the most. By 5 o'clock that evening, I had finally gotten the chance to do most of the back. My captain instructed me to put the lawn mower away. "They will have to finish where you left off tomorrow. It's getting dark out here." He said.

The next morning, "firefighter Brooks to the captain's office. Firefighter Brooks to the captain's office." When I got there, my captain explained that I was going to have to remain at work until 2 o'clock. He said that one of our guys had an emergency and will be at work at about 2 o'clock. As badly as I needed the money, I was tired, and also needed a break from the politics. "Tailboard meeting in the engine room in 10 minutes." Like always, we started with issues about the last shift. And of course, everyone wanted to know why the lawns weren't done. One of our paramedics yelled, "Ask fire-fighter Brooks, she's been here two days, and got nothing done." "That's not true. I was at station one on Saturday. They reassigned me here yesterday, but we were busy. So, we did what we could." I answered. "And all you did was cut the front and only part of the back. That was pretty pathetic. Not only did you not finish cutting it, but you didn't even get around to edging."

Said another firefighter. "The edger was out of twine," I answered. "Excuses, excuses. Whatever. Thanks to you, we're going to have to work that much harder today." Said the paramedic. "Well in all fairness, this is not her regularly assigned station. And she did do the best she could yesterday." Said the station captain. "Whatever." Said the firefighter.

It was moments like this that made me want to haul off and whoop one of their asses! We all knew good and damn well that if I was one of the guys, meaning if I were a man like them, they wouldn't question anything I did. The guys seldom picked on the other rookie firefighters. And hardly ever pulled these stunts on each other. At least not with this kind of malice or vitriol. But since I was a girl, they took every opportunity to mess with me. People taking a whack at me when they were good and damn ready, was getting old fast!

Finally, 2 o'clock came. After briefing the other firefighter, I took my gear off the engine and drove the department pick-up truck back to station one. When I got there, Loretta and K-sue was in the parking lot talking. "Hey kid, how's it going?" Asked Loretta. "It looks like you've seen the devil himself." Said K-Sue. "Wish I would have. Probably would've had a much better time with him." I said as they started laughing. "I was just headed back to Escondido. Why don't you let me give you a ride home?" Said K-Sue. "Thanks, I can sure use one." I said.

On the way home, I filled her in on some of the things I was going through. She said as bad as everything was, she wasn't a bit surprised. She said the same as Loretta, and most of the women I had talked to. "This shit is thick and only going to get thicker as you move along in your career. Make sure you're well nourished, entertained, and more importantly, getting plenty of rest." She suggested. "How's your home life? Is that getting any better?" She asked. "My Home life can be just as stressful as work at times. Hell, sometimes worse." "You have to catch a break somewhere. You can't be under the gun 24/7 and expect to succeed in your line of work." She said. Again, I knew that. But for now, I was in a hell of a way.

As we pulled up to my mothers, we could hear people arguing from outside. And of course, it was my mother arguing with one of my brothers. We sat in the car talking for a few minutes.

She got out of the car and proceeded to help me with my gear. I thanked her for the ride and proceeded to get the rest of my things. "What the fuck! On second thought, go get your shit! You're coming home with me. We've been sitting here at least 15 minutes. And these people have been arguing since we've been here. At this rate, you'll be on top of City Hall in a clown suit with a rifle shootin at folks! Go get what you can. We'll bring you back on your next four-day to get the rest of your things." She said. You bet I did. And in a hurry. She didn't have to ask twice.

I went inside my mother's apartment and got a few select items, and all fire department related items including books. "Where are you headed to old gal?" Asked my brother Walt in a very low voice. "I'm moving to Escondido for a while." I answered. "Yeah, you need to get the hell out of here. Those two have been going at it since this morning." Said Walt. "Yeah, I can only imagine. Here's the number to where I'm moving. Here's the station number." I said. I wrote all the numbers to where I could be reached, and gave them to Walt. We took two big trash bags full of things I was taking and headed toward the door. My mother stopped arguing with Doc long enough to notice I was leaving. "Where you call yourself going?" She asked. "I'm moving to Escondido for a while. Just until I save enough money to get my own place." I answered. "You ain't gone have no blessings, you big booty applejack head bitch." She yelled as I was leaving.

We loaded the car as quickly as we could. "Was that you your mom was in there arguing with?" Asked K-Sue. "Hell Naw! She ain't about to get started with me either. I'm about to go up to the park." Said Walt. "It was good seeing you man. I'm gone have to pick you up and beat you at basketball sometimes." Said K-Sue. "You got it." Said Walt. "Well old boy, I'll visit you as much as I can." I said as we hugged each other. "You stay focused, and take care of yourself. I'm just happy to see you get out of here." He said.

Chapter 6

A NEW DAY

A New Day... Well, kind of

Several months had passed since the move to Escondido. It was a quiet and scenic environment. I woke up to birds chirping every morning and went to sleep to absolute quiet at nights. No sun up till sundown arguments. No gunshots in the distance. No wild police chases to dodge. No helicopters flying over, flashing their lights through your windows in the middle of the night. And since I had finally bought myself a new car, no more buses.

But of course, not everything in my life was going easy. My mother was always calling the house leaving nasty messages. And even though I had agreed to be in an exclusive relationship with Tyson, we never got to see each other. We lived two hours away from each other in good traffic. Plus, we worked totally different schedules. Then, of course, was the ongoing politics at the job. If it wasn't one thing, it was two.

"How are things going? What's up with you kid?" Asked K-sue. "Everything's OK I guess, I'm hanging in there." I answered. "If there was something wrong, you would tell me right?" She said. "Oh absolutely, yes I would talk to you if I needed to." I said. "What you reading?" She asked. "Just going over some notes. We got our half point exams tomorrow." I said. "I hear you've been acing it so far. That's really good; I'm proud of you kid. Keep up the good work." She said. "Thanks. I'm trying." I said. "You sure you don't want to talk to me about something? You seem down." "Naw, I can handle it. Thanks anyway." I said. "Well, I'm off to work. But I want you to remember something. No one does it alone. We all need a little help at times." She said. "You guys have helped me enough. It's time I start figuring things out for myself. Thanks anyway." I said. "All we're doing for you is what someone has already done for us. Even Loretta. I know the way you see it is; she was there all by herself. But that's not entirely true. She had a network of women put in place to talk to. Her mother, her sisters, cousins, friends, you name it. All there to support her. So did I. From where I'm standing, you don't talk to very many people about your job. At least not the politics of it all. That could be a good thing in some situations, or it could go against you. Only time will tell if it's going against you or not. But I don't want it to be too late by the time you figure it out." She said. She was right. My ass was being eaten alive by all the games these guys were playing. And I just did not know what to do. My back was against the wall. And it was time that I come out swinging. The only problem was, how was I supposed to hit back, without getting fired?

The next day, we took our exams. I felt very strongly about my results. When we left the classroom and went to the back of the station, the training team had three different stations of practical simulations set up. Ropes and knots, ladder raising, and the hose advance. The way it worked was, they gave us an allotted amount of time for each event. Then they took all the different times and numbered them from one through four, to see who had the fastest to the slowest time. As long as each firefighter did the event within the allotted amount of time, he or she would pass that particular event. The numbering from 1 to 4 was done purely out of sport. Just a way to measure you against your peers. We all did the events within the allotted amount of time, which meant we all passed our practical exams. But the way we measured against one another was completely different. When it came to ropes and knots, I had the fastest times. When it came to raising ladders, I came in third place. With the hose advancement, I came in dead last. Hey, not that it bothered me. I was a slow runner, and I knew it. I've been a slow runner ever since I can remember. The way I saw it was, different guys had different strengths, and weaknesses. As long as we're all good enough at the job to be paid.

A couple of days later, I was reassigned to headquarters, station one. As I was coming up the stairs, one of the firefighters slammed the door to the men's locker room. He was accusing me of what I presumed, of peaking at the guys while they were getting dressed. He complained to the station captain about my always going past the men's locker room. The problem was, there were only two ways to get to the firefighter's dormitories. We either had to take the front stairs going through the office in the lobby area. Or, go up the back stairs, which meant you had to pass the men's locker room. I must have walked past that locker room a million times by then, with absolutely no incidents. Only to have him accuse me of whatever he was accusing me of that morning. It just didn't make good sense. To me the logical answer to fixing that situation, was to keep the men's locker room door closed, instead of jamming it open as they usually did.

That situation was brought up at the tailboard meeting. The station captain told me to start walking up the front stairs coming from the front lobby, instead of using the back stairs like the rest of the firefighters used. "That's not a problem for me sir. But doesn't the Fire Chief want all firefighters to use the back stairs? I'm only asking because the last thing I want is to be written up for something as small as which set of stairs I'm using, to get to the females' dormitory." I said. "Don't worry about that. I'll make sure I clear things with the Fire Chief and everyone else involved. That way you shouldn't have any problems in the future using the front stairs." He said.

Well, I don't know what fire chief, working for what department he cleared things up with. Because when I came to work about a week later, I was called into the captain's office. "Firefighter Brooks. It has been brought to my attention that you have been coming to work using the front stairs coming from the lobby. Is this true?" Asked the on-duty captain. "Yes sir, it is. I was instructed about a week ago to start using the front stairs." I said. The problem in this moment was, this captain wasn't our regular captain. And had heard nothing about such arrangements. So I took a moment to fill him in on the events that had taken place last week. "That doesn't make any sense. Doesn't the men's locker room have a door? The last time I checked, it did. So why won't they simply close the door to the locker room. Instead of changing the policy to accommodate one firefighter. Or worst yet, having one firefighter follow some unwritten rule. Tell you what, I'm going to look into this. Something doesn't make sense." He said. "Yes sir." I said as I left the captain's office.

At 8 o'clock that night, "Firefighter Brooks to the Captain's office." When I got into the office, "have a seat. As it turns out, the Fire Chief knew absolutely nothing about the situation with the men's locker room. He also knew nothing about your being told to use the front stairs to come to the dormitories, instead of the back stairs like all the other firefighters. As a result of my talking to him, he told me to inform you to use whichever stairs you wanted to use. He also wanted me to make sure the guys always keep the doors to the men's locker rooms closed at all times. We will make sure this information is passed along department-wide. That way, there's no misunderstandings in the future." He said. "Thank you, sir. Sorry about any misunderstandings." I said. "No problem. It's not your fault. The left and right hands sometimes forget to wash each other." He said. Not that this entire incident was that big of a deal, to begin with. To me, the whole situation had been blown out of proportion. If someone was concerned about privacy, the door to the locker room should have been closed. End of discussion. But then again, why miss an opportunity to mess with "her." That was the issue. Take a bunch of little molehills and make big giant mountains every single time when my name was remotely involved. I had only been hired six and a half months. And this shit was old!

The following shift, the captains, had decided to time us putting on our gear. They told us to go to our engines, get our gear, and line up inspection style. I could see the captains and a couple of engineers in a corner in a huddle talking while we were lined up. As all the captains and engineers walked back over, Captain Grizzy lead the pack. "All right, here's what we're going to do. We will time you putting on your turn-out jackets, breathing apparatus, face mask, and helmets. We're not going to time you putting on your full gear." Yeah, I should be able to do this with no problem. I got this. "The way you are going to be graded is, the person coming in first place will get an A. Second-place will earn a B. The person coming in third place a C. And last place, unfortunately, will get a D. Each captain is holding a stop-watch: this is the only way we can time you simultaneously. When you are finished put your hand on the top of your head and yell, 'Time!'. To be fair, before we get started, we will allow you time to warm up. We've decided to give you two timed sections to practice, or warm up. Any questions? No questions, well let's get started." Captain Grizzy said, "On your marks, get set, go!" We all scrambled facemask, helmet, time. What the heck! I came in last.

We got all of our gear ready to go a second time for warm-ups. "On your mark, get set, go!" Got my breathing apparatus, my facemask, my helmet. Time. I came in last again. What in the world is going on? I know I'm faster than these guys! Just then, Chief Hemet walked over and said, "We're going to do this one more time. This time I am going to watch. As you were please." Captain Grizzy proceeded, "On your mark, get set, go!" Again, we all scrambled to put on our gear. And again, I was dead last. But this time, Chief Hemet, said, "I don't recall seeing anyone except Allison tighten their straps. Her face mask, and helmet. The rest of you," as he walked over to the other rookie firefighters and proceeded to knock their helmets off the tops of their heads, "Haven't tightened a damn thing. You're so eager to win that you're willing to cheat to do it. Firefighters don't cheat; they simply get better. Do I make myself clear?" "Sir, yes sir!" Chief Hemet looked over to the captains and engineers timing us and said, "Three of you will time the guys, and I will time Firefighter Brooks. Go ahead Grizzy." "On your marks, get set, go!" Grabbed my turn-out jacket, breathing apparatus, facemask, helmet. "Time!" Well wouldn't you know. This time I came in first. Not only did I come in first. I came in first by a landslide! "Well fellas," said Chief Hemet, "what did you get?" They all begin to give each other the times they had on their stopwatches. One gave a time of 28 seconds, another time of 22 seconds, the other one 24 seconds. "Let the record show." As chief Hemet showed the other guys my time. I came in at 19 seconds! "She didn't just beat them. She stuck a pike pole up their asses and hung them over a fire pit. Fellas, we can all give a lot more attention to details." "Sir, yes sir!" As he walked away. Boy are we in for a quiet night. As usual, the only firefighter who congratulated me was Firefighter Talley.

At about 11 o'clock that night, we got a three-alarm fire. Engines 41, 42, 43, truck 411, 441, LA County 105, Lynnwood 41, on and on and on. Structure fire on the corner of Alameda and Santa Fe. Multiple calls, flames showing. Downey dispatch only dispatched two alarms. Once we were there,

Chief Hemet declared it a third alarm fire and asked for additional equipment. We treated this fire as we would have any other fire. But I couldn't help but notice, during the salvage and overhaul phase, most of Compton's guys, were giving me the cold shoulder. Here we go: I beat them at something. Now I have to pay for it until they win again. And these were not fair one on one contest. It was always me against them. Not just a hand full of rookie Firefighters either, but half of the firefighters in Compton against one girl. A complete ambush! When we got back to the station, Captain Grizzy said he wanted to talk with me before I turn in. "Firefighter Brooks, to the captain's office." Here we go. "The reason I called you here, is I couldn't help but notice you seemed a little tired tonight on that fire." A little tired! What the hell does a little tired even look like for firefighters? "We also had a couple of your peers complain about the way you were carrying your latter." So what the hell were they doing? Standing around watching me while the rest of us put out the fire! "As one of your captains, it is my job to make sure that you're always at your best. It is also my job to make sure that you work in a safe, and professional manner at all times. Brooks, you're at the halfway point on your probationary year. So far your scores are coming in extremely low. You're going to have to make a complete U-turn, or we might not be able to keep you here with the Compton fire department. Do you have any questions? Ok. Apparently no questions. Do you have any comments or statements? Well if you don't have anything to say, that will be all, you're dismissed." I left the captain's office that night feeling completely defeated. After all the hard work I've put in, years of volunteering, this is what it's going to come down to. A bunch of insecure men, making false allegations.

As I drove home the next morning, I thought about every woman in the fire and police service that I had spoken to till that point. What was I going to do? Who was I going to call? It wasn't like I could pick up the phone and call just anybody. Only a few women sincerely get what I'm going through. Loretta used to say, "If it's lonely at the top, it's five times as lonely for girls at the top, and even more lonely for women in suppression." Most female cops, especially depending on how big the department is, usually have another woman nearby. As female Firefighters, when we look around the room, we're usually the only ones in the room. 90% of the times, not only did I have to represent for women, I had to represent for blacks and women.

I got to the house at about 10:30 that morning. When I got inside, there was K -Sue. Just the person I needed to talk to. If anyone would understand what I was going through it was her. "What's up, Rookie?" "Everything." "How are you coming along?" "I need to talk with you; you got a few minutes?" We sat at the dining room table as I told her about everything I was experiencing. She wasn't at all surprised. She was a bit agitated that it took me so long to have that conversation with her. But said now was as good a time as any. "Allison, I'm going to put it to you just like this. I want you to pay very close attention. What I'm about to say, I'll never repeat. First, let's deal with the easy part. You're not failing anything. These guys are trying to shake you up." "You think so?" "I know so. I'm very familiar with your training. I am very familiar with your test and timing scores. I'm also very familiar with the crazy bitch who helped train you. Come on Allison think about it. Why the hell is it that you always beat these guys when their timing you? Why do you think you always beat these guys when you're doing your drills? Because you are good at what you do! You tell me how the hell is it that you're only good when everybody's watching? But then according to some captains, you suck ass in fires!" "Come on; I'm listening." As I sat there thinking about what she was saying, truly digging and trying to find the answers to her questions, it finally hit me. I had what Oprah calls an A-Ha moment. There it was in front of me the whole damn time. "When we're doing skills test and drills. Everybody can see what everybody else is doing. So, if they try to say I failed something, then everyone will know that Captain lied. Which is why they continue to give me low marks in these fires. No one is hardly watching anyone because they're too busy working." "There it is, I knew you had it in you. Allison, you're doing just fine. What they're doing to you is wearing you down mentally, and psychologically. They are intentionally playing with your confidence. That way, they won't have to wash you out. You will eventually do it for them!" There it was as clear as a bell when she said it. I was so busy punching, that I forgot to bob, weave, and block. Any good fighter knows, you can throw all the punches you want. But if you allow yourself to get hit too many times because you're not blocking, you'll eventually get your ass knocked out! "Allison, you've been playing checkers with those guys. Well, I'm about to teach you how to play chess.

You and I both grew up in the hood. You know how we always say you can't bring a knife to a gun fight. Well, you're in a war. And while you're trying to make nice with them, they're shooting at you! Listen up. We're women, which makes us mentally more dominant. Why do you think Tupac said we get our name and our game from a woman? Because it's true: there is not a game on the planet that I have seen my father or brothers run, that I didn't see my mother or sisters run first. In the pimp game, who makes more money men or women?" "I don't know, I've never thought about it." I said. "The average madam makes 10 times more than a pimp. And here's why. Women know how other women think, for the most part. I say for the most part because women are very complicated. No two women think exactly alike. But men. Completely different animal! I don't give a damn how smart or dumb he is. Most of them are controlled by money or pussy, and sometimes both! So that's exactly what you are going to use to bring them to their knees.

You see the position that you're in as bad. I look at your position as unique. How many stations do you guys have in Compton?" "We have four." "And out of those four, how many are you and Loretta allowed to work out of?" "Only two." "From now on, when these guys mess with you, mess with them. For instance, when those hoes call the station looking for them, rock their world with a little something. Most of those guys are married right?" "Oh absolutely." "You know how they always tell other guys, to cover for them. And then other guys pass it along to you? What is it that they ask you to say again?" "They usually tell us, to tell their wives, that they're out on a run." "Of course they do. But you guys know, that's not the case. You guys know that's code for, I'm with some ho. The wife doesn't know about the ho, and the ho usually doesn't know about the wife. So start mixing up messages."

I should have thought about doing what she was saying a long time ago. I could have saved myself tons of trouble and sleepless nights. Only one question left. "How do I do this without them knowing it's me?" "And there lies the beauty. Those guys cannot stand one another. They only keep up that buddy-buddy facade to unite against us. They have so many enemies; they won't know where to start looking. Oh don't get me wrong, they'll know that every time they mess with Allison, something goes terribly wrong. They just won't be able to prove it's you causing it. Key the shit out of their cars, do it all. It's not like they're going to call home and tell their wives, honey I think my girlfriend keyed our car! Think about that. They will be so busy trying to figure out what's going on with their own pathetic lives, until they won't have time to mess with you anymore." "That's pretty brutal." "What? Don't have the stomach for it? Well maybe you have the stomach to move back into that shitty little apartment in Compton with your mother, after these guys finally figure out a way to get rid of you. Stop acting like you don't know the game and open a can of Compton Crip whoop ass on those motha fuckas! Your one brain is better than 5 of theirs put together. You're a very intelligent streetwise girl. But you better start using it before it's too late!"

She's right. And the good thing is, once I get these guys off my back, it's not like I'll have to go and start all over with a new batch. As she said, we only had four stations. But Loretta and I were only allowed to work at two. "The sooner you get started, the better. You only have five months of probation left. Call it, operation save your ass. By the way, keep this between you and me." "Thanks K-Sue, this is a lot." "The whole damn career is a lot. Look, me and you, we're different. Loretta has a tendency to be too patient at times. Especially when she knows she's settin a trap. That's the white half of her, and it works for her." Laughter. "You and I however, or not the let your ice cream melt while we eat our cake types. We like to eat our cake and ice cream at the same time. And ain't a damn thing wrong with that.

Those guys are kicking you for doing the same shit they do. When they win, they celebrate. When they're good at something, everybody knows about it. But when you win, or you're good at something, you have to hide it? What kind of shit is that? Why do you have to fall in the middle, or last, so they can feel like men? Listen Allison; they don't want us. And it's not because we're not good at what we do. Not only are we good, but in some cases, we're better than they are, which makes us a threat. And that's the part they can't handle. To hell with them. Be yourself. And keep being the winner you truly are."

After her advice and pep talk, I felt really good. I feel better than I've felt in months. That was all I needed. To simply be reminded that I was OK exactly the way I came. 'Operation save my ass', will go into effect starting tomorrow.

It's a Glasshouse after all

I went to bed thinking about everything K-sue said. Half of this was going to be fishing from a barrel. The other half, a little more complicated. All I needed to do now, was think about who I would get, and when I would get them.

The next morning when I got up, I felt rejuvenated. Like someone had literally removed a 50-pound barbell from around my neck. Once I was at work, I did things as I would usually do. I cleaned restrooms, I cleaned dormitories, I cleaned any and everything that the guys didn't get to. Everything was going according to schedule so far. No problems to speak of today. But that was part of the problem. Some days would be OK. Some days things would be bad. And other days worse. The problem I had was, I couldn't afford the luxury of thinking about how things were in that moment. I had to move along according to my plans. After all, the career I saved will be my own.

Of course, we received several phone calls for several guys while they were out of the station. So I had a little fun mixing messages. I couldn't believe these guys would actually call a number they weren't familiar with, and start a conversation with a complete stranger. They knew damn well that the woman they were on the phone with, had absolutely no ties to them. But it didn't seem to matter. And like K- Sue had suggested, 50% of them plain didn't give a damn about talking with someone else's girlfriend. It was truly the way my uncle Silky said it was, "hoes are for everybody!"

So far, things were moving along masterfully in that area. Since I noticed how well the mixing of messages was working, I continued to use that strategy for a while. Why switch bait if the fish are biting? "Hey man! Nancy told me your punk ass tried to talk to her last week. She called here looking for me, and you called her house trying to get at her." I could overhear two of the guys going at it; I just couldn't make out which two. "Man I don't know what the fuck you're talking about." "Man you know damn well what I'm talking about. And if you call her again, I'm gone call Valerie and tell her about all the shit you've been pulling." "Man, I wish you would call my wife over some ho." As the two of them started to get heated, guys began running from all over the station to break them up. Looks like things are moving along just fine in the mixed messages department. Oh well. Time to start mixing food.

About a week later, operation mix a dish went into effect. These guys would often bring leftovers from home to eat for lunch or dinner. The last thing another man wanted to see, was some guy eating the food that his wife had especially prepared for him. So quite naturally, I had to switch a couple of meals around. Heat a container full of food and set it on some guy's desk in his dorm. And shamefully, this also worked 50% of the times. "Hey man! I've been looking for that. That's my food. What the hell are you doing eating it?" "I don't know. When I walked into my dorm, it was just sitting here. So, I ate it." "It was just sitting there! Who the fuck do you think you are, Goldilocks?" Once I did that a few times, I had to move on to whatever was next.

A couple of weeks later, I didn't want to do anything drastic, such as key anyone's car. She was right; I didn't have the stomach for it. Plus, I was such a tomboy, I couldn't stand the sight of a scratch on a car. Let alone a nice car, which is what most of us drove. But I had plenty of fun doing other things. Like the time I took one of the guys shaving kits from the sink area and put it in one of the other guy's lockers. A couple of shifts later, he was walking through the dorm only to find the other guys locker open, with his shaving kit sitting right there for everyone to see. "What the hell are you doing with my shaving kit? You thieving ass perv!" A couple of months of this, off and on, was all I needed to get the wheels set in motion for those guys to turn on each other. They were so busy watching their backs from one another until they no longer had time to zero in on me. And there were about 60 of them, versus only one of me.

Months had come and gone. During the first week of August one of our captains announced at the tailboard meeting, "Our department currently has five open and pending sexual harassment lawsuits. And by the way, none of those have been filed by our girls. Go figure."

Say what you'd like. But no one should ever throw rocks in a glass house. No matter what sex or race they are. The situation around here was fragile at best. How else could I have executed such an easy takedown. And it was exactly as K-sue explained. By the time they were done messing with and pointing at each other. They simply had no time left to mess with me. As Loretta would say, "Checkmate, motha fuckas."

In the middle of August. K-sue along with some other family and friends had decided to get together to barbecue for Loretta's birthday. I went outside to tease her while she was working the grill. "Way to get rid of the evidence Detective." "What you know about that, firefighter? Loretta was telling me about some of the department's latest misfortunes. That's too bad, don't you think." We both laughed. "Indeed it is. Too bad it had to go to that." I said. "Now you know how to get a son of a bitch up off of you. Hopefully the next time they start you'll be on a level playing field. In fact, I know you will. Probation is over in the middle of September, right? So you're good to go kid." She said wow flipping a few patties. "Yeah, I'll be fine. You're right. The next time they get around to pulling my card, at least I will be in a position to fight back." I said. "Thanks again. I mean thanks for everything." "You got it kid." She said.

"Listen, I just put a deposit down on a nice little apartment." I told her. "Did you? Well congratulations. Where is it?" "It's on the border of Lakewood and Long Beach. Right down the street from the Lakewood Mall. Really good area. Just blocks away from the ocean." I explained. "That is a good area. Well good for you. When are you moving?" She asked. "September 1st." I answered. "Well, kid. It's been good having you. Just be careful and watch your back at all times. Always pay attention to your surroundings. Got it?" "Yeah, I got it." "And listen. Don't forget to pick up the phone and say hello from time to time." She said. " Always." I said as we gave each other a hug. "But for now, go grab those pans out of the kitchen and bring them out so I can get some of this meat off the grill." She said. "You got it detective." As I headed to the kitchen.

This move was going to be just as scary, as it was exciting. I had never lived alone. There were going to be lots of challenges. All of which I was up to. The first thing I had to do was furnish the place. I had saved quite a bit of money. But I didn't want to spend it all, not in one place. So, I made sure to furnish a little at a time, starting with my living room.

On September 1st, I met the manager of the apartment to get the keys to my unit. Since the utilities were already on, all I needed to do, was switch them over into my name. My furniture was scheduled to arrive on September 2nd. Now that I had a sofa, a love seat, and an entertainment unit, I went out shopping for a new TV. By the middle of September, which is when I was done furnishing my living room, it looked and felt like home.

On September 18, I was off work. But I also knew that I was no longer a probationary firefighter. September 20th, when I returned to work. The other probationary Firefighters were collecting money to throw a party. Didn't know for sure if I would be attending or not. But I gave my share of the expenses just the same.

It had been a while since I last went over to my mother's place. So I decided to swing by after work.

Chapter 7

WHERE THE GIRLS AT?

Where the girls at

I got off at 4:00 PM that Friday because of a work trade I had done for another firefighter. I wanted to go see my mother before I drove home. As I got out of the car, I could hear a bunch of guys in her apartment having a discussion. From the voices, my uncle Silky, my cousin Carlos, Walt, Doc and his buddy Deal were inside. They were in a discussion about women. My uncle Silky got pimp ways and tendencies, but he's not a pimp; well at least not for profit. My cousin Carlos is a Mexican guy with a thing for black women.

I stood outside my mothers' apartment for a couple of minutes to hear what they were talking about. How often do I get to be a fly on the wall anymore? "I'm just saying, that's why I only mess with black women. Most Hispanic women shape like boys with a teardrop butt. And don't let them have a baby on you. Then they're shaped like men. So they go from a small box to a big box!" Said Carlos. "I'm not saying that I disagree because I know sistas be having hella bodies. But they got messed up attitudes." Said Deal. "That's cause y'all be tryin to get with those rats!" Said Walt. "Yeah sistas be havin good looking bodies, I'll give them that. But sometimes man, their faces ain't all the way right." Said Doc. Some other guy that I didn't recognize chimed in and said, "That's what I'm sayin, Hispanic women, be havin OK faces, and fucked up bodies. Black woman be havin nice bodies and fucked up faces. You bump into those fives and sixes, but it's hard to find those seven, eight and nines." My uncle Silky said, "So we got a case of butta body, and butta face."

A butta body, is someone with a nice-looking face, but her body is not quite what you're looking for. A butta face, is someone with a good looking shapely body, but her face is not what you're looking for. Get it, butta body and butta face. That's one of the perks of being in a male-dominated family. You get a front row seat to how their minds work. Well sometimes.

What I knew about every one of those fools in there was, they would take any woman who would have them. I was laughing so hard they had to hear me out here, at least that's what I thought, so I went in.

Once inside, I saw another guy I'd never met. When they saw me walking through the front door, "Hey Alli, what's crackin?" Said Doc. "Hey niecey, long time, no hear, no see." Said my uncle Silky as he stood up to give me a hug. "Allison, how much money you got toward the freaknik?" Said Carlos. They all laughed. "The what what?" "They tryin to round up all the rats to have a broke version of freaknik." Said Walt. "Man, I know you playin." "No I ain't. See, I even made them a flyer. "Calling all rats, calling all rats. If you want to get drunk, take off your clothes, and get shot next weekend, then meet us at Willowbrook Park." Silky was very irritated, "See Walt that's the problem, you ain't got no vision." "Man I got plenty of vision. The problem is y'all ain't got no money."

As they started arguing, or a heated discussion, "Hi Allison my name is Bentley. Just call me Bent, that's what everybody else calls me." Carlos chimed in, "Bent, as in bent over broke. This nigga broker than all of us put together." Laughter. Bentley was properly named. Usually when someone gives you a luxurious name, they're funny looking. How many funny looking kids do you know whose parents named them after very attractive celebrities. It's not fair to that child. That's all I'm saying. Bentley was tall and handsome with long cornrows. Too thin for my taste. Besides, I prefer men to have short and neat hair-cuts. Much more professional looking. But he was a good-looking man. "Hi Bentley, nice to meet you."

I gravitated towards my uncle Silky as I usually did. We had a lot of catching up to do as usual. So that's what we did, spent hours talking about life, Music, and everything between. My mother was out with some guy she was seeing at the time. That was the best time to be at her place, when she wasn't there. At about 8 o'clock that evening Silky, Doc and Deal all jumped in my car, and we went to the liquor store. A bottle of Hennessy, a bottle of gin, a 2L bottle of Coke, and half a gallon of orange juice. That's what I bought. The fellas bought cigars and rolling papers.

When we got back to my moms, Walt was bumpin the music. Silky and I continued our conversation. "So, tell me more about this thing you guys are tryin to put together." "You know how it is niecey; we just want girls, girls, girls. We tryin to put somethin together up at the promenade in Long Beach." He said. "Up there at the park?" "Yeah that's the spot. Doc and Deal know this dude on the street team at 92.3 FM. If they can get him involved it should all come together like butt cheeks." "What all are you guys tryin to do?" "We want to put together something with a few lowriders, some barbecue, and a whole lot of women. We gone have a few rappers come through; it's looking pretty good so far." Sounds easy enough for you guys to mess up.

"But on a completely different note, how's the job coming along?" "It's coming along pretty good, I've got my work cut out. Mostly with the politics of it all." "I bet you do; those dudes are scared of you. They look at you and all they see is a threat. Them cats got plenty of groupies too; I know they do." "Yeah, plenty of groupies, whatever you want to call them. Most those women have absolutely no shame." He starts laughing. "What do you mean?" "A couple of our guys put on Santa Claus hats around Christmas time, so they could get women to sit in their laps and take pictures with them in front of the fire engine." Laughter. "Ain't nothing wrong with that." "Wasn't nothing wrong with that at all, until they wanted to sit in my lap and take pictures." Laughing his butt off. "Ain't nothing wrong with that either Niecey. It's like I always say, hoes are for everybody. Them hoes was just as interested in your wallet as they were in those guys wallets. Most hoes are equal opportunist. Go ahead and let those hoes do their damn jobs. Just don't give em no money." "It's just that I feel very uneasy when they start pulling those kinds of stunts." Laughing again. "That's because you don't know how to handle them. They are around you because they want your attention. Talk with them and listen to em so you can get comfortable around em. Women hold the key to life. The better you learn how to handle them, the better you will learn to navigate through life, you feel me?" That didn't make a lot of sense to me. In fact, it didn't make any sense. "I want you to come to this event we throwin in a couple weeks. I think it'll do you some good. Plus, I need somebody that I can trust to videotape it on my new camera." Oh good, sounds like my kind of place. "Just come hang out with us and kick back."

Here it is; freaknik California style. Or as Walt termed it, brokenik. Doc told me he needed a ride. So I met him at Deal's house. When I got there, Doc, Deal, and Bent were standing there with big Jackson five 2 x 2' Afros each. "See you guys decided to pay homage to Snoop. How am I supposed to see out of my windows?" I said. "We ain't got that far to go." said Doc.

The boys talked about who all they expected to be there. I was merely hoping that everything would turn out OK. No drama, no shooting, not even a catfight.

We drove deep into the park where it was being hosted. When we got back there, wow! This is a good turnout. There were about 300 people there. There were 15 lowriders parked to the side. Several barbecue pits going with hotdogs and hamburgers. They had a DJ on the stage. They even got a couple of well-known rappers to show. And as my uncle wanted, plenty of girls! There were about 60% girls there. Half-naked women all over the park. "Man, I can work with this." Said Deal. "Man, I think everybody can work with this." Said Doc. "I ain't gone lie; I had my doubts. Usually when y'all throw something, it's way too many nuts and not enough sluts. Y'all finally got this shit right." Said Bent. "Yeah, now let's just hope these fools act right." Said Doc. "They should; it's plenty of women here. I don't see why nobody would want to fuck this up." Said Deal. "Man, the only thing I could see breaking out is a couple of catfights. And anybody can live with that." Said Bent. Yes, we literally can live if there's a couple of girls fighting here and there. When dudes get into it, here come the guns. Followed by bullets. Then we all must duck and pray for the best. "Doc, pass out those cups and let's split this Hennessey before we get out." Said Deal. "Way ahead of you dawg." As he gave us all a plastic blue cup.

We were looking for different people we knew. We couldn't find Silky or Carlos. Just as I started talking to this underground rapper I knew, "Hey

Niecey!" It was my uncle, Silky. "We were lookin for you, where are you set up? " "I'm not set up yet. Carlos got the camera in his trunk. We'll take care of that later. I got a couple people I want you to meet." Oh no. Anyone who knows Silky knows that this can go one of two ways: Either he's going to introduce me to a potentate, then expect me to rap to them. Or introduce me to one, or multiple hood rats, then brag about how I'm a Firefighter. Right attitude, wrong plan. "Just go with the flow. Don't think just follow."

He walked me over to a group of girls. Two of them were dressed alike. They both had their breast nearly hanging out of their blouses, and half of their asses hanging out of the short pants they were wearing. "This is my niece, the one I was telling y'all about." Silky said to the girls. He didn't introduce me to them. They walked over; one grabbed one of my back pockets, the other one put her hand in my other pocket. As I put my arms around both girls. "Let's go. Try not to look constipated." He said to me. Even though I didn't know what was happening, it was clear to me that I wasn't in any danger. We walked over to a picnic table that had a big sign that said reserved taped to it. Once we got there, he told the girls to have a seat. "Peep game niecey." We walked about 15 feet from where the girls were sitting. "Kick back niecey. I need you to talk with these girls for a minute. Get to know them." "Why?" "You need to learn to relax around women. Especially woman you don't know. You do OK with the fellas. Its girls you cain't handle." To be honest, I'm not comfortable around anybody I don't know. And up until now, I didn't know that was a problem.

These girls were obviously high. They sat there very patiently, not saying a word. "What are your names?" "I'm Shaquita, and that's Shaquanda." Damn! Those names don't make no kind of sense! Do black people put any thought into what they name their kids? "I'm Allison." "We know who you are. Your uncle told us all about you." Said one of the girls. "Oh yeah, like what?" "Like that you're a firefighter. You're 23 years old. And you're a cool ass person to be around." The one who wasn't talking grab my left arm and put her head on my shoulder. And I was OK with it. I'm sure the Hennessey was doing its part. But I didn't want to get up and run. "So, tell me, what possessed you to want to be a firefighter?" So, I gave her the long version of what sparked my interest in pursuing such a career. When I finally shut my mouth, the girl on my left said, "I admire that. A lot of us don't know what the hell we want to do. But you're only 23 and doin the damn thang." I wanted to ask them their ages. But then again, I thought that would be rude. They didn't ask me my age. My uncle had volunteered that information. "So what do you girls do for a living?" "Nothin." That was open and shut.

Silky finally came back to where we were sitting to get me. "Come on niecey, I got some more people for you to meet." As I stood up to leave, "nice meeting you two." They both stood up to give me a hug. "Allison you got a good heart, don't change." Said the girl who was sitting to my left. We walked over to another group of people. He tried to introduce me to most of them. By this time the Hennessey had me completely relaxed. I didn't even try to talk to anybody. I just nodded my head and stood there buzzed.

My cousin Carlos got on stage, borrowed a microphone from the DJ, and said, "we're about to have a dance contest. Whoever can dance the freakiest, will win $300." Silky took some keys out of his pocket and said, "I need to get this camera right quick." As he went to the car, Doc and Deal came over to where I was.

Before I knew it, three girls were standing on stage ready to go. Silky gave me his camera and wanted me to get higher up so that I could get some good footage. So I stood on a nearby table. As we were getting ready to record, Carlos said, "We are going to have three prizes. First place $300, second place $200, and third place $100. Before they got the music going, there were at least 15 girls on that stage. "The butterfly ah oh that's old, let me see that pussy roll...pussy roll...pussy roll." It was the un-edited version of Tootsie Roll. Hang out with the boys, and you will learn what rap is really saying! As the girls on stage started dancing, the crowd got loud. They were going at it hard. One girl took off her blouse. Then to make sure she wasn't going to be outdone, one took off her blouse and bra! "How long do you think it will take until one of them is completely naked?" I asked

Doc and Deal. "Hopefully not much longer." Said Deal. "You know what the cold part is?" Said Doc. "Them Niggas ain't even got no prize money." "I know damn well you lying." "No I ain't." Laughing our asses off. When he said that, half the women up there had their blouses and bras off. "What are you guys gone do?" "See a bunch of free ass and titties, then deal with the consequences later." Armed with that information, I gave the camera to Doc, and got what we call the hell out of there! Now I know exactly why Walt didn't bother coming.

The day after brokenik

The next morning, I woke up at about 10 AM. I had decided to sleep over at my mothers' since she wasn't there. I was hungry and wanted to get something to eat, but not before telling Walt how things turned out at freaknik. Just then the phone rang, I stood there wondering if I should answer it or not. About five minutes later it rung again. Then about 10 minutes after that, it rung again. "Who the hell is that blowing up the phone?" Said Walt. "I don't know. I was just hoping it would stop." "Yes sir, tell me what happened down at that old freakynik." "They had a pretty good turnout." I told him about some of the people I met. The lowriders that were there. Free hotdogs and hamburgers, free water. Then I told him about the dance contest. First place, second place, and third place, with absolutely no prize money. "Yes lord, oh yes lord, how did that go?" "When they told me they didn't have any prize money, I gave Doc the camcorder and left. So I have no idea how everything ended." "Yes ma'am, so the end of this story is yet to be told."

The phone rang again. This time Walt answered it. "Hello." He immediately put it on speakerphone. It was Silky. "Hello Walt, put Doc on the phone man." "He ain't here." "Man stop playin and put him on the phone!" "Man, I already told you, he ain't here shit!" "Then where is he!" "Shid I don't know.

I thought he was with you." "Man, you ain't gone believe this shit! They had a dance contest. They lied and told them girls they was gone give them some prize money. When the Contest was over, Doc, Carlos, Deal, and Bent got in Carlos car and left me there!" We were laughing so hard, Walt had to put the phone on mute. "Punk motha fuckas! I had to call Pressure Man to come get me." "How come you didn't just get a ride with somebody who was already there?" "People got to fightin and runnin and shit. I didn't have time to ask for no ride. Walt fuck you wit all them damn questions! Come get me from Helen's house!" Walt hung up the phone. I was laughing so hard I could hardly contain myself. "That nigga tryin to get mad at me like I threw that shit! Man, every time they give somethin it backfires! Callin here like he surprised."

Walt and I were both hungry and agreed to go sit and have breakfast. Over breakfast, we laughed about some of the past events that the family had given that didn't go according to plan. In fact, a lot of barbecues, parties, and other family functions were plain laughable. But in the end, we always had a good time.

He also filled me in about the time he, Doc, and a few of their buddies got together to DJ for a function. They got about a fourth of their money before the event started. When the event was over, the clients didn't have the rest of their money. So, they packed their equipment and five guys into one van. One of their buddies had the wherewithal to shoot his way out of there, because he was angry about not being completely paid. Shoot they did! They fired two hand guns in the air as they were driving off! The only problem was, because of a faulty fuel pump, a few other problems the van had, not to mention all the weight it was carrying, the van only got up to about 10 miles an hour. So they had one hell of a time getting out of there. Then of course, most of the people at that event, knew who they were. Talk about a poorly executed plan. "Now you see why I don't mess around with them no more." Walt said, as I was laughing.

On the way back to my mother's place, we stopped over at a liquor store and picked up a bottle of Hennessy in case we wanted it for later. Once we got inside, the phone started ringing. "Don't answer it. We already know who that is." Said Walt. He was right; we knew it was one of the fellas, possibly Silky calling again. "Hello" "Hello Allison, Walt hung up the phone in my face! I need you to come get me from Helen's house." Yep, it was Silky. "I thought you would be back in Lancaster by now." I said as I sat on the couch. "Pressure man got a flat. He went over to his aunt's house in L.A. I walked over to Helen's." "All right, I'll be there to pick you up in a little."

Walt and I rolled over to Helen's place to get Silky. When we got there, he wanted us to give him a ride around the city before going back to my mother's place. By the time we made it back to my mothers', Doc and Carlos were there. We could hear the music as we walked up to the door. "So Silky, which one of those girls did you end up spending the night with?" Asked Carlos. "Helen." Said Walt as the rest of us laughed. "Man fuck y'all! Where is my camera?" Asked Silky. "Man, I gave that shit back to you yesterday at the park." Said Doc. "You didn't give me a damn thing." Said Silky. "Yes he did, then you sat it down on the table." Said Carlos. "Looka there! The camcorder still at the park filmin!" Said Walt. We all laughed. Except for Silky. He was pretty pissed off about the situation.

Later, we cracked open that bottle of Hennessy. We were all in a mellow mood for the most part. "Hey niecey, peep game." Said Silky. So I went over to the kitchen table where he was. "What did you think about yesterday?" He said as I sat down. What was I supposed to think? That wasn't my usual cup of tea. "What do you mean?" I asked. "Well, I know that wasn't quite the norm for you. So, I want to know what you thought?" He asked again. "It was different." I said as we started laughing. "I bet it was. But I wanted you to get around common everyday people for a change." He said while making himself a drink. Common everyday people don't start taking off their clothes the minute somebody starts waving invisible cash around. Maybe your average stripper would for literal cash. "It's been a while since we've thrown a good picnic." He said. Is that what they're calling them nowadays? Don't get me wrong. I'm hardly the one to judge anything that took place yesterday. I've taken my clothes off in some peculiar places. Well, never in public. Don't have the chutzpah. "What did you think about Shaquita and Shaquanda?" He asked. "What about them?" I asked. "They are a couple of working girls, tryin to get out the game, feel me". Working girls? They told me they didn't do shit. And I had cause to believe them. Apparently work meant something different to my uncle, than it did to me. So, I asked. "Working? What do you mean when you say working girls?" Silky answered, "They're hoes Niecey, paid authentic hoes." "Wow, hookers, prostitutes." I said in disbelieve. "Now you hear me." He said while taking a sip.

We got into a variety of interesting conversations, as we usually did. A lot of what he said was mind-blowing. For instance, he believes that men and women will never be equal. When I asked him why not, he simply said, "Women will never pay for sex. And they shouldn't. Why pay for somethin you can get for free? And never give away nothin you can sell. A good percentage of women have sex with attachment on the brain. While a certain percentage of men just want to bust a nut between something that looks good in the moment." "In other words, they don't know how to separate sex from love." I said. "Not all women have that issue. There's enough of them out there who damn well know the difference between a booty call and a one-night stand, from a relationship. They just ain't dumb enough to pay for that shit." He said. You damn right! And why the hell should we!

"Women try their damnedest to marry up. That way, they can lean on their husband's success. The smartest ones usually get their own shit." He said as he looked over at the microwave to see what time it was. It was getting late. Not that I had to work the next day. But I wanted to get home to sleep in my own bed a couple of days before having to go back to work. Walt and Silky decided to ride over to my place with me. To Long Beach we go.

Chapter 8

POLITICAL SCIENCE

Political science

Feels like I spent half the night explaining to my uncle why I wasn't doing more with music. Not only was I busy, I had to set a solid foundation for my career. Besides, music is a nasty business. This bitch doesn't play second fiddle to anybody or anything. Either she was up front and in the center of your life, or she wasn't in the room. Especially the area I wanted to focus on. I had taken some classes in recording engineering, the music business, and musical instrument data interface, better known as MIDI. With music, the more I learned, the more I needed to know. Most artist no matter who they are, have their recording sessions, then they go home. Most recording engineers, music producers, and others in management, eat sleep and live the industry. And since I already had a career, I needed to focus on it. The problem with me at the moment is, I don't have a life. All work and no play. Music is and always will be the love of my life. But for now, I have to let her go.

We spent the entire day watching and critiquing music videos. The three of us, Walt, Silky, and myself all liked Runaway by Janet Jackson. Somehow my uncle truly believed she was saying the one thing missing was him. Walt and I had a nice chuckle at that. "Well fellas, I have to work in the morning. So I need to turn in early tonight." I said as I headed to my bedroom. It was only about 8 PM when I went to bed. I made myself turn in between 8 and 9 PM after my four days off. It was always a lot harder to get up for work after being off four days in a row.

When I woke up the next morning, it was 5:30 on the nose. I usually didn't get up until 6 AM. But being that I had to take the fellas back to my mothers' before going to work, I had to get up a little earlier. To my surprise, they were both wide awake. "You guys are up early." I said. "By the time we decided to go to sleep, it was nearly 4:30 AM. So, we decided it would be easier to just stay woke." Said my uncle. I dropped the guys off at my mother's place and kept going.

When I got to work that morning, I had a message from Tyson. Since when does Tyson call me at work? That's right. We haven't spoken since I lived in Escondido. So he not only doesn't have my new number. He doesn't know I've gotten my own place since we've last spoken. I'll have to call him later this evening.

Our day was moving along at a pretty good pace. At about 10:00 AM, I was called into the captain's office. "You need to report to the fire Chief's office. Something about a special assignment." Said the captain. "Yes, sir." When I got into the Chief's office, there he was sitting with a big smile on his face. "Sir I was told to report to your office for an assignment." "Yes. You are going to escort one of our council members today. You will report to the Assistant Fire Chief's Office. He will assign you a company car and give you further instructions." Said the fire chief.

As it turned out, I spent most the day driving the Council member from city to city for various meetings. I met lots of interesting people. Mostly politicians from other cities. All asking pretty much the same questions, "Do I ever intend to run for office?" I had to ask a couple of them which office. It didn't matter which office or branch of government I would choose. They only wanted to know if I planned to go into politics at some point of my life. And my answer was always, absolutely not.

During the drive back to the city of Compton, the council member suggested that I at least explore the possibilities of going into politics. "Start by taking some classes in political science. You never know where it could take you. You're very charismatic. You're attentive to others needs. And you're an excellent public speaker. All qualities you would need to eventually run for office." Said the councilwoman. Oh, that's just wonderful. Yes. Go ahead and start taking political science classes on top of my already busy schedule. I was about to start taking captains classes, along with other career-oriented classes. The way I saw it was, my ass was spread thin enough. And I had no interest whatsoever in going into politics. "You're awfully quiet. Did I lose you?" Asked the councilwoman. "Just that I have no interest in politics. Besides, I need as many fire-related classes as possible. I'm enrolled starting next semester to start taking captains classes." I said. "For you, those classes will be a walk in the park. You can get through those classes in a year maybe two. When you're done with those classes, you'll have to sit idle to pick up another year on the department before you'll qualify to promote. During that time, it might be beneficial for you to go ahead and start taking some political science on the side. We need to move you through the ranks with the fire department as soon and as quickly as possible. Then you'll come across the street with us, and we'll get you ready for Washington." Said the council woman. "Just think about it kid. There's nothing those broad shoulders of yours can't handle." She insisted.

She gave me a lot to think about. At some point, I not only wanted my captains' classes out of the way. I wanted to get back into music. Even though it wasn't going to pay the bills, it was the great equalizer in my life. Music made everything somewhat normal in my world. And God knows I wasn't going to try to live without it.

At 8 o'clock that evening, I called Tyson. It's been a while since we last spoke. "Hello, how are you? Long time no hear from." I said as I was excited to hear his voice. "I called your friends in Escondido about three weeks ago. They told me you moved on September 1st." He had a lot of bass in his voice. "You know what you are Allison? You're a cold-hearted bitch!" He said. "What the hell is this all about?" "You could have at least called me and told me you had your own place and given me your new information!" "You do realize I just finished probation right after I moved. I've been extremely busy. Which is why I didn't want to get into a serious commitment in the first place. I'm not just sitting on my ass all day watching soap operas. There is no check in the mail for me." "Five minutes. All it would've taken is about five minutes for you to make that call. When we first got together, I told you I would take whatever the hell I could get. Whatever amount of time you had to spend with me, I would've taken it. That turned out to be absolutely none. Well, I'm not doing whatever the hell this is. Take care." He said as he hung up the phone.

There I was again. Same script, different cast. As I laid there in my bed trying to figure out what went wrong, it all boiled down to timing. This wasn't my first failed attempt at a relationship. And I'm sure it wouldn't be the last. I've had at least a couple of guys in the last few years say almost the same things, before breaking off the relationship; or as they say, "whatever the hell this is!" Tyson was right. It wouldn't have taken me any more than a few minutes to pick up the phone and say, "by the way, I've moved. Here's my new address and phone number." The problem was, I was clueless. Not only had I never been in a real relationship, simply put, I wasn't ready for one. Maybe Nikki was right. She said I should start off with something small, like a houseplant. And if I could manage to keep a plant alive for a couple of months, then move on to a pet. Then last, a man. I thought she was only kidding when she said that. Now that I think about it, she might be on to something.

"Engine 41, vehicle fire on Compton and 43rd." Oh well. It's just like the song my mom used to play called the entertainer says, "The curtain is up, and my audience is waiting out there. So walk out in style, and don't forget the smile. The show must go on, cause I'm the entertainer."

When we got there, not only was there a van on fire, someone had run into a power pole causing two wires to be down. Those bad boys were cutting through concrete like butter. There was no way in hell we were going to get that out! Not before calling Edison to deactivate those lines first. Normally it would have taken Edison anywhere from 45 minutes to an hour to respond to wires down. But by there being a fire burning that we needed to extinguish. They were there in about 10 minutes. Thank goodness for small favors.

The next morning. I was called into the fire Chief's office. "Good morning Firefighter Brooks. I heard things went well yesterday." He said. "Yes sir, I suppose they did." I responded. "As you know, the holiday season is upon us. I have various public safety awareness events, along with other speaking engagements I need you to attend." "No problem sir." "These should keep you busy clean through Thanksgiving." He said. Oh sure. And now that

I don't have a boyfriend, I'll have plenty of time to focus on Community awareness. "The way these events are set up: Some you will attend with Loretta. You will attend some with the on-duty engine company. Then there's a couple you will attend alone. Any questions?" "No not at the moment. I suppose I'll be filled in on the details as events arise, am I correct?" I asked. "You definitely will. In some instances, you will be expected to wear your class A dress blues. But for the most part, you will wear your regular uniform." He said. As I was leaving his office, he gave me a list of coming events. The first event was only one week away. It appeared to be an easy enough assignment. It was career day for a local high school.

The morning of the event, Loretta and I put together as much career-related information as possible. The biggest part of the assignment was speaking to a bunch of ninth graders. Of course, Loretta had decided to allow me to speak.

When we got on campus, we met with the assistant principal. She told us exactly how long we were to speak and told us the order in which we should go. Other than the fire department, there was a guy from a pest control company, some lady from California Edison was there, and 92.3 The Beats' street team was there.

The kids recognized a couple of the guys from the street team's morning crew and went wild! We had to go before seven different ninth grade classes. In the first session, the bug guy went first, then 92.3 the beat went second. The Edison lady went third, and the fire department spoke last. Right away, I recognized the order in which we were speaking, was not going to work. We had to do something fast. The kids did not pay attention to anyone after the radio personalities had spoken.

I immediately huddled with Loretta once we were done with the first session. "I'm sure you've heard the phrase, 'no one performs after Streisand'. Well, we're getting our asses Streisand by 92.3 The Beat. Unless we do something about the order in which we are speaking, those kids won't even notice we're here." "What the hell are you talking about? Who gives a shit? We're getting paid time and a half to put up with these little smart asses! They're not going to listen to anyone no matter what order we speak in!" She said. "Since you don't give a damn, then what I'll do is rearrange the order in which we're speaking. You and I both know these kids have a better chance of getting struck by lightning than they do of getting a job with the radio station, or any other facet of entertainment." I said. "What's your plan? What do you want to do? Let's hear it." "First I want you to pay attention to what happens in this next session. Once we're done, I'll speak with the others to make sure they're on board with changing our speaking order." I said. "That's fine by me." She said.

When we went into our second session, the exact same thing happened. They went wild over 92.3 The Beat and didn't notice anyone who said a thing after that. Once we left the room, "Side bar, can we talk for a minute? I noticed none of the kids are paying attention to anyone after 92.3 the beats' street team speaks. They're busy playing with their bumper stickers, T-shirts and whatever else you guys are giving them once you're done speaking. So how about this." I suggested that the bug man speaks first. Followed by the lady from California Edison. Then the fire department to go third. And 92.3 The Beat would speak last. The radio station loved that idea. They thought it was only logical. They noticed in the first session the kids stop listening after they were done speaking. I'm glad they were cool about it. "Thanks, guys. We were getting Streisand by you guys." I said as we all laughed.

When we did it the way I suggested, things worked out much better. The kids who were interested in the various companies once they were done speaking, asked a variety of questions about that company. There were lots of kids who were interested in becoming firefighters too. We also had the girls' undivided attention. I'm sure, the fact that we're girls had a lot to do with it as well. Normally, if girls didn't see women doing jobs that were traditionally done by men, they wouldn't bother showing up to those particular programs. By Loretta and I going out for career day, 3 out of 10 kids who showed up for the fire explores program the following month were girls. Normally, we were fortunate if 1 out of 20 were girls. Smart move by our fire chief for sending Loretta and I to speak after all.

By the way, 92.3 The Beat thanked me for that advice when we were done with that event. They said they were going to suggest that they speak last at all speaking engagements from now on. Yeah, it makes sense to me. Most kids won't eat their vegetables after you've given them ice cream and cake. And that's what the street team was in their eyes…dessert.

I'd been in my apartment now for just over two months. It was fully furnished, with black, white, and silver. I went with a black leather sofa, black leather love seat, black and silver entertainment center, and a black and silver 7-foot curio cabinet. This bad girl had five glass shelves with lighting inside. I used this to house my sports memorabilia which included a Magic Johnson rookie card, a Michael Jordan rookie card, a Larry Bird rookie card, and a Shaquille O'Neil rookie card. The pride and joy of that entire cabinet was my Mickey Mantle and Jackie Robinson rookie cards. Not that I was much of a baseball fan. But I knew who these guys were and what they meant to the sport. I put those two on the very top shelf. The only thing that I wanted for my living room now was a 50-gallon saltwater aquarium. My bedroom was white and silver. I had a second bedroom that I use for an office and a guest room. I had a desk and a futon in that room.

Being that it was early November, it was cold outside. Perfect lovemaking weather. Now all I needed was a lover. I had a black book full of men. But that didn't matter. I had to pull myself together and figure out what the hell I wanted. My career was pointed in the right direction. I even had a set goal for when I was going to start my music endeavors again. But my love life was in shambles. And thanks to my being pulled in five different directions, I didn't see anything promising on the horizon. Do I continue with these hit and runs? Should I zero in on one of the guys in my book? Or should I start over with someone entirely new? Obviously I have more questions than answers. So I'm calling timeout on my love life for now.

Just after 11:00 PM my phone started ringing. When I answered, it was my little cousin Shaunte calling me. Turns out that she, my cousin Charron, and their friend Kendra decided to go to a house party. Not only did they not like the party, but they didn't like most of the people there. So they wanted me to come pick them up from somewhere in Long Beach, to bring them back to my place.

There they were sitting at a bus stop, the three of them, dressed like TLC. "You guys are entirely too young to be out here in the streets this hour of the night. Forget you're too young, scratch that. No one should be out this late unless they have a very good running car. What the hell are you girls doing out here?" I asked. "Well, we're 18 years old, which means we're grown. So we can do whatever we want." Said Shaunte. When our office administrators would pick on me about my age, I get it. At that moment I completely understood what they meant. My cousins might as well have still been five and six years old. They were my little cousins. And they were just kids in my eyes. "2 1/2 of you are 18. Charron might be 17 by now. It doesn't matter to me how old you are. Try explaining to some nut that you're 18 years old! I don't want you girls out here this late anymore." I said. The three of them were very quiet. I highly doubt if it was because they were listening. If anything, they were just too tired and sleepy to argue.

November nonsense

It was cold outside, and enough already. I needed to at least talk to a man. So I looked through my book to choose someone I knew I didn't have to commit to. I decided to call this guy named Stacy. We met a few years ago when I was a casual longshoreman. Stacy was from the East Coast somewhere in New York. He moved here in the late 80s to get a job in the shipping industry. That eventually landed him a job as a longshoreman. Hopefully, his number is still good. I've always enjoyed talking to him. Our conversations were more sensual than they were sexual. And that was all I needed for now. Just some good conversation with the opposite sex. "Hello" "Hello is this Stacy?" "Yes this is he, who's calling please?" He said in a very curious voice. "It's me. Ambulance attendant turned longshoreman, turned security guard, turned firefighter." I said. "Allison. I thought this was you. What's going on girl? It's been a while since we talked." He said. "Yeah. It's been a while all right. I'm surprised you have the same number." "Yeah. I've had this number almost eight years. Why change it now?" "Yeah. I hear you. So what's new at the zoo?" "That's what I need to be asking you. You're the one making all the moves. We're stuck in square one trying to figure it all out. Solomon told me you were with the fire department now." "Oh yeah, who told him." "Probably Mike." "I don't talk with Mike or Solomon. You're the first person I've spoken to from down that way in months." "Well, you know how it is down here. These guys gossip worse than a bunch of 60-year-old women." He said. He was right. All those guys did was talk. If you want your business out there, tell one of them, and by the end of the day, everybody knew your life's story.

"When was the last time you visited the East Coast?" I asked. "Haven't been home in three years. I promise my mom's I would get up there for Christmas." "That's good. How long are you staying?" "I'll be up there for Christmas and New Year, so two weeks." He said. "Oh yeah. Do you guys do the Time Square thing? Or do you watch the ball drop on TV like everyone else." I asked. "Yeah. We usually watch it on TV. It's cold as hell. It's overly crowded. You can't get to the restrooms when you need to. It's wild. So native New Yorkers don't bother." He said. The same way native Californians didn't really do Hollywood. The only time we went, was usually when a relative from out of town wanted to visit the walk of fame, The Chinese Theater or whatever it was they wanted to see down there.

The two of us took a little time to catch up on things. "So I finally got a call from the ice queen." He said. "The what-what? Did you just call me an ice queen?" I asked. "Oh. You didn't know?" He said. "Didn't know what?" I responded. "That's what the fellas down there call you. The ice queen. They say you're stuck up." "I'm stuck up? How is that?" "According to them, you don't speak. You don't go to any company functions. The list goes on." He said. "Did you speak up for me? You know, at least jump in there and block on occasion?" I asked. "Of course I did. But those cats are going to say and believe whatever the hell they choose." "Which is exactly why I didn't have anything to do with them. You know how guys are. You hang out with them at a company function, then suddenly, word is, 'your fuckin'. So quite naturally, I stayed to myself." I said. "You did what you had to do to survive around there." "You damn right! It's always harder for we girls, than it is for you boys." Especially in male-dominated fields, which I always seemed to gravitate to. By the time I was 16, I learned that I couldn't sit still very long. So, I preferred jobs that required a certain amount of labor. That way I wasn't sitting around bored to death, watching the clock.

Stacy was cool. He was an exception to my not having anything to do with male coworkers. He wasn't the typical sitting around telling lies man on the job. The two of us went out for coffee a couple of times. No one ever found out about it, because he never told anyone about it. "Why was I so special?" He asked. "Just that you didn't talk. I never heard you bragging about your weekend with some girl." "You know them cats be making that shit up, right?" "Of course. But that's not the point. If they were hard up enough to make up stories about women, just imagine what they would do if they actually went out with one." I said. "You girls be up to no good too. You're just sneakier about yours." He said. "We do talk about sex. But we don't brag about it. And for the most part, we don't give names." Whenever I talked to any of my girlfriends about sex, it was usually a learning and teaching moment. More like an exchange of information. It wasn't done out of spite, or for bragging rights.

"You guys ain't got to brag about it hell, you're always gettin it. It's a normal part of you guys lives." He said. "Not always." I said. "The only time a woman ain't bonin on the regular, it's because she don't want to. Whatever the hell her reason is." He said. "Now you're startin to sound like my uncle. And I'm not saying you don't have a point." As he cut me off, "Hell yeah

I got a point. Why do you think these rappers are always dissing women? It's because they can't get no pussy! Flat out! When they become famous and get a little money, they finally start gettin some. You can tell when they start gettin it too. Cause their lyrics are less inflammatory towards women." "OK. You made your case. But I still say there's no excuse for bad behavior. And you're right, there are women who are out of line to. They may not be as bad. But I get where you're coming from." We had very interesting discussions, which was why I liked talking to him. It was getting late, and I had to get off the phone. But we agreed to call each other more often.

I was back to work on engine 43. And November nonsense was in full effect. Around this time of year, we started getting reports of stolen cars. And drugs being dumped randomly around the city. The game with the stolen cars was: Upper middle-class and rich people from different areas of California would pay professionals to steal their cars and bring them to the city of Compton. They would park the car, take the stereo out of the car, take any rims or valuables out of the car, and set the car on fire. A day or two later, report it as stolen. All to make it look as if some black gang members from Compton stole their car, then stripped it, and set it on fire. It was a cover-up that worked for several years. Always around this time of year so they could get a new car for Christmas with the insurance money. By the way. Compton fire department wasn't the only department having this problem. South-central Los Angeles, and other high crime areas were having these issues too. Poor and disenfranchised kids had enough to cope with in the inner cities. They didn't need a bunch of extras being put on them. But then again, greed has no boundaries. That saying also rang true for insurance companies. They were the ones who got tired of the same scams being run, and finally started doing their homework. Once they started paying their investigators to dig a little deeper. The game was over. They started arresting these so called white collared professionals for being the thieves they really are.

Last year I didn't have to work on Thanksgiving. But this year I got popped not only on Thanksgiving Day, but two days prior to, and the day before.

Thanksgiving was not a lonely hearts holiday. And if you didn't have any family or close friends, boy did you feel it. A day before Thanksgiving. We responded to two suicides. Both males over the age of 60. On Thanksgiving Day. We responded to four suicides. All males 50 and up. Not to mention our regular stroke and heart attack victims. Then of course, not to be out-done, are the drunks driving around on the streets. Combined, these things made for a tough 72 hours to get through. But we pulled it off as usual.

Chapter 9

GOOD RIDDANCE THANKSGIVING!

The day after Thanksgiving

What a shift. Who knew working Thanksgiving would be so difficult? Finally got a four day. I could use a bit of an uplift after the past week. "Firefighter Brooks pick up line 2, firefighter Brooks pick up line 2." When I picked up the phone, "hey old gal; what you up to this weekend?" She asked. "Stop tryin to sound like Walt," I said. It was my aunt calling to tell me about a party one of their buddies was throwing this weekend. I had never been to one of this parties. But I heard they were good parties. This was my opportunity to finally get a chance to go. She said it was going to be this Saturday from 9 o'clock until. Gotta love those. Until meant, until everybody went home, or passed out. "Yeah, count me in. I'll drive." I told her.

Saturday night at about 8 PM, my phone started ringing off the hook. And of course, it was a bunch of different relatives calling about the party. Some wanting to know what time it started, and others wanting to know where it was. Have to admit I'm pretty excited myself. Didn't get a chance to go out a lot. I spent the last six years working hard and chasing a career. Now that I finally passed probation, I intended to greatly reward myself.

We met up at my aunt's place. There was myself, and two of my aunts. The three of us road there together. We got there at about 10 o'clock. The place was packed. There were very few places to sit. Not that we were there to sit. We were there to dance and have a good time. But of course once tired of dancing, you need a good place to sit and talk. We noticed a table with about eight empty chairs around it. When we went over to have a seat, some 400-pound girl popped out of nowhere and said, "These seats are taken." "All of them?" I asked. "Yes all of them." She answered. It was something about the way she answered and her demeanor that completely pissed me off. So quite naturally I took one of the chairs anyway. "Hey, I just told you these seats were taken." She said in an even more nasty tone than before. "I know you're big as hell, but there's no way you could be sitting in all these seats at the same time." I said as I took another chair and put it where my two aunts were standing. One of my aunts gladly sat down, while the other one looked at me like I was crazy. She looked rather puzzled. So I explained, "There's about eight or nine chairs at that table and only one of her. If she wants these chairs back, then let her come get them, I wish she would." There's always some fat girl saving food and drinks, or tables and chairs. The designated loser of the group. And in this case, the designated loser of the imaginary group.

There were easily 250 people there that night. Some of whom I knew. Some associated me with one of my uncles, others associated me with one of my aunts. Only a couple of people knew me for who I was. Oh my god. Is that Alton? "Hi Allison, I haven't seen you in years." Alton was one of our fine ass neighbors we grew up with in Compton. Lived right down the street from my grandmothers' house. He was between four and six years older than me. And tonight I intended to find out just how much older he was. "I haven't seen you since I was in the eighth grade." I said. Damn, this dude is fine.

Most of the guys in his family looked good too. It's a DNA thing. "Yes, I remember. That's when your mom moved you to the other side of town, next to MLK hospital, right?" He said. "Yes, that's exactly right. So what have you been up to?" I asked. "Just trying to survive and put food on the table like everyone else." He responded. I started noticing boys right around my 11th birthday. By age 12, I had a huge crush on Alton. He was only second to the king of pop, Michael Jackson. "Yeah, I get that. How's your mom and the rest of the family?" I asked. "Allison, can we go outside and talk. I'm sure we'll find someplace a little more quiet." He said. "Sure, I don't have a problem with that," I said as we walked out to the main lobby. We took a stroll over to a seating area. It was much quieter out here. "This is much better. Now we can hear each other without yelling and repeating ourselves." He said. "How's your mom and the rest of the family? Haven't seen anybody in years." I said. "Everybody's OK; we've had a couple of deaths in the family. But we've been dealing with it pretty good, well at least as good as can be expected. How about your family, how is everybody?"

He asked. "Can't complain. Everybody's fine. Believe it or not, two of my aunts are here with me tonight." I said. "I thought I might have recognized a couple of your family members. Wasn't sure though." He said.

We took some time to catch up. We talked about everything from old neighbors to people we both knew in general. "Allison, I used to have the biggest crush on you." When he said that, I was shocked! Understand, that I was the biggest tomboy I knew. Not only that, I was always a chubby kid. And since we didn't have a lot, I seldomly had the latest fashions. "Really?" I said in disbelief. "Yes, but one of my uncles told me I was too old for you. And he was right. You were only in the seventh grade then." He said. And only 13 at the time. The thought of a boyfriend would have gotten me a foot in the ass! "You were only about 12 maybe 13. But you were very developed, and all I knew was I wanted a close-up." He said. "How old were you?" I asked. "I was a junior in high school, so 17." He answered. No use in shying up now. A minute ago, I was ready to whoop some girls' ass over a couple of chairs. But I choose now to tense up. Say something you idiot, speak! "Can I buy you a drink?" He asked. "Sure, in fact how about I buy you one?" I asked. "This one is on me. What can I get you?" He asked. "Gin and 7-Up." I answered.

We bought our drinks and headed back out to the lobby. "Alton, I liked you too." I told him. "Thanks for saying that." He said. "No really, I honestly think you're very handsome. Always have. Alton how old are you?" I asked. "I'm 28. I'll be 29 in February. Since you asked me my age, it's only fair that I get to ask you. How old are you?" He asked. "Just made 24 a couple of weeks ago," I answered. "Really, what day?" He asked. "November 8." I answered. "So I got you by nearly 5 years." He said. "Guess so." "So then I was definitely too old for you." "Back then, yes you were. But not now." I said. Ah oh, alcohol talking! Slow down! "I sure hope not." He said. He asked me what I did for a living. "Believe it or not, I'm a firefighter." I said. "No way! For what department?" He asked. "Right here in the city of Compton." I answered. "So you go in to burning buildings and everything? There's something dangerously sexy about that. A real-life Shero!" He said.

"Never heard it put quite like that, but I'll take it." We both laughed. We exchanged information. "Can I take you out for lunch or dinner in a couple of days?" He asked. Hell yeah you can. "Yes, I'd like that." I said. He slightly turned his head and kissed me on the cheek and gently on the lips. "That was 11 years overdue." He said.

We locked eyes and started kissing. Bet it won't be 11 years before we kiss again. "It's getting late; I need to go check on my aunts." I said. The truth was my aunts were more than capable of taking care of themselves. I just needed an excuse to get the hell out of there! My coochie has always had a mind of her own. And tonight was no exception. "Do you mind if I come with you and say hello to them?" He asked. And have my aunts in my business, absolutely not! "Well no, just give it about five minutes before you come over," I said.

As we went back inside, I went over toward my aunts, and he went in the opposite direction. There was a couple of family friends sitting with them. "Where have you been half the night?" Asked one of my aunts. "Somewhere minding my business." I said as we all laughed. "What about you guys? Hope you're having a good time." I said. "Oh yeah, we've been dancing, had ourselves a couple of drinks and everything." One of them answered. Just then, Alton walked over to speak to them. "Hello, I don't know if you guys remember me, but I'm Alton, how are you?" "Yes, we remember you." Said one of my aunts, as we all laughed. "So that's where you was all night, hanging out with Alton." One of my aunts said as they laughed and I started to blush. Well, I tried to hide that little tidbit. But of course, it didn't work.

We were there for about another hour before people started leaving. "Can I walk you to your car?" Asked Alton. "Sure, hold on." I said as I told my aunts that I would meet them at the car. We walked out to the lobby and started holding hands. "I'm glad I came tonight. Had to take off work to be here, but you made it worth my while." He said. When I got to my car, we gave each other another gentle kiss. "I have to work tomorrow afternoon, I get off tomorrow night at eight. Can I call you at about nine tomorrow night?" He asked. "That's fine." I said. Forget cloud nine, I was on cloud 11 or 12. To find out a boy that I had a crush on since I was 12 liked me too. Things were good, and getting better by the minute.

The next day, I couldn't wait to tell my cousins who I ran into at the party. Wait a minute, who was I supposed to tell. My cousins are too young to remember Alton. But I know who should remember him. Let me call Nikki. Nikki was one of my little cousins, second cousins. Over the years, we thought we were first cousins. As we grew older, we learned differently. But by then, we didn't care. We were thick as thieves. There's not a lot Nikki doesn't know about me, and not a lot I don't know about her. We did mostly everything together. Until she up and married some dude right after her 18th birthday. A big mistake we both knew she was making. Sometimes you have to let people do as they choose, then stand back and watch the whole thing unravel. "Hello, Smith residence." As she answered the phone. "Good afternoon." I said. "Who is this?" She asked. "We both know it's been a minute, but you ain't never had a friend like me." I said as she started screaming through the phone. "Oh shit, what the hell? Bitch what took you so long to call me?" She said very excitedly. "Wait a minute ho, last time I checked the phone worked two ways. Don't act like you can only receive incoming calls." I said as we both laughed. "Well shit, I lost your number." She said. "Well who's fault is that?" I said as we started laughing again.

"You know I miss your crazy ass. What have you been up to?" She asked. "Everything; since I've passed probation, I've had my ass into as much as I can get into. Remember old what's her name, discipline. Well, I told that bitch to go sit her ass down somewhere!" I said as we both laughed. "It's about time. I knew you would get tired of being the family mascot. Anybody would get sick of being the golden child. Most of us was out there tearing the city in half, while the closest you could get was nosebleed seats to watch the rest of us fuck up." She said. "Ain't that the truth." I said while laughing. "So you go right ahead and act as big a fool as you want. I'll co-sign that shit." We both laughed.

We caught up on a few things. Then I told her about the party last night. "Do you remember Alton, fine ass dude who used to live down the street from my grandmothers? There was a house with a bunch of men coming and going all the time." I said. "There were a few houses like that on Peach Street." She said. "That's true. But think about some of the finest dudes we grew up with. He went to Willowbrook, while we were at George Washington. Then I think he went to Centennial while we were at Willowbrook." I said. "Snap! Fine ass Alton. Carmel complexion, curly hair, hazel eyes, about 6 feet tall, and dimples that could stop traffic. Hell yeah I remember him! Girl, his whole family was good looking, and buff." She said. "Yeah, they used to keep all those weights in their garage and was lifting all the time." I said. "Guess what, I used to have the biggest crush on his Brother, what's his name again?" She asked. "I forget his real name, but we used to call him Dino." I answered. "Yeah, Dino. And their cousin James. Girl those were some fine ass dudes." She said.

"You ain't gone believe this." Finally got around to telling her about how I ran into Alton at the party last night. Gave her the jest of our conversation. Told her about our exchanging information. Then told her about that kiss. "Bitch, that kiss was 11 years overdue." She said. "That's what he said." I responded. "So when you gone tap that?" She asked. "As soon as possible." We laughed. "I'm still trying to wrap my mind around the fact that this dude actually liked me back then." I said. "Come on Allison, stop playing. You've been wearing a D cup ever since the six grade. You had a well-rounded Bubba licious booty. And big thick legs. Most of us still don't have what you had at 12 years old. Knock it off." She said. "Guess I never thought about it like that." I said. "That's because you didn't have anybody in your ear to school you like that." She said. She was right. I was so busy focusing on what I didn't have, I didn't know what I had. "Think about it. A 12- year-old running around Compton, with a body like yours. You did good that all those hounds did was drool from a distance!" She exclaimed. "Yeah, I hear you." I said. "Not trying to knock on your moms or nothing, because we both know my moms had some fucked-up parenting skills on her too. Just saying that we know God was watching you. That goes for me too. It didn't hurt to have all those uncles either." We both laughed. We talked quite a while before I finally hung up. That was the good thing about

Nikki; she never bit her tongue. She just said what she had to say, the way she felt it. She always had my back, and I've always had hers.

The closer it got to 9 o'clock, the giddier I felt. Then 9 o'clock came, no phone call. Then 9:15, still no call. Then finally at 9:30 the phone rang. When I answered, it was my mother. The last person on the planet I wanted to talk to. She went on as she usually did about a bunch of miscellaneous. She went on about nothing for about 20 minutes. Then finally I said, "Mama I got to use the bathroom, I'll talk to you tomorrow." "One more thing right quick." She said. Then she went on and on about the neighbors for another 20 minutes. "It's getting late. I have to use the bathroom, plus I have to work in the morning." I said. "I thought you said you were off work until Tuesday." She said. "No, they called me in to work overtime." I told her. "Oh, all right. Well it's getting late anyway so I guess I'll talk to you later." As she finally hung up. I didn't have to work until Tuesday as she said. But it took a lot to shake my mother.

It was about 10:30 when my phone rung. If it's my Mother again, I'll kill her. "Hello." "Hello Allison. I hope I'm not calling too late." It was Alton, and I was happy. "No, it's not too late. I don't have to work tomorrow. So I'm Ok." I said. "Just ticked off because I wanted to call you over an hour ago. By the time I got through wrestling my little brother for the phone, and attempting to recharge it, I got frustrated and went out and bought a regular old fashion phone with a cord." He said. "That was a lot." I said. "Not for the chance to talk to you again. I wanted to keep my promise, so I made sure I called you tonight. No matter how late it was." He said. I'm glad he did. When he didn't call just over an hour ago, I was starting to think the worst of him. Like we girls do sometimes. "Well thanks, I appreciate that." I said.

We stayed on the phone for hours, talking about absolutely nothing. But since neither of us wanted to hang up, there we were. "Which one of your little brothers did you say lived with you?" I asked. "The baby boy, Terrence. I don't know if you remembered him." He said. Not really. "There was five of you guys, right?" I asked. "Yeah, my oldest brother, myself, my little brother Dino, then there's Tracy, and Terrence, The youngest two." He said. "No, I don't think I remember Terrence." I said. "Yeah, he just turned 18 this past summer. I told my mom he could live with my cousin Jimmy and I for a little while. You know, just to give him a taste of what it's like to be on his own." He said. "That was nice of you guys. I think I remember Jimmy. Is his name James?" I asked. "Yes, that's him. We've been calling him Jimmy ever since he was about eight years old. You know how it is." He said. "When we were kids, it seemed like there was at least 15 people that lived in your grandmother's house with you guys." I said. "That sounds about right. There was a bunch of us coming and going. My grandmother's health was taking a turn for the worst. So, my mother gave up her place to go live with my grandma." "There was about 10 of us at my grandmother's house." I said. "Sometimes people just did what they had to do." He said. "Yeah, that's exactly what we did. Then in the summers, we would pick up 2 to 3 extra cousins from out of town." I said. "Damn we had some fun summers. Remember those water balloon fights. Red light, green light. Hide and go get it." We both started laughing. "If I ever found you, I would've tried to hit that. I wouldn't have given a damn about what any of my uncles had to say." He said. "I'm glad you didn't find me. Because I would've let you." I told him. "BS, no you wouldn't have." He said. "Yes I would have. All the monsters that felt me up, I think I would have gone all the way with you."

Oh, I meant that. When playing hide and go get it, the ugly dudes always found the girls. If Alton ever found me, who knows what the hell would have happened. Our community was full of guys. Some of them good-looking, some not so good. We had our share of fine ass brothers. Then of course, like with anything else in life, we had a few monsters blended in. Both male and female. On our street, there was usually between 10 and 14 guys that regularly hung out together. There was only about four of us girls that hung out with them. And one of them was only around in the summers to visit her grandmother. There were other girls on our street, just that they were older, and wasn't into what we were doing. Much the same with the older guys. In our crew, the guys were between 10 and 17 years of age. The girls, between 10 and 15. I was 11 when I started hanging out. But 12 when I met Alton.

When I looked over at the clock it was 2:08 AM. We had been on the phone nearly 4 hours. And it felt like an hour at best. "Girl, you got my head all messed up." He said. "Why you say that?" I asked. "Because, if I would have known I could have had somebody like you. Just saying I wish I knew that's all." He said. "It wasn't my fault. It wasn't like you tried to get with me and I shot you down. It was just that, we didn't match. 12 and 17, doesn't match. 15 and 17, now were cooking, depending on who it is." I said. "Yeah I know, it was just one of those things I guess, right place wrong timing. If we played hide and go get it in the future, and I find you, would you let me hit it?" He asked. "What you may or may not know is, the game is rigged. As I got older I learned, the more sophisticated girls told the boys they wanted to be with, exactly where they were so called hiding. So you wouldn't have to find me. I'd simply tell you where I'm going to be. And once you get there, yes, I would definitely let you hit it." I answered. "Damn girl!" He exclaimed. We made arrangements to call each other in a couple of days. It was 2:35 AM when I hung up the phone.

A couple days later

We had a very busy day today. It's about 8:30, and I'm winded. All I could do now is hope I don't get a fire tonight. As I flipped through the channels in the TV room, I ran across a music video I had never seen before. It was 'As I Lay Me Down,' by Sophie B. Hawkins. I had always liked the song but had never seen the video. Boy, do I love music. No matter how my day was going, music always made it better. I sat there in the TV room for an hour simply unwinding.

Just as I was about to head upstairs to the dormitory, my pager went off. Didn't quite recognize the number. But upon calling it, "Hello." It was a voice I didn't recognize. "Hello, did someone page Allison?" I said. "Hold on." Said the guy on the phone. "Hello, how are you." It was Alton. And of course, that head over hills 12-year-old girl showed up. "I'm fine, and you?" "Much better now that I'm talking to you." "What's wrong?" I asked. "Just had a rough day today, well a little worse than usual." He answered. "That's too bad," I said as another firefighter walked in. "Alton, let me call you back in about 10 minutes." I said. "Is everything OK?" He asked. "Its fine, I'll call you right back, bye." I hung up the phone and went upstairs. The last thing I wanted was some nosy fuck in my business. Misery loves its share of company. And unfortunately, a lot of our guys were plain and pure, miserable.

When I got upstairs, I realized I hadn't laid out my bedding. So I went ahead and of course took care of that. By the time I got everything set up and got into my sweats, I realized I didn't have a phone in my dorm. Hopefully, I can get the one in the dorm next door. The phone was sitting right there on the desk. It had a 50-foot cord, as we frequently had to share. "Hello Alton," as I sat on my bed. "That was the longest 10 minutes of my life." We both laughed. "I'm sorry. One thing leads to another around these parts. When I called you earlier, one of our guys walked in to where I was sitting. So I took the liberty of coming up to my dorm." I said. "Oh, I get it. Don't want them in yours." He said. "Damn right. So tell me about your day. What happened?" I said. "No. I want to hear about your day. You're the one with the interesting job. Not me." He said. "After a while, every job is just that, a job. You're right about things being interesting. I will admit, there are no two days alike around here. Sometimes a little too much excitement." I said. "Yeah, like what for instance." He asked. "Like for whatever reason, the fact that suicides, and murder-suicides skyrocketing around this time of year, eluded me." I answered. "That's news to me. Why would someone want to off themselves around Thanksgiving? Isn't that supposed to be a family holiday?" He asked. "That's what I thought. Of all the years I volunteered here, I've never worked Thanksgiving or Christmas. Last year was my first Christmas working as a firefighter. This year was my first Thanksgiving.

And apparently, it's a very lonely time of year for those who do not have a family. Or family who cares about them." I answered. "Wow, who knew." He said. "Yeah, tell me about it. Guess my family is so big, I didn't really think about people who either don't have family, or family who simply don't want to be bothered." I said. "Yeah, I know my family is huge. If anything, there's usually bickering and fighting about who's going to do what and where. But we're all always welcome." He said.

I went on to explain the different holidays and the patterns associated with them. I also explained the different times of the month and the patterns associated with those. As I was already tired, I could barely hold my eyes open. I had to end the call about 20 minutes in. "Alton, I hate to hang up so soon. But I need to get some rest. Just in case I get a fire tonight." I explained. "I can understand that. You want to be at your best." He said. "There's a choice I don't have. I always bring my A-game." I said. This time I made arrangements to call him back. I asked him what time does he prefer. He said anytime he's off work and can get to the phone, being that he had to share with his cousin, and often his little brother. "So how about tomorrow at 10?" I asked. "Tomorrow at 10 AM or PM? I'm off tomorrow." He said. "You are? So am I." I said. We had a brief but exciting moment of silence. "If you're off tomorrow, can I take you out to dinner?" He asked. "Let's do lunch. It will be my treat." He agreed. There was absolutely no way I was going out with that man tomorrow night; being that I had to work the very next day. We decided to meet up at 12:30 at one of my favorite spots in Long Beach. I hung up the phone and fell right to sleep.

The next morning, my alarm clock went off at exactly 7:00 A.M. Wow, can't believe we didn't get any runs after 8 o'clock last night. Is the city still here? Well, after all, it is almost a week after Thanksgiving and just a couple of days before the first of the month. We had to enjoy the quiet times as they came, although seldom they were. As usual, I put on my shoes and ran down to the engine room. When I got there, my relief was already checking the equipment. "Good morning," I said. "Yeah, what happened to this gauge on the breathing apparatus?" He asked. "Why, what's wrong with it?"

I asked. He showed me what appeared to be a broken and much stretched gauge on the shoulder strap of the breathing apparatus. "Did you check it yesterday?" He asked. "Of course I checked it. Not only did I check it, I used it yesterday on a car fire." I answered. "Well, it sure doesn't look that way. If you used this thing on a car fire, you apparently broke it and failed to tag it out of service. So I am not wasting any time on this issue. I've already reported it to your captain." He said. Just as he said that my captain walked into the engine room. "Now, what seems to be the problem?" Asked the Captain. "It's like I told you. The shoulder gauge on this breathing apparatus is broken. I don't want to start anything. I just want to get to the bottom of what happened." He said. The nerve of this bastard! If he wanted answers, all he had to do was speak to me about it. The same courtesy he would have extended to any other firefighter. But since it's me, let's start a bunch of mess, and pretend he comes in peace.

"What do you mean? She just used this thing on a car fire yesterday. When she put it back for reuse, there was nothing wrong with it. So I don't know what happened between the car fire yesterday, and this morning." Said the captain. "That's exactly what I said. I have no clue how this gauge got this way, but I can write it up and take it out of service. Not a problem." I said. My captain agreed with me, then proceeded to ask if there was anything else we needed. As he explained he had lots of paperwork to catch up on before leaving. "Yes, I have a problem with her either leaving equipment that should be taken out of service, or equipment missing altogether. And something needs to be done about it!" He said. This was news to me. "Listen up. If there were any past problems with firefighter Brooks and any equipment, this is my first time hearing about it. Second of all, we have protocols in place in the event of such incidents. These are very strong accusations you allege against your fellow firefighter. So, the question becomes, have you exercised any grievances against her for such actions in the past? Of course not. As I've stated, I have paperwork to finish. Good day firefighters." Said the captain as he left the engine room.

The captain most definitely had better things to do. He didn't even entertain the thought of this nonsense. Normally, I would be standing there at least 20 minutes trying to prove my innocence. I was glad things went in my favor for once. After all, his claims were completely baseless. Not to mention, my captain was absolutely right. We had more than enough guidelines in place for how to handle every situation that could possibly arise. In this situation, he should have come to me, pointed out any errors in any equipment, and given me the chance to correct it. If not corrected by the on-duty firefighter, then you should go to the on-duty engineer. He did neither. He went directly to our captain. Which should have also ticked off the engineer, unless he was in on it.

Since I was officially relieved, I took a shower, put on my clothes and got the hell out of there as quickly as I could. Once home, I called Loretta and filled her in on this morning's incident. "You are not going to believe this shit!" I said. "Oh...try me." She said. "This morning, as I walked into the engine room, my relief was already there doing his equipment check." I said. I continued to explain exactly what happened. When I finished telling her the story, she had an interesting explanation on what could have happened. "He may have very well broken the gauge himself. I wouldn't be surprised. Wouldn't be the first time we've seen or heard of such. You know damn well these guys have no limits to what they will do to get you in trouble." She said. She was right as usual. But this shit was old. And I was tired. I was about half-past tired. "Just stay on your toes as usual, and make sure like with everything else, you document it." She said. "Have you gotten your new calendars yet?" She asked. "No. Not yet." I answered. "I'll make sure we put you a couple to the side." She said. "Thanks." The one thing I could always depend on was Loretta's intuition and insight.

Time for me to set this morning's events to the side, as I had a lunch date in just a couple of hours. Wasn't going to wear anything fancy. I'm a T-shirt, jeans, and tennis shoe girl. Will be till I die. Makeup? For special events only. Purses? Only clutch bags, and also for special events. Perfume? Of course, all the time, no matter what. Used very little. To me, perfume, and colognes should only be smelled when you're in close proximity. For instance, when hugging the person or no more than a foot or two away. My mother taught me to never buy knock-off brands such as from a perfume gallery, a convenience store, or worse yet a gas station. "Go to Macy's, or other reputable department stores, and get the good stuff." I have terrible allergies; So, I have no choice but to follow her advice in this matter.

We met at the lighthouse in Long Beach. We were equally happy to see each other. We gave each other a nice embrace, followed by a smooth kiss on the lips. "Reservations?" Said the hostess. "Yes, for two under Allison." I responded. "Right this way please." She said as she took us to our booth. "This is a really nice place." Said Alton. "It's one of my favorites." I said. It was indeed a really nice place. It was right off the coast with perfect views of the ocean, the Queen Mary, the Spruce Goose and that spectacular light-house after which it was named. If you didn't have reservations this time of year, right after Thanksgiving and just before Christmas, you could for-get about eating here. True, California is a popular tourist destination. But most people just don't cook after Thanksgiving. Guess they're busy shop-ping for Christmas.

"Damn you look good in those jeans. Make a brother want to peel them off of you." Said Alton. That's right. I'm not stupid. Usually made sure those jeans fit just right, and sometimes a little tight. Got to give the boys some-thing to look at. Besides, what the T-shirt and tennis shoes lacked, the jeans more than made up for. "Thanks, you're looking good yourself." I said. "You don't live very far from here, right?" He asked. "No, I don't. I live right off the border of Lakewood and Long Beach. Just blocks away from the beach." I answered. "I don't live too far away myself. I Live right down the street from the Lakewood Mall." He said. "You work at Douglas right?" I said. "Yes, but they are talking mass layoffs in another year maybe two tops." He said. We talked for a while, then had a couple of martinis followed by a variety of dishes for lunch. We strolled along the pier, then finally walked onto the sand. We sat and talked for quite a while.

It was getting late and cold, so he walked me back to my car. "Would it be too much if I call you in a couple of hours, just to tuck you in?" He asked. "Since you asked so nicely," I said as we both laughed. "Yes, that'll be fine." We gave each other a very long passionate kiss, before driving in our separate directions.

When I got home, my phone was ringing. "Hello." "What's up playgirl?" It was Nikki. "Oh, I got your playgirl, where are you?" I asked. "Where I'm always at, home." She answered. "So how are things going between you and Alton? Have you seen him since Saturday?" She asked. "Your timing is impeccable. We just ended our lunch date. He's about to call me in a couple of hours." I said. "Hell yeah, that's how you do it. That'll work. What do you think of him so far?" She asked. "I don't know. Too early to determine. So far so good. But what you're really trying to ask, is when are we gone bone, right?" I said. "That's exactly what I'm asking?" She said as we both laughed. "As soon as possible, whenever that happens to be. I'm not in a big hurry though. We'll get there." I said. "What! You, not in a hurry? Come on Scorpio; we're always ready to fuck." She said. "Hold on. Take your finger off the trigger. I didn't say I wasn't ready to bone when the opportunity presents itself. I'm just not in a hurry. There's a difference." I said. "Opportunity, present itself. What kind of talk is that? You're not applying for a job. He's a man. You tell him you want to fuck. You guys go back to one of your places, and you get busy." She said. "You crazy as hell. As I said, we'll get there, eventually." I said. It took me a while to get her off the phone. Once I did, I packed my bag for work the next day and got ready for bed.

At 7 o'clock on the nose, my phone rung. It was my mother. Another person with impeccable timing, except I usually didn't want to talk to her. She usually called with a slew of problems. Usually about the neighbors. And usually, she was wrong as two left shoes. You would never hear me tell her that. If I did, it would take me weeks if not months to clear the air with her. Besides, the way I saw it, better them, then me. "Hello, Allison. You know Doc got his ass in jail, thanks to Walt." She said. I could tell

Walt, and my mother were in a very heated argument. "You act like I put him in there. You can't blame me for that shit!" Said Walt. From the sound of things, the two of them were hardly done with this kerfuffle. I listened for a couple of minutes, then I asked, "Mama. What is it that you needed me to do?" "You can start by having a little compassion." She said. "I'm sorry, my condolences. I'll get myself, and a couple of other guys started on a fundraiser first thing tomorrow morning for his release." I said. "You know what Allison, I'm tired of yo stanky ass!" She said as she hung up the phone. Good riddance! There's another situation. Not that I didn't care about my brother; just that he had a tendency of being in the wrong place, at the wrong time. And like always, it was someone else's fault; well at least according to my mother it was.

At about 7:25 the phone rang again. Hopefully, it's not my mother calling back with part two of, free her poor innocent son. "Hello." "Hello, Allison." Said Alton. "Oh thank goodness, it's you." I said. "Who were you expecting?" As he laughed. "Never mind. It's a long story. Nothing I care to get into." I said with a sigh of relief. "Not only do you have a very exciting career, but you also have an intriguing home life." He said. Not sure if I would term it intriguing. More like interesting. Just had my share of dealings with undiagnosed crazy people, aka, walking 51 50s. "It has its moments." I said. "Thanks again for today. It was different from most the dates I've been on. I really had a good time." He said. "Oh yeah, what are some of the things you're accustomed to doing on dates?" I asked. "The usual. Movie Theater, a bar, stuff like that." He answered. "What are some of the things you like to do? What are some of your hobbies?" I asked. "Don't really have any of those. Don't have a lot of time. What about you? What are some of the things you like doing?" He asked. "I have a bunch of hobbies: Music, I like building RC's, flying kites, and the occasional horseback riding. I'm all over the place with my interest." I answered. "You said you were into music? I assume you're talking about more than listening?" He asked. "Believe it or not I went to school to become a recording engineer." I said. "Really? that's different… Tell me about it." He said. "Thank goodness the fire department pick me up before I dove in too deep." I said. "What's wrong with music?

Sounds exciting to me." He said. "Indeed it is. Assuming you can make a career of it. The phrase starving artist was definitely coined by an artist. Probably one who found him or herself in near starving situations." We both laughed. "Girl, you are too much." He said.

We talked a couple of hours about a whole lot of nothing. That's the good thing about getting to know someone you like. You never get tired of talking to them. We made arrangements to go out again that following Wednesday. We had to get off the phone, it was getting late, and I had to work the next morning.

Chapter 10

IT'S BEGINNING TO LOOK
A LOT LIKE CRAP!

It's beginning to look
a lot like Crap

The next morning when I went to work, Christmas was on everyone's mind. The guys were discussing what their kids wanted, what their wives bought on Black Friday, and all the overtime they were going to need to work to pay for it. Most of our veteran firefighters, engineers, and captains alike, usually started their vacations right around December 15th, not to be seen again until January 5th at the soonest. My job was to remember to sign up for overtime. That way I could choose the stations and equipment, I wanted to work. Hopefully, that was something I wouldn't have to concern myself with for the next couple of weeks.

Being that it was the last day of the month, and it was a Thursday, I expected things to move a little slow. And they did for most of the shift. So I decided to repair any equipment that needed fixing. After all, tomorrow is Friday, December 1st, and we won't catch a break again until January 10th at the earliest. The way things went around this time of year was; Thanksgiving kicked off family fights, and sadly enough, murder-suicides. Those types of behaviors usually continued until a few days after Christmas. Then came December 31st, New Year's Eve. Which usually kick off drive-by shootings between rival gangs. Those usually didn't end until around the 3rd or 4th of January. Then of course, in the first week of January, was the Christmas tree burnings. Which usually didn't end until around January 10th.

By 8 o'clock that night, we had only gotten a couple of calls, so I went to my dorm and laid out my bedding. I also made sure the phone was in my dormitory on the desk, as I had made a promise to call Alton once he was off work that evening. Just after 9 o'clock, "engine 43, squad 441, traffic accident on the corner of Alondra and Willowbrook." When we got on scene, there was a car that had crashed into a telephone pole. It was bad. The entire front of the car looked like an accordion. There was a hole in the windshield, where someone's head had obviously gone through. The only issue was, there was no one in the car, or near the car. Whoever it was, had to be seriously injured. Talk about strange. Since we couldn't find anyone, we cleared the scene and went back to the station.

About 15 minutes after we got back to the station, "engine 43, squad 441, accident victim at a gas station on." When we got there, PD was on scene. This guy had a huge 7-inch laceration to the top of his head. It was gushing with blood. And he reeked of alcohol. "This is obviously our missing accident victim from earlier." I told my captain and the officer. "Sure the hell is. How in the world did this guy make it this far in this condition?" Said the captain. "In a word, alcohol! Said the officer. Liquor gives fools the added strength they need to do all kinds of dumb shit." Said the officer. "Yeah, but he will definitely feel this for weeks, if not months to come, assuming he survives." Said one of the paramedics. He was right. We have seen many drunks do remarkable things under the influence of alcohol. Once that liquor wore off, some of them was good as dead. Literally!

It was just after 10 o'clock by the time we got back to the station. I wasn't going to bother calling Alton until the next day, being that it was so late. That was at least until I looked at my pager and saw that he had called me twice. The last time being only 10 minutes ago. "Hello, Alton." I said. "Damn girl, what happened to 9 o'clock?" He asked. "Negro don't act like you forgot I was at work today." I said. "Oh I know. You guys apparently had your asses handed to you." He said. "Not really. We only had two calls up until a couple of hours ago." I said. "What happened on that last call?" He asked. "Some drunk ran into a telephone pole. Don't want to talk about it though. We have to see and do this shit all day. My job is the last thing I want to talk to you about. Hope that doesn't sound off cuff in any way." I said. "No. Actually that makes plenty of sense. It's not like people call 911 because they're having a good day and just want to say hi. I'm sure they're calling because they're experiencing an emergency and need you guys to help." He said. "Exactly. And when we get there. They are at their absolute worst. So imagine responding day in and day out, with no let-up, to various emergencies. The only person you want to talk to about any of this is your therapist. I tried to leave work at work, and home at home. Just works better for me that way." I said. Just then, "Engine 41, 42, 43, truck 411, squad 441, LA County 105, Lynnwood engine 41. Structure fire, multiple calls, flames showing." "Talk to you tomorrow." I said "Be careful. Talk to you tomorrow." He said.

When we got there, it was an abandoned hamburger stand. This place was a known homeless, and junky hang out. The parking lot was full of potholes, and by now, being that it was vacant so long, this place should be full of booby traps. And we soon discovered it was. Engine 41 was stuck behind a train, leaving engine 43 the first in Engine Company, which meant I was the first in firefighter. When we got there, my captain told me to do my thing. Normally, I would have pulled about 200 feet of 2 1/2 inch supply line. Being that this place was abandoned, not to mention I needed some flexibility, I pulled my 1 3/4 inch, 200-foot pre-connect line. This was more than sufficient for what I needed to do.

Since I was first in, I was at the tip of the nozzle. Once I was inside, a paramedic came in behind me. I thought he was going to back me. As it turned out, he attempted to take the hose away from me. He pulled the hose as hard as he could from behind me. When I felt this motion, I held on as tightly as I could. He pulled a second time even harder. So, I shut the water off, stood up, and rammed his ass out the front door and proceeded to fight the fire. Once the fire was out, he was extremely upset. "Are you crazy, what the fuck is wrong with you?" He said. "No asshole, what the fuck is wrong with you. I'm in front of the flames, at the tip of the nozzle, and you are trying to take away my only defense. Have you lost your raggedy ass mind!" I said. That's right. I was off of probation. Tired of being fucked with. And had enough whoop ass to go around twice.

"It's about time somebody put that turd in his place." Said firefighter Talley. From the looks and expressions, most of our guys agreed.

The next morning, my captain wanted to talk to me about the incident that had occurred last night. "Sure, as soon as you get that bastard down here we can talk. The days of me doing a bunch of he said she said is over. Get him here so we can handle this like grown folks, or I don't have a damn thing to say." I said. "Well, if anybody asks, I gave you a good talking to." He said. "Of course you did." I said as I left the captain's office.

"Firefighter Brooks, Report to the captain's office, firefighter Brooks report to the captain's office." Now what? When I got to the captain's office, "Pick up line one, it's the fire marshal." He said. "Firefighter Brooks speaking, how may I help you?" "Hi Allison, relax it's me, Colton. How soon can you get to station one?" He asked. "In about 20 minutes. Why, what's going on?" I asked. "They were about to mandatory you for engine 41. But I told the Fire Chief I needed you for something. I'll explain it to you when you get here." He said. "All right. I'll see you in a bit." I said. I took all of my things, put them in the trunk of my car, and drove down to station one. Whatever Colton needed, I'm sure it was a lot better than working an entire shift at station one. Today was Friday, December 1st. And let's face it. Every weekend was hell in the city of Compton. Now let's add the fact that it's the first of the month, right before Christmas. A triple disaster!

When I got to station one, "Thank goodness! You must be my relief." Said the on-duty firefighter. "Nope, I'm here for a completely different assignment. Sorry." I said. As much as I liked that firefighter, I liked myself a lot more. When I walked into the front office, there was a couple of office administrators, Fire Marshal Colton, and hazmat officer Chandler. "What's going on? You guys aren't even supposed to be here today." I said. "It's called playing catch up." Said Loretta. "Oh yeah? I thought catch up around this time of year was reserved for slackers. Ho chasing slackers at that." I said. "Well don't you have all the answers?" Said an administrator. As we all laughed. "Come here. I heard about what happened out there last night." Said Loretta. "Happened, what?" I said. "I know your ass. And you're a bad liar. Spill it." Said Loretta. So I told her my side of things as they happened last night. She laughed feverishly. "It's OK to defend yourself. But be careful. I don't want to hear about anything else like that." She said. "OK, so," I said as she interrupted. "You heard me. I made myself very clear. Now go see what Colton wants." Loretta was the one person I never argued with. Well at least not successfully. She was always getting my ass out of trouble. Even when it looked like I was headed in the wrong direction, she would put up roadblocks forcing me to turn around. By now she was so good at it, half the times, I didn't know she was doing it.

"Fire Marshal Colton, how are you sir?" I said as I walked into his office. "Just fine Brooks, how about yourself? How are you holding up out there?" He asked. "I'm doing OK sir." I answered. "Good. The reason I called you in this morning is, remember that strip mall that burned down a few weeks ago across from the airport?" He asked. "Yes, I remember it." I answered. "Well I need you to get some aerial shots of it. And when you're done with that, we need you to also get some pictures of all three of the high schools in the city." He said. "Sure, no problem. Anything for you guys." I said. "Wonderful. The pilot is waiting for you at the airport at helipad three. I will call and let them know you're on your way. Oh, Brooks. We got you four hours pay at time and a half. Thanks again for helping us out." He said. "No problem. Thanks for getting me out of being mandatoried on 41's." I said. We went into the safe and got the briefcase with the camera and telescopic lenses. "Here, take a couple of rolls of film. Make sure to remind the pilot to leave the door off your side of the chopper." He said. "Insurance doesn't want to pay huh?" I said. "Yeah. You know how it goes. They want to pay the absolute minimum if anything at all. That's why you need to make sure those pictures are spot on." He said. "You got it. See you in a bit." I said as I left for the airport.

When I got to the airport, the pilot had the chopper warmed up, and ready to go. "I'm assuming they've already briefed you on this assignment." I said. "Yes ma'am, about a week ago. So you assume correctly. Door off or on?" He asked. "Off. Thanks." I said. "Insurance doesn't want to pay huh?" He said as we laughed. "They should. But we want to be ready for the commissioner's office just in case." I said. When you've been around as long as some of us have, certain gaps start to feel themselves in, depending on how the situation is being handled.

It took us all of two hours to complete that assignment. Once we landed, I again thanked the pilot and headed back to station one. When I got back, I gave the camera to fire marshal Colton, thanked him again for everything, and headed home.

December Shuffle

When I got home, I worked on my calendar for the month of December. Being that we had a 72-hour rule for overtime, I played the game to my advantage. I highlighted all the days that I was going to sign up for over-time clean up till and past Christmas. Since I knew my shift had to work Christmas Day, there was no way I could get around working that day. So I strategically maneuvered my days to work to my benefit. We would just be coming back from a four day on the 25th, which meant that I had to work on the 25th, 27th, and 29th. Which gave me the 30th, and 31st of December off. Also, the 1st and 2nd of January off.

Just as I was planning my overtime sign-ups, the phone rang. "Hello." "Hey, old gal, what you doing?" It was my aunt. She was calling to tell me about another party their friend was giving for New Year's Eve. "Yeah, count me in. I just looked over my calendar for the month, and I'm off on the 31st. I'm glad you called, now I know to make sure to be off for the 31st." I said. "Make up your mind child. I thought you said you was off on the 31st." She said as we both laughed. "I am off; I just need to make sure they don't try to make me work overtime that night." I said. "Yeah... Make sure, because I don't want to have to go up there and punch somebody in the nose." As we both laughed again. "All right, let me get off of here so I can plan my schedule." I said. "All right old gal, see you soon." She said.

With a party on New Year's Eve in the mix, I really needed to plan my schedule. If most of our family guys wanted Christmas Eve, and Christmas day off to be with their families. The same was true as it applied to New Year's Eve, and New Year's Day for our single guys, which included myself. There I was, highlighter in hand, planning my days. Here it is: I would sign up for the 23rd and the 24th for overtime. Hopefully on truck 411. That way, I would only have to worry about fires and heavy rescues for a couple of days. Then I would return to my regular assignment on engine 43 come Christmas Day. Then, I'll sign up again for the 28th, which will give me 72 hours worked by the 30th. That way, even if they do make me stay on the 30th, they will have to let me go on the 31st. Perfect. Now that I've planned my work, all I needed to do was work my plan. The rest of the day was spent making sure that everything I needed for the next couple of weeks was put together.

At 7:30 the phone rang. "Hello." "Hi Allison, how are you?" It was Alton. "Hi. I'm good, how about yourself?" I said. "Just fine. How did your night turn out?" He asked. "Interesting at best. The last time I was on the phone with you I was dispatched to a fire." "Yes, I know. How did it go?" "It was OK. Just another day on-the-job." "Come on. You can be a little more specific than that." He said. "I could. But I don't want to." We both laughed. "That's not fair." He said. "What about you? How did your day go? By the way, how is it that you're calling me this early? Aren't you supposed to be at work?" I asked. "No. Remember I told you I work from 10 until 6 on Fridays." "Yes, you sure did." "You work tomorrow right?" "Yes, I do. Then I'll be on a four day until Wednesday. I go back to work on Thursday." I said. "Nice, that's what I like about you guys schedule. Ten days a month. I think I could learn to live with that." He said. "Yes. But don't forget its 10, 24-hour shifts a month. Well, could be 9 days, or 11 days, depending on how the days fall." I said.

"So, what are you doing?" He asked. "Other than talking to you, sittin here watching videos." "Oh yeah, what's on?" "Janet Jackson 24 play." I said. "That's a good one, a lot of thought went in to that." "Indeed. It was nicely done. Well planned. But then again, her work is usually different." "Would you like some company?" He asked. "Would love some company. But I can't. Have to work in the morning. I'm trying to be on my best behavior. December is a busy month for us." I said. "The entire month. That hurts." He said. Little does he know, it was going to hurt me more than him. But what was I supposed to do. I had to take every opportunity to rest. "So, when are we going to see each other again?" He asked. "As soon as our schedules line up again." I said. "Hopefully soon. Are you going to the dance? The one on New Year's Eve?" He asked. "Yeah, plan to. My aunt told me about it today. How about you, are you going?" I asked. "Yeah. Especially now that I know you're going. I'm gone make damn sure I'm there. Hopefully, we'll see each other before then though." He said. "Oh yeah, I don't see why not. What days are you off next week?" I asked. "I'm off next Tuesday, and Wednesday. Can we lock those days in?" He asked. "Let's do it. I'm supposed to be off both days. So, if I don't get any mandatory overtime, we'll hang out." I said. And like usual, we stayed on the phone a couple of hours before hanging up.

The next morning when I got to work, it was business as usual. Today was Saturday, so that meant we had to cut the lawns. Being that it was Saturday, December 2, that meant we were going to be extra busy, and have to make sure the lawns still got cut. The first call I got, was to assist PD with getting inside of a house. The neighbors called because they had not seen one of their neighbors in a couple of days. One person told us, she sees him going to work every morning, but had not seen him in the last couple of mornings. Another neighbor told us they get together every Friday night to play dominoes. But when they came over last night, his car was here, but he didn't answer the door. So quite naturally they were concerned. It didn't take a genius to figure out this was going to be more of a recovery effort, than a rescue. There was a bar door on the front of the house, with what appeared to be a two-way dead bolt. There were bars on most of the windows.

We walked around the house looking for other ways to get in. Finally, we discovered one of the windows that did not have a security bar. "We'll climb in through this window." I said to the officer who was with me. She had been with the Police Dept. just over a year. As I proceeded to walk back to the engine to grab a few tools to open the window, "where are you going?" Asked the officer. "To get some tools. You don't expect me to get it open with my bare hands, do you? Don't get me wrong, I could, but why should I." I said.

She followed me back to the engine and waited for me to put on my turnouts, then helped me carry a few select tools. As I reached for my breathing apparatus, "would you like to borrow a respirator?" I asked. She continued to stare at me and finally asked, "Why would I need a respirator?" Really! She hasn't been around long, I'll give her that. But this is the city of Compton. One year of service here, was the equivalency of 5 years served anywhere else. There was no way in hell, this was her first time having to break into someone's house to find them. But then again, maybe it was. So, I asked. "Is this your first recovery?" "My first what?" She asked. Just then, another officer I knew pulled up. "You guys haven't gone in yet?" She asked. "No. We just found a window with no bars. Got all of the tools I need. We are about to go in now. Care to join us?" I said. "No. I'll hang around and do my thing once you guys finish doing yours." She said. Just then, the officer who was with me initially held up my respirator and asked the other officer, "Why do I need this?" "Don't tell me this is your first recovery." She said as the other officer stared at her. There's that dumb ass look again. I said to myself. "Well, you got to get your cherry popped at some point." She said.

Once I got the window open. I could tell right away he was in there. So, I put on my breathing apparatus, and told the girl from PD to put on her respirator. The other officer told her what to look for once we were inside. "You have to find the keys to the front door. There appears to be a two way deadbolt on the bar door. So, you won't be able to simply go inside, unlock the door and walk right out, not without a key." She said. "I'll help her. You climb in first, you're the one with the gun." I told her. The window that we climbed through was his bedroom window. As we walked toward the living room, there he was in the middle of the living room floor. I could tell he had been there a couple of days. The officer reached for her respirator as if she was going to take it off. "Don't you dare!" I said as I reached around her head and covered the respirator with my hand. "As bad as things look, if you take this mask off, things will get ten times worse! I fucking guarantee you! Now let's find these keys and get the hell out of here!" I said. I opened the front door to let some light in. When I did that, wouldn't you know; the key to the deadbolt, was in the deadbolt. All we had to do was turn it, and let ourselves out.

When we got outside, I called the officer I went in with to a quiet little corner and talked with her. "You can take the respirator off now. You'll be all right. Apparently, you've never smelled a dead human before. It's bad enough we must carry countless images around with us, for God knows how long. If you would have succeeded in taking that respirator off inside the house, not only would you see his body for weeks, you would smell that odor for weeks." I said. "Thanks. Thanks for everything." She said. The other officer walked over and asked, "How did she do?" "As good as can be expected for her first body recovery." I said. "That bad huh?" She responded. "Let's get together over coffee one morning, or whatever you girls pleasure." I said. "You got it." She said. "Keep an eye on her; she's going to be sick." I said as I walked back to the engine.

We often found ourselves in very nasty situations. And the sad thing was, often the guys wouldn't back you. If there was no other female around, you were on your own. Now true, they could make the argument that what we did was a one-man job. Usually, only one officer was supposed to climb in, after the fire department open the door or window for them. Now ask me how many times I have seen one of the guys go in alone. Usually, there's three and four of them going in to recover a body. If I wasn't there to open the window for her, then assist her once she was inside, things would have gone entirely different. Once the fire department opened the window, she would have been on her own. Forget a respirator. Forget any detailed instructions. They would have allowed her to go in, discover that man's body, puke all over the place, then hazed and put her down for months. Just as those guys had each other's backs, I made sure to look out for the hand full of girls that was around. And made sure they were smart enough to have each other's backs.

When we got back to the station, I could see no one had gotten started on the lawns. The squad was there, which meant both the firefighter/ paramedics were there. The truck was there, which meant the truck firefighter was there. Never the less, no one was doing any yard work. So I got the lawnmower, gassed it up, and got started in the front. But let's face it, the 911 calls were not going to stop because I was cutting the lawns. Like always, we had to work it out the best way we could.

After running calls all day, and trying to get the lawns done by myself, it was 6 o'clock when I finally finished cutting the grass. No one had bothered to help, which meant none of the edgings was done, none of the weeds were pulled, and none of the bushes were trimmed. And all I know is, I wish a motha fucka would get in my face, about what all I didn't get done by myself! The next morning at 7:30, I was called down to the captain's office. "You're being mandatory on truck 411 today. So get your things off of 43, and put them on the truck." Said the captain. "Yes, sir." I said. The mandatory overtime had started early this year. How in the world could I have possibly ended up on the truck without signing up for the truck? Whatever went wrong, I'll take it.

We had our morning meeting in the TV room, instead of the engine room. When the station captain told us about the situation with the lawns, one of the firefighters automatically started complaining. To my surprise, one of the paramedics asked me what went wrong. "I'm not sure. But I'll tell you this. I did what I could. We had lots of calls as I'm sure you guys can imagine. By the time I was done mowing the grass, I didn't have any daylight left to do anything else." I said. "So in a nutshell, she was out there trying to do all the yard work by herself. And of course she couldn't get it all done, not by herself. Hell, wonder woman couldn't get all that done." He said. "All I know is, let those motha fuckas pull this shit again next week, and see what happens!" Said one of our veteran engineers. "We have already been down this road with Loretta. These bastards would leave her out there to do the yards by herself. Then of course, when she couldn't finish it by herself, they would try to place all the blame on her, instead of getting their asses out there to help her like they were supposed to." Said one of our captains. "The last time I checked, everybody, Captain all the way on down to fire explore, is supposed to help with lawn detail, at every station, every Saturday." Said the other paramedic. "Sounds like what needs to happen to me is, you guys need to remind your peers, that whenever they leave these girls hanging, to do the yards by themselves, all in the name of messing with them, they're messing with everybody. Because we all have to get out there the following Sunday, to play catch up on something they didn't do. So not only is that shit old, it's over. Starting now!" Said the veteran engineer.

Hell yeah! It's about time. I did not expect things to go that way at all. Not in a million years. It's not as if they're just figuring this out. They were pulling this stuff on Loretta long before I got here. They can't get to her anymore because she's in hazmat, tucked away from most of their bullshit. That meant I had to pay for both of us. Looks like they weren't going to be able to use the lawns against me anymore. So, let's see what other sadistic shit they would pull.

Next on the docket was, what are we going to have for dinner tonight? "It's a Sunday; it's cold outside, why don't we cook soul food." Said the station captain. "Man stop trying to be slick. You just know that Allison's here and you want her to cook." Said one of our medics. "You damn right. What's wrong with that? By the way, will you throw in a peach cobbler for dessert?" Said the station captain, as we all laughed. Being that they took a stand for me earlier, the least I could do was cook. We decided to make red beans with oxtails, collard greens, cornbread, baked chicken and peach cobbler for dessert. As we were working out the details for dinner, the phone rang. One of our firefighter/paramedic's answered it. "Excuse me, captain, this is the captain from station one on the phone. He says that there was a mix-up, and the firefighter at station one is supposed to be on the truck." So that's what happened. I knew something was wrong. I didn't sign up for overtime. And you never get put on the truck unless it's your regular assignment. Or if they needed to hire someone for overtime, who signed up to be on it. Oh well, station one here I come. "Unless whoever it is down at station one can make a peach cobbler, they can keep his ass right where he is." Said the station captain, as the rest of the guys laughed.

Looks like I was staying on the truck after all. In that moment, I was thankful for two things. One, that I had agreed to cook. And two, I knew how to make peach cobbler.

Chapter 11

DECEMBER MADNESS

Just get through December

We had a decent shift yesterday. We had a structure fire just after 2 o'clock this morning. The fire kept us out of the station until about 6:30 this morning. The senior engineer said, "You can expect a big fire after a big meal." Especially if some idiot leaves Christmas lights on his house for three consecutive years, never checking for blown fuses, to suddenly plug those puppies up and have embers from the arching wires set the insulation inside your roof on fire. Now that combined with a big meal, makes for a big fire.

As I was briefing who I thought was my relief so that I could go home, "Firefighter Brooks report to the captain's office. Firefighter Brooks report to the captain's office." When I got there, "You're being mandatory for engine 41. Get your things and report to station one for duty." Said the captain. "Yes sir." I said as I left.

The thing about station one, was although it was busy I had the girls. Office administrators and Loretta in hazmat to talk with to help offset things. At least I had them until 6 PM. After that I was on my own again.

We had a couple of calls before having to go to station three to pick up a few things. When we got there, the captain on engine 43 came out and told me to go upstairs and clean the kitchen. Not only was I baffled, but my entire engine company was also puzzled. "That's right, you heard me. You guys left a dirty kitchen up there last night!" He said. "No, I didn't leave a dirty anything. I was the cook. Cooks are not supposed to help clean the kitchen." I said. "What's going on?" Asked my captain. "The firefighters from the last shift left a dirty kitchen last night. My guys don't think it's fair for them to have to clean it. So she needs to get up there and get the kitchen cleaned." Said the captain on 43. "But if she was the cook, we all know that cooks are not supposed to clean." Said my captain. "Well that's too bad. She's the only one still here from the last shift. So it falls on her before my guys should have to do it!" He said. "Just go and take care of it Allison. We don't want any trouble." Said my captain. "Yes sir. I'm on it." I said.

When I got up to the kitchen, the firefighter from engine 43 who was on duty last night, and the reserve firefighter from Squad 443, were both still there. If anybody should have been doing the kitchen it should have been the two of them. Being that not only was I the cook, I had more seniority than them. The reserve firefighter doesn't have a leg to stand on when it comes to kitchen duty. The fire reserves know that the kitchen is their responsibility no matter what. I spent five years proudly doing the kitchen as a volunteer firefighter. When we were going back to the engine to leave the station, I noticed the two guys in question in the engine room sitting around laughing. They set me up; and was getting away with it unless I said something. So I told my captain about them being there last night, and the two of them being on duty now. He simply said, "Don't worry about it. You've already taken care of it. So let's go." If I was one of the guys, instead of a girl, you bet things would have been handled much differently. Not only was I tired of rolling over and playing dead, I was sick of everyone else treating me like I didn't matter.

As soon as I got back to station one, I told Loretta exactly what transpired. "Oh really. Who was your captain last night?" She asked. So I told her not only who the truck captain was, but also who the captain on engine 43 was. "Give me a minute. I'll be back in about 30 minutes." She said. We both walked out of the female dormitory. Loretta heading back to her office, me heading to the engine room.

We were dispatched to a slip and fall in a grocery market down the street. By the time I got back to the station, Loretta was ready to talk with me. "Guess what. Those guys are in serious trouble! Your truck captain from last night just happened to have been assigned to engine 42 for overtime today. He said, before he left this morning he instructed the firefighter and the reserve firefighter to clean the kitchen. He also told me that squad 443 was dispatched to a heart attack last night while they were in the middle of cleaning the kitchen. Since they knew it was going to take a while to return to the station, they left the reserve firefighter behind to help the firefighter on engine 43 complete the kitchen. Apparently when the medics left the station, the two of them did nothing. So when you guys got back from that fire this morning, the captain ordered the two of them to clean the kitchen. He also told them once they were done, that the reserve firefighter was to report to station one to work on squad 441. Not only did the two of them not bother cleaning the kitchen. The reserve is obviously hanging out at station three, riding along with his buddy on engine 43, instead of doing what he was told." She said. "The shit you find out once you open your mouth." I said. "Exactly. Also keep in mind stress levels are always higher around this time of year. Look; just do your best, and get through December." She said.

The two of them were in serious trouble. Little did they know that our station captain from last night would be at work today. As a result of their insubordination, the firefighter on engine 43 received a written warning. The reserve firefighter was suspended from the program indefinitely! Not only was he being insubordinate by not cleaning the kitchen. More importantly, he didn't show for his original assignment for today. Which caused him to be AWOL. Since he had been written up previously, once this calendar year, and AWOL twice this calendar year; the department was no longer interested in keeping him as a part of its volunteer firefighting program. The truck captain from last night, called the captain assigned to engine 43 for today, and told him exactly what was to happen with those two guys. Justice was swift this time. And I needed it to be. I felt very bad about how I was treated earlier. To be kicked or messed with once in a while was to be expected. But someone constantly yanking my chain was starting to weigh me down. And now, some of them had the nerves to get the reserve firefighters in on the act.

That reserve firefighter had some chutzpah. Written up this calendar year, not to mention the write up he would have received today. AWOL twice this year, not including today. In my five years as a volunteer, never was I once written up. And AWOL! I wouldn't dream of being AWOL. If I did, I would wake up and apologize to my superiors. There's usually enough politics to go around. But as a volunteer, hell as a firefighter period, you try not to get involved. Yeah, he was asking for it all right. And today, he got it.

Later I got a chance to talk with Alton. Being that I was coming off a 72-hour stretch only to be off one day, then come right back for 48 hours, I wasn't sure about our plans. "Can I at least come over and cook for you tomorrow?" He asked. "As long as you promise to behave yourself." I answered. "I'm not making any promises." He said. "Then you can't come over." I said. As badly as I wanted this man, I couldn't have him just yet. "We've liked each other for the past 11 years. Why not make it official?" He said. "Believe me when I say, I wish we could. But I'm burned out. And I got this sort of recipe that I've been following for a couple of years as it pertains to my body." I said. "Really? Care to elaborate?" He asked. "Yes... simply put, I don't have sex when I'm tired." I answered. Then to turn around and come right back to work the next day, that was a no-no for me. The guys did it all the time. Not that they were so much stronger than us that they could pull it off. The fact of the matter was, they would show up and do a half-assed job all shift long. If one of the guys questioned as to why they weren't pulling their weight, they would simply brag about their sexcapades the day before; While all the other guys sat around listening and drooling at all the lies they were telling. For one of us girls to get away with something like that...Dream on!

We agreed to meet tomorrow at 2 o'clock, my place. "Dammit you. Can I at least bring my lips?" He asked. "Yes. Please do. We'll just have to make sure our lips stay on each other's lips. PG only. OK?" I said. "Alright... I'll behave." He said. If we were having this much trouble agreeing to keep our pants on over the phone. It was going to be an even bigger challenge in person.

Home for a Day

We didn't get any calls after 11 o'clock last night. I got up at 7 AM sharp. While walking past the captain's office, I couldn't help but overhear that they were having scheduling issues. The good thing about my situation was, I had just completed 72 consecutive hours. Which meant they had to send me home. Besides, I was signed up to work overtime tomorrow on truck 411 followed by my regular shift the next day on engine 43. I briefed my relief and got out of there as quickly as I could.

When I got home, I noticed my neighbor's son looking at me through his bedroom window. "Hi, shouldn't you be in school?" I asked. "Yes. But mom asked dad to take me. He said he didn't want to. So I stayed home." He said. "All right. But don't make a habit of it. You don't want to get comfortable being at home. You'll get lazy and end up dropping out of school altogether." I said as we both laughed. He laughed a little too hard for a 9-year-old kid. It was as if he knew exactly what I was talking about. The sad thing was, he probably did.

Once inside my apartment I followed my usual, haven't been home in a few days routine. The first thing I did, was open all the windows. Next, I needed to empty the dirty laundry from my duffel bag, into my dirty clothes hamper. I repacked my duffel bag with clean underwear and T-shirts. Now the only thing left for me to do was take inventory of what I needed for this afternoon's meal. We had agreed on spaghetti. It was simple and easy. He was going to cook the spaghetti. I was going to make the salad and garlic bread. Being that we were cooking an Italian meal, he thought that a bottle of red wine would go nicely with it. The last thing I was concerned with was my liquor and wine inventory. You learned very early in your career as a firefighter to become a lush. So I kept a fully stocked bar, with plenty to choose from. And even though I wasn't a wine drinker, I kept a couple of bottles of Merlot to the side.

Alton got to my place at 2:05 PM. When I open the door, he walked in with two brown paper bags full of groceries. "What market did you go to?" I asked. "I went to Ralph's, right down the street from here." He answered. He put the bags on top of my kitchen counter, then proceeded to look around my apartment. "This is nice. The community is nice, the building is well kept, and your place is macked out." He said. "So I've been told." I said as we laughed. "Come here girl, bring it in." He said as he reached for my hand. We wrapped our arms around each other for a hug, then started kissing. I put my hands on his chest and gently pushed him away. "We will never start cooking if we keep this up." I said. "Yeah, no kidding. Let's get started." He said as we walked to the kitchen.

He emptied both bags onto the kitchen counters. From looking at the ingredients, he knew what he was doing. While he was cooking, we did a lot of talking and laughing. We also had our share of kissing and playing touchy feely. In total, it took us about two hours to make that meal.

When we sat down to eat, "You know what, I forgot the wine." He said. "Don't worry; you didn't need it." I said as I pointed to the bottle in my liquor cabinet. "Damn girl, you must have at least $1000 worth of liquor in here." "That sounds about right." I said. The spaghetti was on point. He knew what he was doing after all. We talked so much while having our meal, it took us nearly an hour to finish it. Once we were done eating, I showed him my remote-control cars. We recalled other kids in the hood having them. But neither of us could afford to have one as children.

We turned the TV to music videos. "You said you had some musical experience. What exactly does a recording engineer do?" He asked. We talked about the difference between various positions in music management, and other music-related positions. "What can't you do?" He asked. "I'll let you know when I find out." I said as we started kissing again.

There we sat, on the middle of the sofa, kissing the night away. I wanted this man with everything in me. The fact that I haven't had sex in months wasn't helping anything either. "Shit, I want you bad." He whispered. "I want you to." I whispered. He put his hand down my pants. I pulled it back out. "I'm sorry." I said. "Promise I won't hurt you." He whispered. "We will next time, I promise." I said. "You promise?" "Yes…I promise." I said. As we were laying on the sofa fully embraced, Anytime, Anyplace, by Janet Jackson came on. Talk about playing dirty. You know what Janet, fuck you and everything you stand for! I thought as I laid there with my head buried in Alton's chest; starving my black ass off. "Speaking of starving." Alton said as he reached for the remote and turned the volume all the way down. "Thank you." I said as we fell to sleep.

The next morning, my alarm clock went off at 6 AM. We were still laying on the sofa in each other's arms. Even though it was a close call, we managed to keep our clothes on. We had a cup of coffee and watched the morning news together. "I'll call you later." I said. We gave each other a soft peck on the lips before leaving. He walked me to my car, where we gave each other a hug before driving off in separate directions.

December Madness

No matter how good my nights were. My days always came back to bite me in the ass! I showed up to station three bright and early, put my gear on the truck, and proceeded to do an equipment check. Once I was done, at about 7:55, in walks a firefighter telling me he had been assigned to the truck. "Naw Buddy, that can't be the situation. I signed up a few days ago to be on the truck. Besides, before I left last shift I was told that my spot was secure." "Well, the battalion chief just told me I was on the truck today." "We'll have to straighten this out with the station captain." I insisted. The situation was, we had both possibly been assigned to the truck. The problem was, I'm sure I had the right per department policy to be on the truck rightfully. Not only did this guy work overtime as much as he could stand to. Plain and simply put, I had more seniority than him as well. So either way, I should rightfully be the one working on the truck today.

When we went into the captain's office to resolve things, the other fire-fighter continued walking upstairs. So I explained the situation to the station captain myself. The station captain recited the department policy on the issue and made a few phone calls down to headquarters. Once he spoke to the captain at station one, the issue was resolved. "Firefighter Brooks, you are to stay right where you are. I will let the other firefighter know." He said. "Thank you, sir." As I walked back to the engine room.

About 20 minutes later, in walks the battalion chief. The firefighter in question was following close by. "Firefighter Brooks, report to the captain's office. Firefighter Brooks, report to the captain's office." Once I was in the captain's office, there stood the battalion chief, the station captain, and the firefighter. "Get your things off the truck, and put them on 43. You're working on 43 today." Said the battalion chief. "Excuse me, sir. But under what theory is this firefighter able to work on the truck instead of me? We both signed up for overtime. Of which, I've worked very little this year. And if we are using the ranking system, I out-rank him." "It doesn't work exactly that way." "From my understanding, it's worked exactly that way for decades now." "Go get your things and put them on engine 43, and that's a direct order." "If you're not prepared to explain to me, which system you're implementing to put this firefighter on the truck instead of myself. Then I am more than prepared to call my union representative." I said. We all stood there anxiously quiet for about 10 seconds. The battalion chief oddly enough turned around and walked right out of the Captain's office with his crony following nearby. In that moment, I felt like Clint Eastwood. Now all I needed was a pistol, a pair of boots with spurs, and some fog to disappear into.

The station captain looked relieved. "Well played firefighter Brooks, well played." "Thanks, but I wasn't playing." I said as I headed back toward the engine room.

They were absolutely planning to punk me. That's precisely why it pays to know your rights. Apparently, he expected me to lay on the floor and start kicking in screaming instead of simply taking a stand for myself. When under attack, especially by your superiors, the first rule is to remain poised. Damn it feels good to be a gangsta.

Things had quieted down rather nicely for the rest of the morning. About an hour after we had our lunch, the firefighter who wanted to be put on the truck came to me with a bunch of accusations. "What I don't understand is, why was it a few shifts ago when I was supposed to be on the truck, you got to be on it instead." "This sounds like something you need to take up with your superiors." "No, I'm taking it up with you. I don't know who the hell you think you are, but you bumped me from the truck. And I plan to get you back!" He exclaimed.

So this is what all of this is about. As usual, a bunch to do with nothing. Even if I didn't sign up for overtime when I was last on the truck, I still out-rank this idiot. So I could have easily requested to bump him from the truck; which I did not. It was a move made by my captain in exchange for a peach cobbler. But the way it was interpreted by this dinosaur brain, was that I was out to get him. And he intended to get his revenge. The sad thing to me was, he didn't have the chutzpah to handle the matter on his own. He had to go and get the battalion chief involved. Which not only showed a lack of respect for our rank and file. It also put our captain in an awkward position. The battalion chief had to know that he was not only out of line for getting involved, but way the hell out of line! The rank of battalion chief is one of upper management. Hiring practices for overtime, is a lower management issue. So not only did he take it upon himself to put his nose where it didn't belong. He was dumb enough to show up and do it in person.

We usually only saw our battalion chiefs at second alarm and larger fires. Or over at city hall, handling more important issues. Why this guy would climb down from his horse to get shit all over his shoes was beside me.

Guess I'll make a few phone calls before the shift is over to do a little digging. Why not? I'm sure something interesting is bound to turn up.

The next day, I was back to my regular assignment on engine 43. The entire day was a debacle. We started our day with a heart attack patient, who was dead an entire day in his home before anyone noticed he was dead and not sleep. "Brooks go ahead and get a pulse on this guy. Our medics are running a little behind schedule." Said the Captain. I know damn well he's playing. The only people we need to call at this point is the corners office. This guy was way past pooling. PD thankfully told us they had the corners office in route and we were free to go.

Next up was a murder-suicide. Neighbors told us that the couple was up arguing most of the night. Then early this morning, they heard four gunshots coming from the apartment, so they called us. When management let us in, there they were, both laid out on the floor. He had shot his girlfriend three times in the chest. Then he blew the back of his own head off. There was brain matter scattered all over the walls behind him.

The next call I got was the all-too-familiar kitchen fire. Kitchen fires were usually very simple for me. When we got there, the owner had poured water on what appeared to be a grease fire. Typical reaction. The only problem with that was, the fire usually spread. Fortunately this time it only made a mess. My captain and engineer went back to the engine and told me to handle it. "No problem. This is simple enough." I said. I took out a respirator and a multi-purpose extinguisher, went back into the house, took the pan that was still burning full of grease, and put it in the oven. Once I shut the oven door; that took care of the burning pan. Now all I had to do was hit a few spots that were burning thanks to the owner splattering grease and fire in different spots. The entire incident only took about two minutes to extinguish.

Before I knew it, a couple of weeks had gone by. All I did was work. And when I wasn't working, I was at home preparing for work. Most of my family was looking for me. So I called my mom and a couple of my aunts and told them where I was. "Do you think you'll be off for Christmas?" Asked one of my aunts. "No, I'm already signed up to work the 24th and 25th." I told her. "Well, be careful out there. Love you." "Love you too. Say hello to everybody for me." As I hung up the phone.

Next on the list to call, was Alton. The timing of our situation couldn't have been worse. On one hand, I was happy to be back in touch with someone like him. On the other hand, this time of year was just plain old nasty for us as firefighters. Let alone a Compton firefighter. "I feel abandoned over here. When are we going to see each other again?" He asked. "I don't know. Hopefully soon. I miss you too." I said. "Damn girl." "Yeah, it's hard for me too." This was exactly the reason I wasn't in a relationship. Up until this point, I was 80% work and 20% play. My life in a nutshell was, high school graduation, followed by part-time school and a full-time job. Followed by the Compton Jim Shern fire Academy, intertwined with other training academies. Followed by full time jobs, intertwined with volunteering. By the way, I also had to find time to work out. All while riding the bus. "So far it's all work and no play with you. Has it always been this way?" "Yes, it has. But I'm about to change all of that. Hopefully, I can get it down to about 50 50." I said. "Hopefully you will. For now, I'm one horny ass man." "I'm hot my damn self. So I get it."

His situation was a lot better than mine's. He could have easily gone and satisfied himself with pretty much anybody. Me, of course not. I had to work. If it wasn't for my schedule, I would have hooked up with him by now. He was obviously not going to go and have sex with just anybody. He was waiting for me. And I was damn sure gone give it up when the time came.

December 24, Christmas Eve. What a damn day. A bunch of crack heads decided to set a Christmas tree on fire in an abandoned building to keep warm. We managed to keep it down to a one-alarm fire. We had to work our asses off to do it, but we did it.

Later that day, we were dispatched to assist PD with getting into a house. That can only mean one thing. Someone was waiting to be recovered. The surprising part was, the fact that they were sending the truck out to help with it. Every engine and squad in the city was running.

When we got there, it was a murder-suicide situation. Not only did this guy kill his wife and himself, he killed their two children. That was always the most challenging part of the job for me. Watching children be stuck right in the middle of grown folks problems. They didn't ask to be here. So, the least parents could do was give them love and protection once they were here. Let alone become their worst nightmare!

Parents. Please stop stressing yourselves over a day. A pagan day at that! Christmas has absolutely nothing to do with Jesus Christ. Why would such a beautiful Lord and Savior, have anything to do with someone offing themselves, simply because they didn't have the money to keep up with such nonsense? He wouldn't! Christmas like all other holidays, is good for business.

Please remember. Children need love. Feed them. Clothe them. And provide them with a safe, clean, and secure place to live. It's vital that both parents not only tell their children they love them, but more importantly, show your children how much you care about them. By being there.

December 25. Before I could get my gear on engine 43, we were being dispatched to a GSW. Being that this was done so early in the morning, there were lots of questions surrounding this situation. The young man was still alive when we got on scene; the detectives were able to get lots of information from him. The victim couldn't have been a day over 16. Thank goodness for the older citizens of our community. An older gentleman went outside on Christmas morning to water his grass, only to look across the street and find a young man lying in a pool of his own blood. From the sounds of things, one of our veteran detectives knew exactly who the shooter was. "Go kick that motha fuckas door in and beat his ass until he's woke. Book him for double homicide. I'll be back at the station in 30 minutes to an hour." He said as he rode away with the paramedics. Two things were very clear to me. One, this shooter had apparently shot someone else earlier this week. And two, they were not expecting this young man to make it. All I could do was what we call a hose down. This was done when so much of the victim's blood was left on the pavement; it was considered a biohazard to leave it.

Later that day. There were several drive-by shootings. These were obvious retaliations from the previous shootings. It was a few days early to be shooting. Drive-bys usually didn't start until December 31st. When we arrived on scene, the paramedics were on the way to the hospital with the first victim. The other guy didn't make it. He was laying on the sidewalk with half his head blown off. All we could do was Cover him and wait for the corners office to arrive. "Hey Brooks, will you help me cover this guy?" "Well if it isn't one of my favorite officers. Hey you. Long time no see. How are things going?" It was the officer that I had assisted some weeks back with a body recovery. She appeared to be just as nervous covering this guy. Not that anyone could blame her. It's just that we see these things all the time. She should be...I hate to use the expression, getting used to it. But this was a part of our routine unfortunately. "Whatever happened to that cup of coffee?" She asked. "I left those arrangements up to you girls. But it doesn't matter. Let's go get a cup tomorrow morning." "You got it. Thanks for helping. See you tomorrow morning. Well, let's hope I don't see you again until then." She said. "See you in the morning."

Things had finally quieted down by 6 o'clock that evening. My mother came to the station and surprised me with several plates of food. She had one plate of food that she cooked. One plate of her desserts. And another plate of my aunt's desserts. "We know how much you like your sweets, so we made sure to bring you two plates of dessert. You wouldn't want none of that dry ass food your aunt made anyway. I wouldn't feed that shit to the homeless." She said. My mother couldn't help herself. She just didn't have a filter. She said what was on her mind, the way it was on her mind. No apologies. "My refrigerator was out about two weeks ago. Thank goodness the man fixed it before I needed it today." She said. "Yeah, Walt told me about that. Don't spend another dime on that thing. The next time it blows. Call me. I told you I wanted to buy you a new refrigerator. When you got that thing almost ten years ago, it was used. I'm surprised it lasted this long." I said. It blew out again about two months later. And of course, I took her down to Circuit City and bought her a brand-new refrigerator.

December 26. It was a horrible month for the city of Compton. But we got through it. The laughter coming from the kitchen indicated that the guys were having a good morning. So I went down to join the fun. "Good morning fellas." "Good morning Allison." "Why didn't you put on a pot of coffee for us girl?" Asked one captain. "No, you guys don't want my coffee. At least not the way it turns out in that thing." I said as we all laughed. We had one of those industrial sized, aluminum coffee pots. The problem with me was, I just started drinking coffee about a year ago. I had just learned how to make coffee in a regular sized pot. Now there I was fumbling around with a pot big enough to serve 50 people. Let's just say the first time I made coffee in that thing, was the last time I made coffee in that thing!

"There was some overtime on the truck this morning. I was going to ask you if you wanted it. But I noticed you've been here 48 hours. And you have to turn right around and work your regular shift tomorrow. Which would put you in violation of the 72 hour rule." Said the truck captain. "Yeah, I know. That's why I didn't sign up for today. I have to work the 27th and the 29th. So it was my plan to work the 27th, sign up for the 28th, then work the 29th and take my happy behind home." I responded. "Yeah, I hear you." He said.

As soon as I was relieved, I drove down to the coffee shop most of us frequented in the middle of town. The officer was already there at the table. "Hey you." "Good morning. How long have you been here?" "Not long. About five minutes." "Cool. Let me get my coffee right quick." I said as I went over to the cash register. As I sat at the table, "How are you handling things Brooks?" She asked. "I suppose I'm doing OK. I'm taking it as it comes. All we can do is our best. Things can look very ugly around here at times. But then we have our good days, when things are quiet, and I get to whoop the guys at dominoes. How about you? How do you think you're handling things?" I asked. She sat there staring at the floor for a while before she answered. "Not too good. I don't think I'm handling some of the things I see around here well at all." She started staring at the floor again. "Do you get with some of the other girls and talk things over with them? It's vital that you have someone to talk to other than a good therapist. Try to find a couple of officers to reach out to. Even if they are from other departments. But it's important to get all the women you can to talk with on the regular." I said.

It was clear to me that she didn't have any support. The last thing you want to do when you were in our line of work, was keep it all in. We need others who understood what we were going through. Not just one or two people, but a network of people. Some of whom you can pick up the phone and call anytime, day or night. You never knew when all hell was going to break loose. So you wanted plenty of people who had your back no matter what. "Yeah. These are times I talk with different family members. Sometimes they get it. Sometimes they don't." She said. "That's going to be the problem with family. Even though they mean well, and you do need them, you must keep in mind they're not out here. So sometimes, they just don't get it. I stopped telling my brothers about stuff I see when I was a fire explore. They only wanted to hear the stories for the sheer horror of the story. And that only goes so far for therapy. My mother of course being a girl, I didn't want to gross her out with any of the stuff I was seeing. There were times she would ask. But if she didn't ask, I didn't say anything". I said. "You're right. I need to get myself a team put together. Starting right here, in my own department." She said. "Definitely. Try asking around. Invite them for coffee or whatever it is you girls enjoy doing. Then eventually branch out to other departments. Find out what kinds of programs the girls are involved in. Become a part of whatever it is you girls do. You don't have to necessarily like it 100% of the times. Just get involved for the socializing, and see where it goes. Even if you don't get that intimate one on one right away. But you have to keep swinging at it. You have to socialize. Don't keep all this bottled in. This career of yours will eat you inside out, if you let it." I said. "Thanks again Brooks. Thanks for everything. For the time you didn't allow me to snatch that respirator off when I was about to puke. And for helping me understand how vital it is that I open up to the other girls." "You're welcome. Here, take my phone number and the station number. You can start with me. Call me anytime. Day or night. I get it." I said as I gave her a piece of paper with my numbers.

We hugged each other before driving away. Now let's just hope she listens.

Chapter 12

AULD LANG SYNE

Auld Lang Syne

December 30, 1995. We managed to make it through another December without killing each other. I just got off work at 8 AM this morning, and I was dog tired. I had meticulously managed my schedule to make sure I would be off the next four days untethered. They could call me if they wanted to, but good luck. Starting with my mother, I had told practically everyone in my life not to call me for the next couple of days. And that I would call them. If there was an emergency, please page me and I would call you back. That was all except the fire department. If they called, it didn't matter because they would have to leave a message. If they paged, again, it wouldn't have mattered. All I had to do was tell them my pager wasn't on. The game that I was now playing was the very game that they spent years teaching me. Now all I had to do was keep this up, until the 2nd of January. The beauty in everything I was doing was, these were my actual off days. It wasn't like I was calling in sick, leaving someone else hanging when I should have been at work.

My aunt and I had made plans to go shopping when I got off work today. Being that I had worked so much overtime, in such a chaotic month, I was feeling it. So I called her and made plans to go shopping later in the evening. We agreed to get together at 6 o'clock that evening. That way I could take a 4 to 6-hour nap, and be rested enough to deal with those after Christmas shoppers.

When I woke up from my nap, it was 3:30 PM. Felt a little groggy, but nothing I couldn't handle. I got a diet Coke from the refrigerator. This usually gives me enough caffeine to push through a few hours. I was fine after drinking half the can.

The first person I need to call at this point was Alton. We were being very mushy on the phone. The last time we saw each other was on Tuesday, December 15th as he reminded me. And thanks to all the overtime, and running ragged across the city, we were doing good to catch each other on the phone more than a couple of times a week. "So let me get this straight. You're off until January 3rd right?" He asked. "Right. And before you even ask, yes, we are going to spend very well deserved, hot and passionate time alone." I answered. "Hell yeah! Just the thought of what I can do with you in three days is driving me crazy." He exclaimed. The feeling was mutual. On one hand, I was excited to be able to finally have sex with someone I had so many feelings about for so long. Not to mention I haven't been this sexually tensed since I started having sex. At least not that I can remember. On the other hand, I was nervous. What if it turns out we're not sexually compatible. Hell, the chemistry had to be there. You don't kiss for hours at a time unless you're feeling some connection. Right? So many thoughts were going through my head, I had to stop thinking. That's exactly what I needed to do, so I did.

When I got to my aunts, two of my little cousins wanted to come shopping with us. Didn't matter to me one way or another. They were well-behaved kids, and I enjoyed being around them. "You guys bet not ask for nothing. All that stuff you guys just got for Christmas. Don't ask for a damn thing." Said my aunt. I could see their little eyes from my rearview mirror, they looked very disappointed. But of course, I was going to do what the hell I was going to do anyway. So, when we got to the mall I called the two of them over and said, "If you guys promise to be good, and not get lost, here's $20 each." "Thanks, Allison." They said with excitement in their voices. "Now don't forget, you have to keep up with us." I reminded them.

As always, I knew precisely what I wanted to wear. I also knew that I wanted black and silver. "Hopefully there's no dress code for this thing is there? Because I want to wear jeans." I said to my aunt. "Dress code! Ain't like we going on a job interview! It's supposed to be a party. You and your damn jeans. That blouse is cute, so are those boots. But child, you need to let me help you find some other pants." She said. We went to every store in the mall, searching high and low, for some pants to match the rest of my outfit. Preferably black. Finally, we found some black dress slacks. She had me put the entire outfit on together. "That looks really cute on you. You're right;

you do know what looks good on you." She said. "That's what I was trying to tell you." As we both laughed. I got a few other accessories. Didn't know if I was going to wear everything. But I wanted to have them just in case.

December 31, 1995. The clock said 1:15 PM when I woke up. Last night I didn't leave my aunts place until...actually I didn't leave her house until about 12:30 this morning. After we left the mall, we went to a burger stand and bought a bunch of chili cheese fries, pastramis, and other junk food we like to eat. So I didn't get home until just after 1 o'clock this morning. At least I finally got some well-deserved rest. And for the evening I had planned, I was going to need it. Being that I overdosed on junk food last night, I decided to make myself a vegetable and fruit smoothie, with a tablespoon of instant coffee. And in true military fashion, I turned on the news. The day was just starting, but people were already getting their asses into trouble. Speaking of getting in trouble, I think I needed more condoms. Not that I was completely out, but I liked keeping a few different sizes. To the drugstore I go. If I didn't think this was a good time in my life for a steady relationship, how the hell was it going to be a good time for an entire baby. Usually, I kept a box of lifestyles, with nonoxynol 9. But those were too tight on the average sized brotha. So I started buying three different sizes. The way I saw it, I was investing in my own well-being.

While at the store, I stopped by the cosmetic counter and picked up a few things. By the time I got home, it was 5:30. I decided to go ahead and lay out my clothes for the evening. Since it was cold outside, and I was tired of wearing a ponytail, I let my hair down and wore it in a wrap.

Other than my brand-new black outfit. I wore my big silver hoop earrings, my silver necklace with a silver lightning charm, a silver bracelet on my wrist, a silver ring on my left thumb, along with a silver ring on my right ring finger, and a pair of brand-new black leather boots with a small 2-inch heel. By the time I was finished playing around with my outfit and putting on makeup, it was time to go pick up my aunts. They had decided to ride back with my uncle, just in case I left early.

It was a quarter till nine when I got to my aunts place. By the time we got to the facility where the party was being thrown, it was 9:30. One of my aunts thought it was entirely too early to go inside. My other aunt said no it wasn't. "Especially since tonight is New Year's Eve. We might mess around and not get in at all." She said. "We already have our tickets. They should have to let us in." Said the other aunt. "Not really. Remember last year, when they had to give some people their money back. They oversold their tickets. And the maximum occupancy is 400." She said. She was right. There was already a line to get in for people who had tickets. So we stood in line with everyone else. By the time we got in, it was 10 o'clock, and the place was packed. "It's a good thing we did bring our behinds in." Said my aunt. "This is one time I'm glad I listened." Said the other aunt.

We all stood in line and got our drinks. As we were walking around, we noticed some friends of theirs at a table and sat with them. Time was ticking, and Alton was nowhere to be found. One of my aunts had to use the restroom, so I went with her. By the time we got back, it was 20 minutes till midnight. The DJ was on fire. So we decided to get up and dance before the stroke of 12. Between the DJ, the liquor, and my aunts, I was having a wonderful time. One of my aunts looked behind me and said, "Allison, look behind you." It was Alton. He was walking over to where we was, but I wasn't sure if he had seen us or not. "I don't think he sees us." Said my other aunt. "He doesn't." I said as I started walking towards him. As I got closer to him, he looked down at his watch. "Yes, believe it or not its 10 minutes till midnight." I said as I stood in front of him. "Wow...you look amazing." He said. "So do you." I said. He gently took both of my hands into his hands, and gave me a kiss on the cheek, followed by a kiss on the lips. "You have no idea how much I've missed you. And to make matters worse, I didn't think I was going to get in. We've been standing out there since10 o'clock. They were starting to give people their money back when we just happened to run into our uncle. He's working security tonight in the main lobby. If it wasn't for him, we wouldn't have gotten in." He said.

We embraced each other, then gave each other another kiss on the lips. Just then his cousin Jimmy walked over and handed him a drink. "Here you go man. Hi Allison. Long time no see." We had not seen each other in years. And these men appeared to be aging very gracefully. "Hi Jimmy. Long time no see is right. How are you?" I asked as the DJ announced two minutes till midnight. "I'm doing good. It's nice to see you again. I better leave you two at it. It's only a couple of minutes till midnight." He said. The two of us walked over towards the floor. The DJ started the countdown, as everyone else joined in. At midnight, the DJ played Auld Lang Syne. The most popular song associated with new years in America. Possibly around the world. Alton put his arms around my waist and said, "Happy New Year's Allison." We locked eyes and immediately started kissing. We continued kissing until the DJ finally played 1999 by Prince. "We need to leave." He said. "Yes we do." I responded.

Before we left I made sure to find my long ass uncle, so he could give my aunts a ride home. "Describe your uncle, I'll help you find him." He said. "He's about 6' 8" tall, permed hair. Possibly has on a black and white plaid suit, with a matching overcoat, and black and white Stacy Adams shoes." I said. Alton looked at me as if I had too much to drink. But once we found Silky, he saw exactly what I was talking about. "Oh, I remember him. Ain't your name Alton. Man, I know your whole family." Said Silky, as I interrupted and said, "That's nice. Got to go." Then he gave his cousin Jimmy the keys to his car. The two of us got in my car, and went straight to my apartment.

Once we got in the door, we locked it behind us, and started what would turn out to be, two days of hardcore, passionate sex. We very patiently removed each other's clothes. But we never made it to the bedroom. There we were, buck naked fucking in the middle of the living room floor. We fit each other like a very snug hand in glove. We never stopped kissing, and he never took his hands from the arch of my back. When he took off his underwear, I could see he was packing. Since we were on the floor, and he was one of those slow and low brothas, I could feel every inch of him. How could something hurt and feel so damn good at the same time? We had sex for about an hour before stopping. This was a record for me. I had never come close to anything like this before. Both of us were thirsty, and damn did we drink! When we were done, I was so tired all I could do was roll over onto my stomach and go straight to sleep. He laid on the floor next to me and did the same thing.

Love hangover

When I got up to use the bathroom, it was close to 11:00 AM. I could smell breakfast cooking. Alton was in the kitchen cooking what smelled like bacon and other food. As I attempted to stand up and go to the bathroom, I slipped and fell right back down. I tried again, only to slip again. What the hell? I wasn't drunk last night, to be hung over this morning. On my way back to the living room I felt wobbly as hell.

There were clothes everywhere. So, I went to my bedroom to get my housecoat. Once I made my way back to the living room, Alton had a plate of food waiting for me. "Here, have a seat. Let me feed you." He said. "Ok, just a few bites, then I'll finish the rest myself." After a few bites, "where's your plate?" He headed back to the kitchen, "got it." He said. When he was on his way back to the living room, I paid closer attention to him. He had on his pants, socks, and no shirt. I've always known he was a good-looking man and worked out. But to see him up close was entirely different. This was going to take some getting used to.

Tuesday, January 2, 1996. By the time we rolled over and got out of bed, it was 11:30 AM. Being that we both appeared to be having some serious love hangovers, we decided to go out for breakfast. As we were talking over breakfast, he took my hand and started slowly kissing my fingers. "You know you started something." He said. "What do you mean?" I asked. "I like you. I'm starting to develop feelings for you. This might seem sudden, but we can't ignore the fact that we've known each other for a long time." He said. When he said that, I felt like shit! Not that I didn't like him. But I could tell he was somewhere in the relationship that I wasn't. "I like you too Alton. But timing is everything for me. So can we take our time, and see where this goes?" I said. "I know you're a career woman with a lot on your plate. So take as long as you need. Just do me one big favor; be honest. Even overly honest. But please don't lie to me. If this is not what you want, or if you're not feeling me, I need to know. And I don't want to be the last one to know; I want to be the first to know." He said. Wow. Now I feel nervous. "You got it. I don't play games. Especially not with people's hearts. And please believe me when I say I'm not going to start with yours." I said.

We left the restaurant and decided to go grocery shopping. "Since you cooked for me the last time I saw you and yesterday, I thought I would return the favor." I said. "Oh really? What did you have in mind?" He asked. "All right. So here's the plan from beginning to end. I want to cook dinner for you. Then send you on your way sometimes tonight." I said. "Send me on my way, what's up with that?" He asked. "So that I can get some unfiltered rest." I answered. "That's right. You have to work tomorrow." He said. "No. I'm going to call in sick tomorrow. I need a couple of days." I said. "Oh, do you?" "Yes, I do." I said, as he grinned. "What?" I asked. "Say it. Go ahead, be a big girl and admit it." "Admit what?" "I wore your ass out. Come on, say it with me." He said. "OK. You wore my ass out. Now stop beating your damn chest before I change my mind and take your ass home now." I said. As we both laughed. He was having a little fun with me because he knew he could. I'm not one of those women who gets easily offended. "What can you cook?" He asked. "I can cook and bake pretty much anything." I answered. "But I would like to keep it as simple as possible. That way there's not a lot of cleanups once I'm done." I said. "How easy would it be for you to make Mexican food?" He asked. "Tacos, only about 20 minutes." "I'll take the tacos. That should leave us plenty of time for other business." He said. I looked upward and shook my head. "What?" He asked. "Shameless." I said.

When we were done having dinner, he called his cousin and arranged to be picked up at 10 PM. We were watching music videos when he whispered, "Can you go another round?" As he started kissing my neck, "Come on." I said as I pulled his hand to go to the bedroom.

We sat in the living room watching music videos until his cousin got there. "When can we see each other again?" He asked. "I'm kind of on a Wednesday, Friday, Sunday schedule for right now. So I'll be off on next Tuesday and Wednesday when you're off." I said. "Cool, so let's get together next week." He said. "That sounds good." I said. We kissed until his cousin got here. I had a wonderful time. Now that's how everyone should start their year.

The very next day I called Sam. It's been a while since the two of us talked. "Captain Sam Jennings, how are you? Or should I say, Officer Sam Jennings? In either case, how the hell are you?" I asked. "It's official. I'm Officer Sam Jennings. Finally got through that six months' probation." She said. "I thought probation for the sheriff's department was one year. Like the fire department." I said. "It is. But don't forget about my units because of my bachelor's degree, and credit for other services. By the way, congratulations on getting through probation yourself." She said. I had made it through one year of service in the middle of September "95." Meanwhile, Sam was finishing what turned out to be her six-month probation in October. "When we gone celebrate?" I asked. "When we both find some matching downtime." She said.

"How's life? How's everything going kid?" She asked. "Since when the hell do you get to call me kid? You're only two years older than me stretch." I said. "And don't you forget it ass munch." She said as we both had a good laugh. "That's what I was calling you about. Life. Mostly sex and men." I said. "You know I'm the love doctor. So, let's hear it." I told her all about Alton. How we had pretty much grown up in the same neighborhood. How we re-connected. And more importantly, how we had something between us now. Then I finally hit her with that question that has bothered me for two days now. Why the hell was I so wobbly on January 1? If anybody knew the answer, it was going to be her. "From what you just told me, you doin good to have been alive on January 1. You let this chiseled athlete, marathon fuck you on the floor. Yeah, you should have at least been in a coma." She said as we laughed. "Listen, kid. A lot of what I tell you guys about sex, I learned from my sister and her fast ass friends. But some of it's through experience. From what I know about you, you just became sexually active at 21. Most of us started fucking between 12 and 16 years old. Especially if you grew up in the hood or in the south. And that kiddy 'hide and go get it' stuff doesn't count. Even now you're not in a steady relationship, so you're only bonin about five or six times a year, which still ain't shit! Don't get me wrong. That's good in some ways, but bad for what you were trying to pull two nights ago." She said. "I get it. I was out of my arena." "Not so much that you were out of your element. It's just that he had you on the floor. Don't make that mistake again. At least not with him. But it sounds like this guy really cares about you. So he's not going to pull that again. He only did it because he didn't know how much experience you had. But now he knows." She said.

"Let me remind you of something. Girls like us don't get away with shit when it comes to sex. Tomboy, athletic, career woman. We're good at almost everything we do. There's only a certain kind of man bold enough to get with us in the first place. Usually men who want a challenge. They're usually cocky as hell and will take every opportunity to remind you that you're still just a girl to them." She said. I'll give it to Sam. She was like having my own personal Dr. Ruth. She knew what she was talking about. And she didn't mind sharing. For most women, the subject of sex is taboo. Either they were having sex, and not talking about it. Or, not having it and not talking about it.

Bulletproof facts
about women

When it comes to sex and relationships with women, there are six kinds:

1. Gold-diggers. Those who use their bodies to get what they want. These women have no boundaries. They usually go with the highest bidder. That is the highest bidder at the time. Unless you are made of money, run!

2. The needy girl. This is the girl who confuses sex with love. This one can't wait to get into a relationship with no matter who it is. This one is a real ball and chain and can become number four on the list.

3. The boring woman. Can be good looking or average. All dressed up with nowhere to go, because she has no life. This kind wouldn't know fun if it hit her upside the head. Be careful! Even when she does settle down and have a family, she still manages to not have a life. The kind who doesn't know when to stop popping out babies. In her head this is what life is all about. She too can easily become number four on the list.

4. The desperate woman. She's not the best looking girl in the room and she knows it. Or, she might be a very attractive girl, and have a bad attitude. In either case, she's usually lost more than her share when it comes to relationships and love. Sooner or later, if she's not careful, she will become a very bitter woman, making her nearly impossible to deal with. Run like hell if you ever come across her!

5. The Tomboy. She's the original party girl. She's not usually loud and crazy, but can be. She's lots of fun to be around, especially in familiar surroundings. She knows herself very well and can usually fit

into any scenario. She's into her tennis shoes and T-shirts because she likes being comfortable. But when she decides to dress up, she usually steals the show. She's good at almost everything she does. She usually loves sports, loves physical and mechanical activities, along with other challenging activities which earned her the name tomboy to begin with. But be careful fellas, only 1 in 15 Women usually fall into this category, which makes them high in demand. Sometimes they can end up becoming playgirls. But also understand, when she chooses to settle down, she's a very loyal and outgoing companion for life.

6. The Man Eater! Simply put. She loves them and leaves them fast! She's good in one room, the bedroom. But when she's done, usually out of boredom, it's over! On to the next man she goes. This one has no intentions of settling down. Thank goodness there's even fewer of her than the tomboy. Only 1 of 20 women fall into this category.

FYI

This information is for both men and women:

Most women, 70% of them, only dress up to compete with other women. They don't give a damn about what their spouse thinks or has to say about the way they look. It's purely a competition for them.

Some women pretend to be into sports. This is usually to attract an outgoing athletic man. If she's really into sports, do a little digging. Try asking her which teams, and some of her favorite players. If she doesn't have any specifics, she's lying! Plain and simple! Especially if she's never played any sports herself.

Sometimes men take dancing, cooking and other exercise classes simply to pick up women. Be careful, once he gets the girl, you'll never see him in these activities again.

The above information works for both men and women. Both sexes can fall into any category on the list. And just as men can pretend to be into something to catch the opposite sex, so can women. When dating to meet someone of common interest and goals, just remember, we are what we practice. If they're pretending to be something, you should see them actually doing what they say they're about. And always remember, the knife cuts both ways.

Chapter 13

TREE FIRES AND HEARTBREAKS

Tree fires and heartbreaks

Friday, January 5. As I headed back to work, talk about walking on sunshine. The last six days were ones for the books. But I'm sure these jackasses will find a way to mess it up in a matter of minutes. When I got to station three that morning, I was told by the station captain that I had been reassigned to engine 41. "Is it until further notice, or just for today? Because the last thing I want to do is clear out my locker and all my belongings for one shift." I said. "On second thought let me recheck that. You're right; you shouldn't have to clear out all your belongings for one shift." Said the station captain. About an hour later, I was called into the captain's office. "Firefighter Brooks. There has been some kind of mix up. You are to report to station one for today only." Said the captain. "I'll get my things." The bad thing about station one was, this area of the city was busier than the area around station three. But by this being Headquarters, the guys were less prone to pulling their stunts. Not that they didn't. They were just less likely to.

We had our usual Christmas tree fires for the most part. Those, we could expect. They usually didn't stop setting those on fire, until about the 10th. Things were going pretty good until some genius decided to set his Christmas tree on fire up against the palm tree in his front yard, as opposed to out in the open like everyone else. This caused the palm tree to catch fire. We could see that bad boy burning from clear across the city. When we got there to put it out, apparently every idiot who saw it on fire decided to drive towards it until they found where it was. So, there we were, on traffic patrol with a 50-foot palm tree burning. Embers were flying everywhere. And smoke was everywhere. But there wasn't a damn thing I could do about it until we got every last one of those cars off the streets. My captain wanted me to use the deck gun on the top of the engine to put the fire out. That would have been a wonderful plan. The problem was, by there being so much pressure coming out of that gun, it was knocking even more embers through the neighborhood. So I had to give up reachability, for a wider pattern on the tip of my nozzle. Which meant I could safely extinguish the bottom half of the tree and down, while allowing the top half and up to burn.

I asked my captain and engineer if they could inform everyone on the side where the tree was burning to move their cars. They had to ask everyone within five houses of where the tree was, to move. Either one of two things was going to happen. The tree would obviously burn itself out, but we didn't want to take any chances of it snapping and falling onto cars, fully engulfing those next. Or, I would safely extinguish it. Took us about an hour to do. But we finally got it safely out.

Firefighting 101. Not everything we do is written somewhere in a textbook. And for the city of Compton, about 30% of our calls were unique to our environment. No matter where you work, you're going to run into that situation that's unprecedented. That something you've never seen before. When you do just remember, do everything you can to help stabilize the situation. If you give it your best every time, things usually work out.

The next morning, I was called in to the captain's office and asked if I wanted the overtime on engine 43 today. "Not really. I'm all over timed out for a while. But thanks anyway." I said to the captain. They were clearly having scheduling issues. But it wasn't my problem. At least not for now. I got in my car and got out of there. With all the fires we had last night, I wanted my rest. And I fully intended to get it.

When I got home, I had a message from Alton on my machine amongst other messages. Once I dialed his number, it dawned on me that he should be at work today. To my surprise, he answered the phone. "Hello, Alton." "Hello, how are you? Thanks for calling me back." He said. "Aren't you supposed to be at work today?" "Yeah. Supposed to be. That's why I was calling you. My job is talking about layoffs. Do you mind if I come over and talk to you in person?" He asked. "Sure, Come on by." I said.

Once he was there, we were excited to see each other. There we were. Acting like we hadn't been together in weeks. Of course, we had to make out before he told me what was going on with his job. When we finally stopped kissing, and feeling each other up, "What's going on? Are you OK?" I asked. "It's my damn job. They've been threatening layoffs for quite some time now. When I went to work Thursday, I found out they're only going to keep about 30% of us. And the ones they do keep will have to transfer to either Texas or Missouri." This reeks! Just when I was getting used to the idea of being his girlfriend. "Are you one of the guys they're planning to keep? Or do you know yet?" I asked. "Yes, they're keeping me. But I'll have to move to Texas or Missouri to keep my job. My supervisor told me they're talking about training me for level one management. If that happens; I'll get a five dollar raise. But again, the drawback is I will have to leave the state." He said.

We both sat there in the middle of the sofa, quietly staring into space. We both felt awful. He didn't want to go, and I didn't want him to. But what was he supposed to do? When life deals you a bad hand. You can't fold and walk away. You have to play that hand no matter how bad it is. "Allison. If you were in my situation, what would you do?" He asked. "You have to make your own decision in this matter. But if it was me, I would take the job. Work is hard to find as it is for black men in California." I said. We both sat there continuing to stare into space. It's like someone told us we only had a couple of days to live. And that's exactly what it was. A death sentence on our relationship. "When is all of this supposed to happen?" I asked. "By the end of January. We're supposed to be given official notices starting next week. But they want everyone moved out and in their new positions by the beginning of February." He said.

"What does your family think about this?" "I haven't told my mom yet. She will hate that I have to move. But I'm sure she'll tell me to do what's best for me." He said. "She would be right." I said. "What are we going to do? You obviously have a wonderful career. Mines is not the best, but it pays the bills." Talk about a situation that completely sucks. "What I don't want to do is sit around moping. This situation is beyond our control. Let's make the best of what little time we do have to spend together." I said. "It's not fair. We were separated because of our age differences when we were kids. Now we're being separated because of our careers." He said. We sat there holding each other and watching music videos. Music always made me feel better. No matter what I was going through, the right song would make it much easier to deal, or cope. We fell to sleep holding each other. We didn't wake up until 4 AM the next morning. We said good morning to each other and started kissing. One thing led to another, then we found ourselves in my bed, instead of getting ready for work. "Let's call in sick today." I said. "Done." He responded. I've used two sick days, and we were only seven days into the New Year. Believe me, when I say, they were well spent.

I called in sick for Sunday. Which of course took care of 8 AM Sunday, through 8 AM Monday. Monday morning through Friday at 8 AM I was on a four day. Which meant that I didn't have to go back to work until 8 AM Friday morning. Alton's situation however was a little different. He called in sick Sunday and Monday. His normal off days were Tuesday and Wednesday for this week.

We spent the next four days not only being lovers but being kids. There is a bowling alley/arcade not too far from my house. Which is where we spent Sunday afternoon until Sunday evening. "You're competitive, aren't you? You've been kicking my ass all day." He said. "Yeah, I got a little something every now and then." I answered. He walked behind me, put his arms around my waist and whispered, "Not in the bedroom. That's my show all day and night." He was right, and I wasn't ashamed to admit it. One thing about being a girl was, the pressure wasn't necessarily on me to be good in bed. I lacked experience, but I didn't mind learning. And I damn sure didn't mind practicing. If it felt good, I went back to it. If it didn't, I immediately called flag on the play and scrapped it. Bottom line.

Sunday night through the early hours of Monday morning, we spent having as much sex as we could stand. We made love like it was our last time every single time. Our days together was coming to an end. And we knew not to take a moment for granted. Since Alton had to go back to work on Thursday, the last day we spent together was Wednesday. We stayed home that day playing dominoes, board games, watching music videos, and of course our favorite, sex. He didn't have to be to work until 12 noon. So I got up and made breakfast before he left. We made arrangements to spend next Wednesday together when we were both off again. But everything inside of me told me that would be the last time I saw him. And it was. Turns out that his job needed him in St. Louis as soon as possible.

When he got to work Thursday, the majority of his coworkers were getting pink slips. His boss gave him a one-way ticket from LAX to St. Louis. His flight was scheduled to leave on Wednesday at 2 PM. And as life would have it, I got popped for mandatory overtime that day. Thank goodness I was on the truck. I spent most of the day hiding from the guys and crying my eyes out. I was sick for weeks after Alton left. We talked on the phone almost every night. But it just wasn't the same. He asked me how I felt about long-distance relationships. I knew that wasn't going to fly. If I had problems with men right here in the same town with me, how the hell was long distance supposed to work? As unfair and frustrating as it was, I had to let him go.

Messy and tragic

It was Valentine's Day. Several weeks had passed since Alton went to St. Louis; I was missing him like nobody's business. Since I didn't have anything planned for the day, I went ahead and signed up for overtime on Truck 411. We were having a peaceful day, so I took care of a few repair tickets.

Later that day I called my cousin Nikki. "What's going on with you? I've been trying to call you for weeks." She said. "All kinds of things started and stopped since I last talked to you." I said. "Oh yeah. Like what?" I filled her in on me and Alton's situation. "Do you think you love him?" She asked. "I think I do. How else can I describe all these emotions running through my mind and heart? On one hand, I wasn't sure because we haven't been together long." As she interrupted. "Your situation with Alton is unique. You've been knowing this man literally most of your life. You can't act like he's some random dude you just met a few months ago and shouldn't have any feelings for. If he was willing to try a long-distance relationship he probably loves you too." "Yeah, but that's not the point. The problem is we're two worlds apart. We can't do anything about that." "Why the hell not? Lots of people make long distance situations work." "Come on. Nikki. This is me you're talking to. I've been known to mess up some shit right around the corner from me. You know damn well I ain't got no business in no long-distance nothin." I said. "Yeah, but I never heard you sound sad over nobody before. Just saying. You know I know you. And your ass sound cut. How long has it been since he left?" "Just over a month now." "How often do you guys talk?" "That's the thing. We used to talk almost every night. But I've been trying to avoid calling him." "Why? That doesn't make any sense." "It does if you're trying to get over somebody." I said. "Yeah, you definitely love this guy." She was right. With anybody else I wouldn't have given a damn if I broke up with him, or if he broke up with me. It usually didn't matter, because I didn't give a shit about them. "And you're sure the long-distance thing won't work?" "Come on boo, if anybody knows my record it's you. You know damn well that's not gone work for me."

This was truly a messed up situation. But it was time for me to move on. So, I decided to take care of a few things I've been thinking about. Number one on the list was buying me a bigger and better car. I had my eye on a nice SUV. I'd also like to put sounds in it. Then I wanted to start taking some music classes along with my captain's classes. Hopefully, between my career, my hobby, and my classes, I would be distracted enough to get over Alton. God knows my career and captains' classes wasn't gettin it done by themselves.

At about 10:30, we were dispatched to a drive-by. "What the hell kind of drive-by requires the truck company?" Asked my captain. "The kind we're about to find out about." I said. Engine 43, squad 441, squad 442, and truck 411 was dispatched to the same drive-by. When we got there, we soon discovered why. There was a drive-by all right. But apparently, some-one was ready for them! There was a total of about nine people hit. Four of which witnesses say fled the scene. And with the carnage that was left behind, I'll say it was probably a good idea to get the hell out of there. Three of the four shooters in the car was obviously dead. The guy that they had run over when they lost control of the car was obviously dead. The driver of the car was shot twice. Once in the chest and once in the head. When they shot him, he lost control of the vehicle, causing him to run through someone's brick and iron fence. When he did that, not only did he trap the passenger side of his car shut, he ran over one of the shooters standing on the sidewalk. Then according to witnesses, the other shooters walked up to the car, and completely emptied their pistols on those guys. After that, they apparently got into two different cars and drove themselves to a hospital.

What will happen is, they will drive miles outside of the city of Compton, just to land at some non-trauma hospital somewhere in the suburbs of Los Angeles. When they get their dumb asses there, and the emergency room informs them that they have no trauma center in which to treat them. They will then alert the authorities and have them sent right back to the inner cities where there are plenty of trauma centers. By the time they arrive. Compton's detectives will have every trauma center in the neigh-boring areas on the lookout. Those guys will have either been arrested by tomorrow morning. Or, have turned themselves in out of desperation to receive treatment.

We cleared squad 442 from the scene to return to their perspective station. Things looked entirely different for the remaining squad, engine and truck company. We had a situation and a half on our hands. We were considering using a number of hydraulic tools to free the one surviving patient. The problem with that was, not only was his door trapped by the brick wall, the gas tank was also on the passenger side of the vehicle. Not that we wanted to. But we had to open the door on the rear driver side of the vehicle and remove one of the gunshot victim's body from the vehicle to save this young man. Once we got him out of the car we could see he was bad off. He had been hit once in the chest and once in his abdomen, with two extensive exit wounds on his upper and lower backs. If he survives chances are he would live out the rest of his life as a quadriplegic. His friends were hardly that fortunate. Two of them had brain matter splattered all over the car. The one guy in the backseat with him that we had to move to relieve him, was complete gelatin from the waist up. He had taken so many bullets, we were taking a chance of decapitating him from just moving him. Which is why we don't like to move people when they are obviously dead. We usually let the coroners office get there and do their jobs. We simply assist them if we have to. But given the situation we didn't have a choice. Once the coroners office did arrive, we needed to use our hydraulic bags to get the car off of the victim that had been run over. He had obviously been shot in the back of the head. Because his entire face was blown off when they turned him over to put him in a body bag.

It was apparent to us that PD was going to be there for quite some time. They told us to go back to the station, and we would be informed when they needed a hose down of the scene.

Chapter 14

IF IT ISN'T LOVE

If it isn't love

Several weeks had passed since Valentine's Day. I was working my assigned shift on engine 43. It was Saturday, so that meant lawns needed to be cut. For whatever reason, our station lawn mower was red-tagged out of order. When I informed my captain, he told me to do the best I could with what I had. Since the edger and the trimmers were working, I edged the front, back and side lawns at station three, along with trimming the bushes. The guys didn't bother helping me. So, I only got around to pulling weeds in the front.

Later that evening, I received a page from Samantha. What the hell! She was paging me 911. When I called her back, she was very upset about a situation that had transpired between herself and some of her male colleagues. "Allison. I promise you I want to kill one of these motha fuckas! Sick of this shit!" "What happened? Where are you? Are you at work?" I asked. It sounded as if she was crying. I've never known Sam to be anything but tough. She always had a very thick skin. Especially when it came to work. She had to. Hell we all did. Showing these guys any signs of weakness, was like showing a hyena the belly of an antelope!

"Sam, are you OK? Where are you?" "I'm at home now. I'll be OK. Just so damn mad." "Do you want to talk about it?" I asked. "Yes. But not right now. What are you doing tomorrow?" She asked. "Nothing too important to cancel. Let's do breakfast tomorrow morning. It's on me." I suggested. "OK. Thanks." We made arrangements to meet up at this nice cafe in Long Beach not too far from where I lived. I told her that I also wanted her to meet my cousin Nikki. "If it's all right with you that is. I think you will get a kick out of her. She's me on steroids." I said. "As long as she understands bullshit and politics, it's fine by me." She said with a little bit of a chuckle. It was a relief to hear her spirits were slightly up. "Thanks, Allison. Thanks for returning my call, and for understanding." "Please don't thank me for something you would have done for me two times over." I said. "Well, I might have done it once, maybe." She said as we both laughed. "I'll see you tomorrow morning at 10. Crazy ass girl."

When I got up the next morning, I was being paged to the captain office before my feet could hit the floor. I know he can't be calling me for overtime. I worked yesterday and the day before that. Plus, I've got my regular shift tomorrow. If I work today, I'll be in violation of the 72-hour rule. Once I was in the captain's office, "Firefighter Brooks. We just borrowed a lawn mower from station one. I need you to go out there and finish the lawns before you go home today." I know damn well this motha fuckas playin with me! Ain't no way in hell I'm about to cut a damn thing before I go nowhere! "Absolutely not! I edged all the grass, front, back, and side by myself yesterday! I also did all the hedging. I pulled as many weeds as I could. There is no way I'm doing anything else to those lawns." I exclaimed. "It's not about you as an individual. It's about us working together as a team." He said. "Team! What team? I was out there by myself yesterday while the team was in here watching basketball! I'm not doing another damn thing." I went into the engine room. Briefed my relief on the equipment, got my stuff, and went home. If they want the grass cut, they betta flip a coin and get busy. My black ass is in the wind!

Myself along with Sam and Nikki met up at the cafe at 10 AM. Sam and I got there at about five minutes till. We hugged each other with a sense of urgency. Neither of us wanted to let go. Here it was; we had worked so hard over the years to get the careers we wanted. Just to be treated badly and taken for granted at every turn. Nikki was pulling up to park just as we got our table.

"So what's going on with you playgirl." She said. "Playgirl? That's you right there. And you know damn well it is." I said. Just then Nikki walked up. "Playa, playaaa! What's up with you girl?" Said Nikki. "Now. There it is. What did you just call her?" Said Sam. "Oh, that's the playgirl right there." Said, Nikki, as they both laughed. "Thank you. Now." Said Sam. "Both of y'all full of shit. If I am a player, then I've learned from the best two I know. By the way, Samantha this is Nikki, Nikki meet Samantha." I said as we all laughed. "Just call me Sam." She said. "I've heard a lot about you. It's good to finally put a face on the picture. All good of course." Said Nikki. "It's got to be all good. That's all I got going on my end. Nothing but good." Said Sam, as we laughed. "In case I didn't mention it before. This bitch is hella cocky." I said as we all laughed. "But on a serious note, how are you? How are you handling things down there?" I asked Sam. "When I first started, I had my good days and my bad days. My good days have become fewer, while my bad days have become more prevalent." She said. "Allison has mentioned a few things to me in the past about the way they treat women in her industry. But what are some of the things you're going through? If you don't mind my asking?" Said Nikki. "The same bullshit. Just PD specific. I don't live there 24 hours. So, take away the cooking and all the chores, but I've got the same politics." Said Sam.

"Can we talk about what happened yesterday? Or do you want to wait until another time?" I asked. "No, I'm good. We can talk about it now." She said. "There's a string of events that led up to yesterday." "I'm sure. It usually is." I said. "These guys have been hinting around for months, about not appreciating the fact that I was only on probation for six months. Now mind you, I wasn't the only one in my class to have this honor extended to them. But I was the most qualified of the four of us who only had a six-month probation." "And let me guess, the only female, right?" I said. "Of course." Said Sam. "So let me get this right. There's a program that allows certain cadets to complete probation early?" Asked Nikki. "Exactly." Both Sam and I said.

As it turns out. Those guys have been leaving nasty messages about Sam, not only around the station. But a few of them even had the nerves to now be prank calling her house. The messages were mostly sexual. Spreading absolute lies about who all she slept with, and gave blow jobs, to not have to complete one year's probation. To mess with someone at work, is asking for trouble. To mess with someone at home was begging for trouble! If there was a new low, this was definitely it!

She took a couple of minutes to explain to Nikki how the program works. The bottom line to me was, she was seriously overqualified for what she was doing in the first place. The sheriff's department should have been glad to have her. And for the most part, they were. She had a four year degree from an Ivy League school. She served two years in the Air Force. Not to mention all the other training she received prior to becoming an officer. To say her resume was impressive was an understatement. If I was considered a threat, then Sam was a triple threat. To me she should have been working for NASA, making a minimum of six digits a year. Why the hell she would bother messing around with the sheriff's department is beside me.

"From what you just told me, your feathers are entirely too bright to even be in your line of work. Why did you choose to become a cop of all things?" Asked Nikki. And that was the million dollar question. "All right. Here it is. I never talk about this. So please keep this under your hat," as she looked over at me. "I'm planning to go into politics someday. Sooner than later." Fuck! Now it all makes sense! Most of Samantha's coworkers wondered why someone with her education and background would become a cop. I completely forgot the political aspects of it all. Somehow, I knew Sam was too competitive to let her older sister outshine her. Nothing wrong with a little friendly competition. "What do you think about that?" As she looked over at me again. "Sounds great. We knew something was up. Had no clue what it was. But I'm glad you finally said something. It makes a hell of a lot more sense than you're simply being a cop." I said. "Thanks. I'm glad you understand." Said Sam. "You and politics. That makes all the sense in the world. It's the cop thing none of us get." I said as we laughed.

After we finished eating, we decided to meet up at my place for some spades and dominoes. "This bitch is clowning." Said Nikki when we walked in to my apartment. Sam headed straight for the liquor cabinet. "So how many hundreds of dollars' worth of liquor is this, about 8, 900." "Yeah, about that. Give or take a few bucks." I said. We agreed to have Long Island Ice-T's, with a shot of Jack Daniels. "Jack goes good with everything." Said Sam. "Negro. You from the south. For you guys, Jack Daniels is a staple." I said as we laughed. I put on Freddie Jackson and broke out the bones.

"So what's up with you and lover boy?" Said Sam. Once I got her caught up on the latest news with Alton and I. "Love? Don't you think it's a little soon to be throwing the L word around." She said. "But it's not like they just met." Said Nikki. "Yeah, I get that. But I know your conceited ass. You don't love that man. You just got some good dick and don't want to let it go." Said Sam. "I don't know Sam. I've been knowing Allison my whole life. And she was hurt when this man left town." Said Nikki. "You girls are closer than two bears in a phone booth. I'll give you that. But I know you. I've been paying attention to you. Especially when it comes to how you handle men." She said. "You got my undivided attention. Go for it, I'm listening." I said.

"Let me tell you some things you don't know about yourself. You can have anybody you want. Men and women. But you don't want them because you're conceited as hell. Not that you're even trying to be that way. The funny thing is, you're oblivious to it. You're used to a certain amount of attention. You're also used to ignoring that attention. I picked up on that when we first met. Now me. Because of the way I was groomed, I'm a narcissistic, self-centered bitch. My parents, with a little help from my sister fucked me up bad. But at least I'm aware of it." She said. That's the one thing about Sam. You didn't mind her putting her foot up your ass. Because she was just as hard on herself. "You've been plucked right out of the ghetto and put into a career unlike any other... firefighting. You've been taught ever since you were 17, to get in, fix the problem, and get out. All without becoming one bit attached to the people you help. But again, it's not your fault. It comes with the territory. Now check this out. Not only are you attractive, you've got the complete package kid. And that's alluring for most people. Especially women. Look, attention can be a very tricky thing. Be careful how you handle it." She said.

"I've always told you, you've got a dangerous combination going. Sexy tomboy, with money, a good education and street smarts. Sam's right. There's something very attractive about that. And I'm sure that uniform ain't helping a damn thing either." Said Nikki.

"I'm gone leave it just like this. My grandmother used to say. The best way to get over a man, is to get under a new one. When you find somebody new. And you have sex with him. If you're still thinking about Alton. You'll know you're in love with him. But I got $50 and a minor in psychology that says you don't. Your ass is hardly in love. You're in lust." Said Sam.

I was in no position to argue with either of them. Both women knew me exceptionally well. Not that I've been knowing Sam forever, but let's face it, she was a quick study. We also had a lot in common. Half of the stuff she said about me, was also true about her. Which is why she was so quick to pick up on certain things when she saw the same traits in me. Nikki was also right. When I put that uniform on, I got just as much attention from the girls, as I did the guys. But I never allowed myself to become spoiled or conceited by any of it. Now the whole love versus lust thing, the sad thing is, I've never been in love before. So I had nothing to compare it to. Only time would tell which one it really was.

Taken for A Ride

When I got up the next morning, I had a lot on my mind. I thought about the conversations we girls had the day before. Sam was probably right. Hell, she was usually right. My bottom line was, I had to figure this thing out for myself. But until then, I had lots of other things on my plate.

When I got to work that morning, I follow my schedule as usual. Immediately after the tailboard meeting, my captain wanted me to clean the backboards in the back of the station. "Sir, I don't know if you realize it or not. But those backboards have been there ever since Friday." I said. "We are not going to get into this today. It doesn't matter how long they've been there. I'm telling you to clean them. And that's a direct order." "Then today must be the day that I get my black ass written up for the first time; because I'm refusing to clean those boards. You and I both know there was at least three shifts of medics between now and Friday. How the hell they didn't get cleaned is beyond me. But I am not about to clean them now." I said. "Have it your way. I will go directly to my office and prepare your write up." He said.

About an hour later he called me to the captain's office. When I got there, "I need you to read over this and sign it when you're done." He said. When I read the write-up, not only was he writing me up for not washing the backboards. He also tried to include the fact that I didn't finish the lawns before I went home on Sunday morning. He attempted to make me look as if I was insubordinate. "I'm not signing a damn thing. The information in this write up is completely bogus and you know it." I said. I went back to the engine room and continued with my day. Apparently, this incompetent son of a bitch thinks I'm crazy because he is.

At least two hours had gone by since I refused to sign the write-up. I was called into the Captain's office a second time. This time when I got there, everyone from the Fire Chief all the way down to my captain was there. What it was exactly they thought they were going to pull was beyond my understanding. "The reason I called this meeting is because, you refused to sign this write up. All we need you to do is sign the paper, and this will all go away." Said my Captain. "As I explained before. The information in that write up is bogus. I refuse to sign that paper." I responded. The four of them got into a huddle and started to discuss the situation as if I wasn't there. I thought to myself, "I need to get a union rep involved." So I did. "I need a union rep." I said. "What you need to do is sign this write up. We're not asking you to agree with the information in it. We're telling you to sign it." Said the assistant Fire Chief.

I left the captain's office. As I was walking down the hallway; out of nowhere, was one of our union representatives. I immediately explained to him what was happening. When I was done talking, he looked at me in disbelief. "No way. You're telling me as we speak. The Fire Chief, the assistant Fire Chief, the Battalion chief, and your captain are all sitting in that office." He said. "That's exactly what I'm saying." I said. He couldn't believe it. We both walked back into the office. "Well I'll be damned. I just knew what Allison was saying couldn't be true. First of all. Why are you guys here." Asked the union rep. My captain had the audacity to attempt to explain what was going on. "All we needed her to do, was sign the write-up." Said the captain. "You guys are way out of line. First of all, you guys have no business being here. The only two this concerns is Allison and her captain." Said the union representative. "Well, they wouldn't be here if she would have signed the paper as I told her to do initially." Said the captain. "What you mean to say is, they wouldn't be here if you weren't so incompetent." Said the union representative.

They all started to disagree. The mood in the room shifted from bad to worse. "This is about to get ugly. Allison, can you please leave the room for a minute." Said the fire chief. "This is already ugly. And Allison I agree, can you please leave the room for a little while. I will come out and talk with you in just a little bit." Said the union rep.

As I went to the TV room and waited until I was called back to the captain's office, I could hear arguing and disagreeing down the hallway. Finally, about 15 minutes later, I was called back into the captain's office. This time, when I went in, there was no one there but my captain, and the union representative. "Allison, here's the situation as it stands. We are going to forget all about this write-up." Said my captain. Really! I wonder who or what could have changed their minds. "Ok." I said. "Let's just call this one a draw." Said the captain. "You can go back to the engine room and finish up whatever it was you were doing before this debacle started. I'll be out to talk with you in a few minutes." Said the union rep.

When the union representative came out to talk with me, it was just as I thought. These guys were more wrong than three left shoes. There was no way in hell, anyone should have been there for a write-up but my captain, and myself. "The problem is, sometimes Allison, when people can't see the light, you have to bring the light to them. And that's exactly what we had to do today. I don't think these guys will be messing with you for a long time to come." Said my union rep. He gave me a few of his business cards. He told me to tape one inside of my locker here at station three. One inside of my locker at station one. And keep one at home. That way if I had any more trouble, I could just call him. And he would make it disappear. "Continue to do the stellar job you've been doing. I don't think you're going to have any problems for a while. If you do, you know how to handle it." He said. And just like that, he was gone.

As long as I stayed on top of things, he was right; I shouldn't have any problems. These guys knew the policies as well as I knew them. They just figured they would try me at every turn. The lawns had to be done on Saturdays, by all on-duty personnel. And if everyone pitched in, it wouldn't take but a couple of hours to handle. Let alone carry over to the next day. Backboards were supposed to be washed by the medics on the same day they picked them up from the hospitals. If the medics were too busy to get to the backboard because of the number of calls being run for that day, then the firefighters would step in and help. The problem was, I was the one who always had to step up and wash backboards. And when I wasn't there, they were simply saving the work until I returned. Same situation with the lawns. They had grown comfortable with me filling in most if not all gaps. This was obviously unfair. But who cares about being fair when you have more important things to do, like chasing skirts. I was taught day one to keep my personal life at home. It seemed to me, several of these guys could use that same lesson.

Once I was off work the next morning, I went and picked up my little brother Walt. The two of us went shopping for that SUV I had my eyes on for a few months. We went to one dealership; they had a couple to choose from. Neither SUV was fully loaded. Nor did they have the color I wanted. If I was going to pay for something, it was definitely going to have all the bells and whistles I wanted, as well as the color I wanted. We finally went to a dealership that was recommended by one of the reserve firefighters. He said that his older brother was a manager down at this particular dealership. They had exactly what I wanted. The SUV, the color I wanted, and of course it was fully loaded. We got to my mothers' at about 8 o'clock that night to show it to her and my brother Doc.

The very next day, we went shopping for sounds. I'm ghetto. So, I intended to have the absolute top-of-the-line stereo for my car. Walt knew a lot about sounds. Not only did he know about stereos. He knew which speakers to match with whatever stereos. He knew what brands worked best together. He even knew the exact size wiring to install to make it sound top of the line, without spending top dollar. Like he explained, some guys spend 8, 9, even $10,000 on sounds, thinking it's going to sound good because they've paid a lot of money. When no matter who you are, you have to know what equipment works well together. There was no getting around knowledge of the equipment you intended to purchase.

When it was said and done, I had an Alpine stereo with a built in EQ, Alpine amplifiers, 2 2 inch Pioneer speakers in the front dash, 4 inch JVC speakers in the doors, 2 JVC 6 x 9's, 2 12 inch JBL subs in a custom built speaker box, a pioneer sound processor wired into the dash, 4 gauge wiring, and of course two extra gel cell batteries to run it all. That's right. $2,500 worth of sounds. And like Walt said, it sounded like it was worth at least $10,000.

A day after we had the sounds installed, we had it cop, and thief proofed. Initially, I wanted the alarm installed before I got the sounds installed. But as both the dealer and my brother explained, you never take the chance of a stereo guy messing up the alarm. Normally, if there was going to be a problem with the two interchanging. It was usually the sound guy getting in the way of everything else functioning properly. It was rarely the other way around. Since it had only taken about an hour for the alarm guy to install the products I purchased from him, it left us an entire day to cruise the Shaw. Being that it was a Thursday, Walt and I decided to wait until the next day, Friday. We bought a few CDs to bump, then went up to Hollywood Boulevard, and Sunset Boulevard.

Friday night, it was all about The Shaw. Crenshaw Boulevard between the 105 and 10 freeways. Make that 30-minute drive, stop at Leimert Park for

30 minutes. Turn around at the 10, then head back to the 105. You never knew who could be on the Shaw on any given weekend. Not only was there a bunch of common everyday people with nice cars hanging out. There were lots of professional athletes; The Lakers, The Clippers, a bunch of rappers and other celebrities with their low riders, all bumpin their systems. But of course, we had to figure out where we placed amongst the best of sounds in southern California. Of about 20 systems that we heard that night, Walt decided that I was in the top three. Not bad for a $2500 sound system.

Now that I was done buying my SUV, and putting sounds in it, I needed a little R & R. I could also use some companionship. I was over the guys in my black book, at least for the moment. I wasn't about to call Alton. The last time we spoke, which was a few weeks ago, he wanted us to visit each other in person. He was going to fly out to Los Angeles for a few days. Or, I could fly to St. Louis for a few days, and he would pay for it. The problem was, I was ready to move on. As it turns out, I'm not in love after all. Love, at least what I know about it, is not selfish. And I was having a very selfish moment. Now all this bullshit about being conceited, Sam could go to hell with that. It was just that I was not about to attempt to do something I knew I would be bad at. Having one man at a time was plenty for me. I was not about to embark on this bicoastal playgirl stuff that some of my friends were into. The truth is, to be a good player, you have to be a good liar. I'm a terrible liar, and that sounded like too much work. Nikki pointed out that the guys were doing it too. "So don't worry about hurting anyone's feelings." Not that I was overly concerned about anyone's feelings. The fact of the matter is and always will be; I only have one life. And I'm living my life for me. To hell with what everyone else was doing.

When I get off work Friday morning, I'll give my girl Leak a call to get up the mountains for a few days. That should hopefully help me to clear my head.

Chapter 15

GIRLS AND BOYS

Girls and Boys

It's 10 o'clock already. Where the hell is this cat? They said I only had to be here for the next 30 minutes two hours ago. These guys should know better than to mess with me by now. "Phone call for Firefighter Brooks on line three, call for Firefighter Brooks on line three." What the hell? They bet not be tryin to pull no last-minute shit. As far as I'm concerned, I got off work two hours ago. It's Friday, I'm on my four day, and I want to get the hell out of here! Fuck overtime! I need to get as far away from Compton as I can. Shouldn't even pick it up. "Station three, firefighter Brooks." "Alli Wali from Cali, what up nigga?" "Leak Leak! What up bitch? You the main person I need to talk to. What's going on?" "Listen. I've got a favor to ask. What time do you get off work?" "I was supposed to have been out of here two hours ago. As soon as my relief gets here." I said. "I need a ride back up the mountain. I came down here a few days ago with Buddha and them to take care of some business. But now I'm over my father's friend's house. And as you know, he doesn't really drive like that. So I need you to come get me." "That's cool. I'm glad you caught me. I was about to call you anyway to see if I can get away for a few days. So where do you want me to pick you up from? Are you still at your pops friend's place?" "Yeah. But I'm about to walk around the corner to the liquor store. The one on the corner of Crenshaw. Next to the Magic Johnson Theater. So when do you think you can get here?" She asked. "As soon as this guy gets his ass to work and relieve me." I answered. "Cool. See you in a bit." We made arrangements to meet up at 12 noon in the parking lot of Crenshaw liquor.

Just as I hung up the phone, "Firefighter Brooks, report to the captain's office. Firefighter Brooks, report to the captain's office." Oh my goodness, I hope they're not trying to keep me here. As I walked into the captain's office, Captain Grizzy said, "Listen up, buttercup. You can go ahead and take off. Firefighter Johnson had a family emergency. I got Edwards coming in to cover his shift. I would have offered it to you. But I know how you girls like your four days." Yes! I'm out of here! You can call me whatever the hell you want to call me, as long as I get to leave. "You're free to go, have a nice four day." "Thank you, sir. Be safe, and have a good shift." Bye! See you when I see you! That's what I wanted to say. Not that I got anything against making money, me or Loretta. It's just that we believe we work hard, so we should play just as hard. Loretta taught me, if I was going to work any over-time, try to work those middle days. That way I would have my four days to myself. And God only knows I usually needed all four days to empty my head of all the BS around here. Firefighting was very stressful. Especially if you had a vagina, instead of two balls and a bat between your legs. Being a woman, you tripled your stress by simply walking through the doors.

"Good morning Allison." "Good morning BJ." "You out of here girl?" "Yeah, I'm gone." "You on a four day?" "Yeah, thank goodness." "Be safe. Don't do anything I wouldn't do." "That sounds too boring for me." As we both laughed. "I heard that. Have a good one." He said. "You too." I said as I got in my car and got my happy ass out of there.

It's a beautiful day down here. I hope it's nice when we get up the mountain. "Leak Leak!" "Alli, what's up?" As we hugged. "You got all your stuff with you?" "Yeah, I didn't feel like being bothered with going back around there to get it. So I brought it with me." As we got in the car, one of her hands went for my stereo, and the other hand went for my CD book. "What are you bumping nowadays?" "Same thing I was bumping the last time I saw you." "Stop playing. You haven't bought any new CDs since I last saw you?" "Yeah, I bought a couple of things. All I bump is oldies anyway." "That's cool. Roll the windows down." "Don't get too crazy. You know we in ticket giving ass LAPD's area. They ain't stopping a whole lot of crime. But they sure write a whole lot of tickets." She put on 2pac all eyes on me CD. "Here take the remote. If you even think you see a cop, push this red button. It will shut all this shit off. To turn it back on, just push this blue button. It will come right back on." "Oh, that's dope. Where did you get this?" "My little brother Walt hooked me up." "How's he doing, with his fine ass?" She asked. "He's OK. His job is trying to work him to death. But he's all right."

"Speaking of your little brothers. I ran into Doc and Deal a couple of days ago." "Where did you see them?" "Up at Hollywood sounds." "Oh yeah."

"Yeah. We was all up there chilling for a minute. That's why I came down here. Buddha wanted me to do some ad Libs, and some overdubs on a couple of tracks." "Oh yeah. What was Doc and Deal up to?" "They said they were working on a few things themselves. El was with them." "Crazy El from jumping jack records?" "The one and only." She said. "I thought they said they was done with him." "He said he was done with them too. Last time I checked everybody was done with everybody." She said as we laughed. "Doc and Deal ain't gettin along worth shit either. They both talking about going solo." "Solo! They need to focus on gettin this first project out. Them Niggas ain't even got an album out yet. And they got the nerve to be talking about goin solo!" I said. "I told El he should have put you in charge of managing them. That way they would've had an album on the table by now." "Naw bitch. I can think of much better ways to waste my time. Them Niggas ain't about to have me stressed the fuck out! My job covers that department quite thoroughly." I said.

When I pulled over to get fuel, Leak motioned for some young dude to come over to the car. "How old are you?" She asked. "20." "Do you know where I can get some bud?" "No, not really." "All right." "Can I get your number though?" He asked. "Naw. You a little young for me. With your fine ass." She said. "Are you sure?" He asked. "Yeah. I'm sure." She said. When I got back in the car, "What the hell was that all about? Bitch, are you trying to go to jail?" "He looked a lot older when he was walking up. But when he got up to the car, he was clearly about 16, maybe 17 years old." She said. "Let me get the hell out of here. Got that little boy lying about his age." I said as we laughed.

We hopped on the 10 freeway. We was bumpin the music, and choppin it up. Just catching up on things. She turns the music down and said. "Before we go back up the mountains, I need you to take me over to your uncle's." "My uncle's, which one?" "Winston." "Winston? What the hell do you want with Winston?" I asked. "Weed nigga. What else?" She said. "Let me ask you something. How the hell do you even know about Winston?" I asked. "That motha fucka the biggest weed dealer in Compton. Not to mention he's fine as hell. If I was around back then, and old enough to mess with him, I would've given your aunt a run for her money. Just saying." "Yeah, he is one good looking dude. Well since you know so much, does he still live in the same house? Over by that burnt restaurant?" "Yeah, it's the same one. When Doc took me over there, I remembered a burnt restaurant being over there. When they gone finish tearin that thing down?" "Who knows? Money moves slow. And around these parts, it moves even slower." I said.

"I'm thinking about doing my own thing. I'm getting tired of Buddha and them. They are starting to get on my fuckin nerves." She said. "What's wrong? I mean, if the money is right who cares?" I said. "Well, that's the problem. The money could be a whole lot better. If they would stop playing and drop the album, instead of trying to shelf it, the money would at least be what it should." "Are they talking about shelfin it? That's a dumb idea! Hell, that's the best album I've heard at holiday productions. Honestly, it's the best album I've heard on any label lately. Ain't no good female artist out right now. There's only one or two in the industry that can even hold a candle to yo ass. That's why I nicknamed you Lady Pac." She sat there quietly staring into space. "Look. If those motha fuckas are dumb enough to shelf that album, we need to figure out how to get our hands on it, and put it out our damn selves! The way I see it, just fewer people to pay when it's all said and done."

"That's what I wanted to talk to you about. I was thinking about starting my own label. And I want you to be in charge of my A&R department." She said. We know lots of talented people. So, I better get to the bottom of why she wants me to run her A&R department. "You know I'm flattered. But I also want to know why you chose me?" I asked. "Believe me. We thought about this long and hard. We do know a lot of people. Some with some pretty good ears too. But none of them are as well rounded as you. Most of them only listen to R&B and Rap. You have a tendency to listen to music in every category. How many black people do you know who listens to Paul Anka, Pat Matheny, Neil Sedaka, and Fleetwood Mac? Because I don't know one, except you. Most of them don't even know who the hell those artists are, let alone listen to them." She said. Yeah. No argument there. We had the same problem with white people. They didn't know many black artists outside of Michael Jackson, Prince and Whitney Houston. "That's why we chose you. You got the most to offer. Besides, I talked to D about it, and she thinks it's a good idea. She thought it would be a very smart move to put a female in charge of A&R for once. Especially one with your ear for music and talent." She said. "Wow. She did?" "Stop acting so surprised. We need somebody with your temperament and discipline. Look at Doc and Deal. With a bit of your drive and focus, they would have had two or three albums out by now." The only problem with that is, you can't tell Doc or Deal shit. And this whole discipline and focus thing. That's not just a Doc and Deal problem. That's an industry problem.

"Go handle your business boo. We got a three-hour car ride ahead of us to talk about this. Tell Winston I said hi." "Get out and tell him yourself. I know you haven't seen him in months." She said. "Naw, I'm good." Wow. I can't believe she wants me to run her A&R department. That's a hell of a compliment coming from her. It would definitely be a nice change having a girl in charge of A&R for once. The first thing I would do is get rid of that casting couch. Either your ass got talent, or you don't. And like she said; I will definitely bring some discipline and structure to the table. They better make sure they want me. I can be over the top anal, while Leak and D are two of the most untamed women I know. Yeah, that's a lot to think about. I would definitely have my work cut out.

"Really bitch! A trash bag? What the hell is wrong with you? If we get pulled over, we goin to jail for distribution!" I said. "Calm down! What the fuck you worried about? We're in your city, you know these fools." "It's not the whole two minutes we'll be in Compton that I'm worried about. It's the remaining two hours and 58 minutes it's gone take us to get to Arrowhead I'm concerned with. Niggas and flies. Neither one is happy unless they're surrounded by shit!" I said. "Dude. Want me to drive so you can finish pulling your panties out of your ass?" She said. "Oh yeah, I'm the one out of line! You're right it is me!" You can't make sense, of nonsense. So I closed my mouth and stopped trying. The good thing is, I'm about to get back on the freeway. So I'm avoiding about 15 to 20 cities full of cops. Now all I have to worry about is CHP. And in California, you have to be fuckin up really bad to get pulled over by the highway patrol.

As we pulled up to her house, "Got new neighbors?" "Yeah. They tryin to squeeze us in a little." As we walk through the front door, I noticed she had a new stereo. "Got a little something to play your music on huh? Cool." "Yeah, it was about time that I got some decent sounds." "So what we gone get into?" I asked. "Oh, I was about to call this dude I know. I'm gone tell him to bring one of his friends for you." She said. "Oh, I was talking about tomorrow. I'm tired tonight." "Well I got needs. I've been thirsty for days now. Do you want him to bring somebody for you or what?" She asked. "Go ahead, ain't nothing wrong with talkin. I'm too tired to do anything else." "Damn, why you tryin to go into sleep mode on me?" She said. "In case you forgot, I just got off work this morning. And I'm the one who drove us up here." I said as she walked into the kitchen to make the call. "Make sure you bring one who's as fine as you." She said as she walked out of the kitchen. "All right see you in a few. Bye. Well, they'll be here in a few." She said.

"So how did you meet this dude?" I asked. "Hanging out on a video shoot with these cats we tryin to work with. You know how it is. A bunch of ugly ass dudes. The finest ones are always gone stand out." "You ain't lyin. What about the cat he's bringing for me? Because I promise you, if this dude is funny looking, I'm going to politely excuse myself, go to my car, and take my ass to sleep!" "If he brings the guy I think he's bringing, you'll be thanking me for weeks to come. He might bring his cousin though. I never met him. But D said he's fine." "Oh, so D met him?" I asked. "Yeah, she met his cousin. But she never met the dude I'm talking to, Aaron. She said she seen him before, but they never spoke or anything."

She took out a sandwich bag full of weed. "Help me roll these joints before they get here though." She said. She sat the bag on her coffee table. "Hold on, I'm trying to find those zig-zags I had last week." She looked over at her fireplace mantle, "Oh yeah, here they are." One of the few sides effects of weed, forgetfulness. "Here, roll up about three." I didn't know what the hell I was doing. I was putting stems, seeds and everything in the paper. I was wondering why the paper kept tearing. "What the fuck! Why didn't you separate the Stems and seeds first?" She asked. "You know I don't know shit about this. I told you, I don't get high. I've never been high a day in my life." "You grew up in a family full of men. Most of them smoke this shit. And I know damn well your brother Doc do. And you never paid attention to how they rolled it?" She asked. "Well excuse the hell out of me for not paying closer attention to how to roll a joint." I said. "Joint rolling 101 is now in session. First, separate the stems from the seeds. Set my seeds to the side. I like to smoke them when I run out of weed. See, just like this." She gently rub the weed between her fingers to separate the stems and seeds. "OK. I think I got it now." Wow, I can't believe I'm actually doing this. "All right, I'm done." "Cool, now just dampen the end of a zigzag with your tongue just like this. Then, put the other one on top just like this. This is about how much weed I like to put in one joint. Now, just roll it. Just like this. Some people like to twist the ends. I like to just crimp mines." She said. "I've seen that done, but why?" I asked. "So you don't end up with a mouth full of weed and fire when you inhale." Oh, that makes sense. "See, just like this. You got it?" "Yeah, I think I got it." I said. "Here, now roll two more." She said.

It only took her all of about five minutes to separate the stems from the seeds and roll a joint; all while showing me how to do it. It took me 20 minutes to roll two joints. "I'm done," I said. "Took you long enough." Just then, the headlights from a car flashed into her windows. "Perfect timing. I think the guys are here." "Cool." I said. She went over to the window, slightly peaked out, and said, "Damn. I think I ordered your flavor." "So who did he bring?" "He bought his fine ass friend, Diego." She walked over to the door, opened it, and met them outside on her front patio. "What's up girl?" "Hey boy." "Hey how you doing, long time no see." I heard someone say. "What's up Diego? I haven't seen you in forever."

As they made their way into the house, both guys stood at about 6'4", slender build, caramel complexion and obviously had gym memberships. This never happens, I must be dreaming. Two good-looking guys rolling together. It's usually one fine, and one ugly, or short, fat, somethings usually wrong. But not tonight. Both of them looked good. Aaron looked like Ginuwine. And his equally handsome friend, well let's just say I couldn't think of a celebrity fine enough to compare him to.

"This is my friend Allison. The one I was telling y'all about, the firefighter from Compton." "Damn girl, you don't look like no firefighter I've ever met." Said Aaron. Why the hell did she tell them I was a firefighter. I never tell guys what I do for a living. Don't want them to have some weird expectation or fantasy they expect me to live up to. "Hi Allison, nice to meet you." Said Diego as I stood up. "It's nice to meet you too." I said as we gently embraced. Guess I'm not so tired after all. "What are you girls up to tonight?" Asked Aaron. "Just chillin. We just got home a couple of hours ago." Said Leak. "Oh OK." "Yeah. Allison just got off work this morning." Said Leak. "Wow, how long were you there?" Asked Diego. "I worked my normal 24-hour shift. Just that we were really busy yesterday." I said. "So how does that work exactly? Do you guys live there?" Asked Aaron. "Not really. We work something called a 3/4 schedule. We only work 10 days a month. Sometimes 9, maybe up to 11 days, depending on how the shifts fall for that month." I explained. I took a pocket Calendar from my duffel bag and showed them what I was trying to say. I told them what shift I was on so that they could see for themselves exactly how it worked. That was always less complicated than trying to explain how it works. Once they took a look at my calendar, "So you work three 24hour shifts every other day. Then you're off four, 24hour days in a row." Said Diego. "Exactly." I said. "I'm in the wrong damn profession." Said Aaron, as we all laughed. "Not to mention firefighters make serious bank." Said Leak.

"What do you guys do for a living?" I asked. "We're in the construction industry. I'm what they call a general foreman." Answered Diego. "I'm what you would call a very temporary worker looking for a new occupation."

Said Aaron. Well, that explains the masculine build. "I'm looking into the music business. Trying to hopefully get something going with that." Said Aaron. "Yeah. That's a good little side hustle if it's handled correctly." I said. "Allison is about to help us do a little something." Said Leak. "Damn girl. You make the rest of us look lazy." Said Aaron as we all laughed. "Allison is serious about her paper." Said Leak.

We all sat there talking for a little while, getting to know each other. "So you girls got any music to put on?" Asked Diego. "Allison, go get your CD book out of the car." Said leak. "What kind of music do you listen to?" Asked Diego. "Everything. I listen to all categories of music." As I picked up the keys. "Oh yeah." Said Diego as we walked out to my car. When we got to my car, "So this is your SUV? Nice." Said Diego. "Thanks." "Not many Sisters drive SUVs. You and Leak are definitely different." "So I've been told." I said as we both laughed. "Is that your truck?" "Yeah that's me." "Not too many brothers drive pickup trucks either. Especially nothing that nice." "Yeah, I'm a dirt devil; I got to have a way to transport all of those tools. If I'm gone be paying for something, it might as well be something nice, right?" "You got that right. That's the way I feel. One of my uncles taught me, a car can cause you to lose your job if you're not careful. You'll be busy calling in making up excuses for a car that doesn't run, and mess around and lose your job." I said as he agreed. As we were walking back to the house, "Can I look through your CD book? I'm curious about what you listen to." "Mostly oldies." I said as I gave him the book. "Smoky Robinson, Stevie Wonder, Luther Vandross, LTD, Stephanie Mills, Tina Marie, Anita Baker, the four tops, the Isley brothers, damn girl. You're a serious lover. Paul Anka, Chicago?" He said as we both laughed. "You do listen to everybody" "Do you know who Paul Anka is?" "Yeah, I do." "I'm sure you know who Chicago is." "Yeah, I know them too." As he continued to flip through my CD book. "Help me. I was thinking of starting out with your smoky Robinson's quiet storm CD, and moving into some LTD, followed by the Isley Brothers. What do you think?" "Doesn't matter to me." Just as we were walking up to the front door, Leak was coming out. She grabbed me by my arm and started whispering. "Peep game, can you guys kick it out here for a little while?" As Diego walked into the house, Aaron pretty much did the same thing to him. "We just need a little bit of time to smoke this joint and kind of get things going." She said. "It's cold as hell out here. It's got to be about 40°. It's probably gone drop down to about 30 within the next few minutes." I said. "Be cool. I'm gone bring you a blanket." Oh I'm gone be cool all right. More like cold. "All right, let me make a drink right quick."

As I walked into the kitchen, Diego asked, "Do you drink?" Hell yeah. "Indeed I do." "I got some Hennessy and Coke. Can I make you a drink?" "Thanks, but I'll make it. You might not make it strong enough." As we both laughed. "Hey Allison, peep game." As Leak called me over to the living room. "Hold on, sounds like my beepers going off again." I said to Diego as we both laughed. "Here's the blanket. You guys only have to stay out there until we go upstairs. I'll leave the door cracked so you'll know when to come inside. You still got those condoms in your glove compartment?" She asked. "Of course I do." "I'm going to need a couple of them." I gave her the keys to my car, then went back into the house to finish making my drink. "Oh, there you are. Looks like we're being kicked outside for a little while." Said Diego. "Yeah, I got the memo, and a blanket to go with it." I said as we both started laughing. In that moment I thought, "That's who he looks like, Prince. A tall masculine version of Prince."

Ebony eyes by Smokey Robinson and Rick James came on as we got our drinks and headed outside. He took my drink and sat it on the ledge. He took his drink and sat it on the ground. "Yeah, don't want to mix those up. Yours might be too strong for me." He said as we laughed. As I sat down, he took the blanket I was holding, folded it, and wrapped it around me. Then he gave me my drink, got his, and sat next to me. "Yeah. The one thing I can say about Arrowhead, is its cold as hell around this time of year." This was the last week of April. So the temperature could still drop down as low as 30° at night. "It's cold, but it's a nice night." I said.

"So can I ask you something? What made you become a firefighter? The only other black woman I've ever seen who was a firefighter was on TV. She was in Mozambique, or the Congo. Somewhere in Africa or something like that. And she blended in with the men. They literally had to say she was a woman, before I knew she was a girl. She didn't look a thing like you. No curves, no nothing. Just looked like a man." He said. "I might have seen that documentary. I understand where you're coming from." I said. "So when Aaron told me that you were a firefighter, and he had never met you, I have to admit, I was a little nervous. Curious, but nervous." "Oh I definitely get it. Believe it or not, I know lots of female firefighters. And a few of them will give me a run for my money. In fact, the one who helped train me is a very good looking girl." I said. "Oh yeah... well I've seen lots of police officers who were women. Just not any who are firefighters."

He was absolutely right. There wasn't a lot of us out there. And only 2 out of 10 were black. "My turn. Now let me ask you something? What is it that you do with music?" "Nothing right now. Aaron wants to get something going. He wants to open a recording lab, and see where it goes from there." He answered. "Sounds good." "I'm also taking a class on Wednesday nights, trying to learn how to get into publishing. I've been meeting some interesting people. In a few months from now, Aaron and I should have enough money socked away to open that recording lab. But the real money is in publishing from what I've been told." He said. "Yeah, that's right. If I had the patience and wasn't so lazy about reading, I would go into publishing myself. But as it stands, I don't feel like being bothered with all that comes with that. It's too boring for me." "Bet it is. You're more of an action girl. You have an outstanding career anyway, being a firefighter. What do you do in the music industry?" "Believe it or not, I went to school to become a recording engineer. But I knew music wasn't going to pay the bills, at least not right away. So I also continue to pursue my career in firefighting." "How long have you been a firefighter?" "When I was in high school, I started as a fire explore at age 17." "Wow, that's awesome. Can't believe I'm sitting here talking to a real live Shero. And you're a beautiful woman. How old are you? If that's not being too forward." "No, it's not, I'm 24." "I'm 26." He said. "Allison, do you mind if I put my arm around you?" Oh please do! "No, I don't mind."

By then, I noticed Leak and Aaron were apparently upstairs. But I felt so good sitting out here with Diego, I didn't want to move. "Diego, you are one handsome brotha. Do you have anyone special in your life?" "No. Now let me ask the same about you. Do you have anyone special in your life?" "No." Hell, I was talking to a couple of guys. The only one close to being special was Alton. And his ass was becoming a distant memory. Guess Sam was right after all. "I do have a three-year-old daughter. I don't know where she is. Don't know if she's even in the country anymore. Her mother is from Belize." He said. "Wow. What happened with her?" I asked. "Don't know. My mom used to say she was homesick. The homey's used to say she was trifling." "What do you say?" I asked. "I don't give a damn anymore. I just want to see my daughter." You can never know what happened in that relationship. It was none of my business to begin with. So, I made it my business, to stay out of their business.

"You just got off work this morning?" He asked. "Yeah, I had to work a couple of hour's overtime, so I got off a little after 10." "So when do you go back?" "Not until Tuesday. I'm on a four day." He started massaging my shoulders. "Am I being to forward?" "No, that feels good." His hands were perfect. "We can go inside now. I think they went upstairs." He said. As we walked inside, the Isley Brothers sensuality was playing. We used to joke and say, that The Isley Brothers and Teddy Pendergrass was responsible for half the black population in America. And that Smokey Robinson, and Luther Vandross was responsible for the other half.

He closed the door and locked it behind us. I took the blanket and laid it across the couch. We went into the kitchen and made another drink. We stood there staring at each other. "Did you want another drink?" I asked. "Yes. Right after this." He slowly, but firmly put his hands around my waist as we begin to kiss. My ass is in trouble now. This man knows exactly how to hold me. And he was handling my ass like I weighed 90 pounds. My heart was racing faster than two rabbits. I wasn't planning on having sex tonight, but plans change. What am I saying? I left my condoms in the car. Ain't no way in hell I'm having sex with this dude. No matter what happens, I'm not going all the way. Not to mention, my dumb ass could end up with something. Something I could very possibly not get rid of. So my mind is made up. I'm not going all the way. Just then, he stopped and said, "Don't worry. I'm not gone to try to have sex with you. But I damn sure want to romance you."

We went over to the couch, he picked me up and laid me across it. Then he straddled himself between my thighs, took my hand, and strolled across his penis. Oh shit. This dude is hung like a horse.

There we were, kissing and grinding the night away. Suddenly he whispered, "Dammit you. I want to tear those sweats off and fuck the shit out of you." OK, this is where we stop. It's hard as hell, but we have to stop. I was hotter than a jalapeno. But I was just as tired. Besides, I was not about to let this man kill me on Leaks' couch. "I want you just as bad. But I'm tired. And I won't be able to hang." "OK. I understand. You did say you was tired. And I don't want to hurt you." "Let's give it a while, we'll be OK." I said. We fell to sleep with Michael Franks playing in the background.

Chapter 16

GIRLS AND BOYS — PART 2

Girls and Boys - Part 2

"Good morning Alli, rise and shine." She's in a good mood. And rightfully so. "Why are you bothering me so early?" I asked. "Early? You don't realize it, but it's almost 12 noon." "Wow. I slept damn near 12 hours!" I said. "Don't trip, we knew you was tired, that's why we let you sleep." As I looked around, I noticed Diego and Aaron wasn't there. "Where are the guys?" I asked. "Oh, they had to leave. Aaron had to go to his job to handle some paperwork. But they said they was gone try to get back up here tomorrow." Oh well. I am supposed to be leaving tomorrow. "Diego's ass is on point, ain't he? I knew you would like him. I'm glad Aaron brought him. He left you a note, it's right there on the coffee table." She said. That was good of him. "So I'm about to get way out of line. Did you guys bone last night?" She asked. Yeah, that's out of line all right. "No, we came pretty damn close though. Girl if I would've boned him, I would be in here with two hands and a flashlight looking for my ovaries." I said as we both laughed. "I wanted him bad to. Ain't no tellin when I might get a chance to bone a dude that fine again." I said. "Then why the hell didn't you?" "Because I was tired. And I'm sick of singing this shit, but I don't have sex when I'm tired." "Yeah, I definitely get that." "I wouldn't have messed with some average dude on a night like last night. And Diego is hung like a horse." To be honest. I would be doing good to hang with Diego on my best day. I wasn't trying to get my ass pulverized in here last night.

"What do you want for breakfast?" "Whatever you feel like making, I don't know; I just woke up, I need my coffee first." I said. "I was thinking about making us some pancakes." "That's cool." "You want blueberries in yours?" She asked. "Wow, I don't think I've ever had blueberry pancakes. All right, I'll try them." "What about bacon and eggs?" She asked. "Two pancakes, two strips of bacon, thanks." I need to hurry and take care of my hygiene, so I can read this note. "I'm about to hit the shower right quick Leak." "All right, go for it." On second thought, I'm about to sit down and read this note. I'm too damn anxious to see what it says. "Good morning Allison." He's got beautiful handwriting. "We had to head back down the mountain to handle some business. I told Leak to give you this note. Thanks for a wonderful time last night. I don't meet many women of your caliber. Wish I had more time to spend with you. I'll call you later, at about 2 o'clock." What time is it? It's almost 1 o'clock now. Let me get my black ass in the shower.

As I was walking to the kitchen, I overheard Leak talking to somebody on the phone. "Hold on." As she looked over to me and said, "Your food is in the microwave. The syrup is on the counter next to the refrigerator." "Thanks." "Guess who I'm on the phone with?" As she started to smile. "Diego." She said. Looking over at the clock on the microwave, it wasn't even 1:30 yet. But I was happy just the same. "All right, well here she is, I'm about to give her the phone." She said. "Hello." "Hi Allison." "Hi Diego." "Did you sleep well?" "Apparently so, I just woke up a little over an hour ago." "That's good. Did you get my note?" "Yes, I got it." "Cool. We drove all the way down here for nothing. Well, we didn't do what we came down here to do. So we ended up going to the guitar center to look at a few things. We decided to buy this recording counsel Aaron had his eyes on." He said. "Oh yeah, that's good. You guys will get there. You'll look up again and be running a full recording studio." "Yeah, that's the plan. What are you girls about to get into today?" "I'm not sure yet." I said. "We was talking about coming back up there between four and five today." "Oh, I thought Leak said you guys was coming back up here tomorrow." "That's the way we were talking at first. But since Aaron didn't have to go to his job, we wanted to head back up there. Leak said it was cool with her. But I wanted to make sure you were good with it too." "Yeah, I'm cool with that." "Can we cook dinner for you girls?" "So you cook too?" I asked. "Yeah, I'm a southern boy. Cooking is not optional for us." "OK, what can you cook?" "Pretty much anything." He said. We decided to fry fish, since none of us had any last night, Friday night, fish night. "What kind do you girls want?" He asked. "I like fillet of soul. What kind of fish do you want?" I asked Leak. "I like fillet of soul too. Get some red snapper too. If they don't have snapper, get some tilapia." She said. I asked Diego if he heard her. He repeated what she said. Just then, I could hear Aaron talking in the background. "Put Leak on the phone. Who the hell eats fillet of soul and tilapia together? They're practically the same fish." He said. "Leak. Take the phone. Aaron wants to talk to you." I said as I laughed. "All right Allison, we'll see you girls in a little while." Said Diego. "OK. See you in a bit." I could hear Aaron through the phone. "Hey girl, who the hell eats tilapia as a backup for snapper?" He said. "Well then you figure it out. Just make sure to bring some fillet of soul, or tilapia with whatever else you decide. You ain't about to stress me out over no damn fish!" She said. Finally got a chance to eat my food. "I got a freezer full of fries. Just bring the fish, and the grease to fry it in. Oh yeah, bring some hot sauce." She said. This house ain't got no hot sauce? So let me get this straight. She got blueberries, and tartar sauce, but no hot sauce. Yeah bitch, yo ass is definitely half white.

At approximately 3 o'clock, "This, is how, we do, it." As I heard Montell Jordan blasting through the stereo. Leak started dancing to the music with a joint in her hand. "This is, how we, screw it. Make yourself a drink. You look tense as hell." she said. "Not right now, I'll make one later." "I want you to hit this joint with me." "You know damn well I don't smoke weed." "But you've never been high before. You don't know what the fuck you don't like unless you try it." "That's the point; you can't miss what you never had." I said. "OK. So fuck the firefighter for now. Just go ahead and be a normal everyday citizen for once. I want you to hit this shit one good time. Just get high with me today. You might like it. In fact, I know you will." She said. I thought about it, and I was curious. "You're telling me that your uncles, your brothers, most of your cousins and pretty much everybody we know, has been high at least a couple times. And you ain't even curious?" "Oh, I'm definitely curious." "Well here. I'm about to light it. We about to smoke it. End of discussion."

She sat next to me and explained how it works. "After I light it, I'm gone hit it twice and pass it to you. You hit it twice, and pass it back to me? Thus the phrase, puff puff give, get it?" "Bitch, be quiet. I ain't that green." She started laughing. She lit it, hit it twice, and passed it to me. I held it between my fingers, looked at it, smelled it, then finally, I slowly inhaled it. "Do it again, this time hold it." She said. I hit it again and held it. As I was passing it back to her, I started violently coughing. "That's because you got those virgin lungs." She said as she took two puffs and passed it back. "Hit it again, you gone keep coughing, but that's OK. It will open you up; you'll get high faster." I took two more puffs and passed it back to her as I continued coughing. "Just relax. Here, finish it." "All of this?" "All of what nigga? Ain't shit left. Besides, you'll be too busy choking to even finish this." Yeah, she was right about that. "Can't believe this is your first time getting high. I'm glad you tried it while you're still young. You hung in there with me, even though you damn near coughed up a lung."

She walked over to the front of the fireplace and stood on the platform of it. "I'm a little stressed because I'm not used to being with a dude more than one, maybe two days at a time." "Then how the hell was you married for two years?" As I started to laugh. "I don't know, that was one of the hardest things I ever did." I started laughing feverishly. "Nigga you fucked up!" After she said that, I started laughing even harder. Seems like no matter what she said, I just kept laughing. Yeah, I'm high all right. But it's nothing like I thought it would be. I'm feeling pretty damn good. Just really laid back. Not a care in the world and everything is funny. "Nigga, you didn't hear shit I said." Sure the fuck didn't. "Well, you wanted me to get high with you. And I did. But now everything is funny. Shit bitch, we can't have everything." I said as we both started laughing. "I can handle a few hit and runs here and there. But I got a black book full of dudes. I just call them when I need them. And they leave when we're done. That's all I want for now. I just got my divorce finalized not even two years ago. I damn sure ain't ready for no commitment, not right now." What the hell are we even talking about? Sounds like I missed an entire conversation. "Well, you gotta do what you gotta do. You'll eventually snap out of it. It just sounds like a whole lot of obligations to me." I said. "What the fuck? We hit that shit damn near an hour ago, and you still high?" I don't know if I'm still high. But I know I feel good, and I'm not about to let you fuck it up.

"You bonin Diego tonight?" "Huh, what time is it?" "It's about a quarter after four." She said. Time be flyin in these mountains. Time flies when you're having fun period. Ask Janet. "Yeah, I want to. I'm scared though." "Scared of what?" She asked. Of ending up sprung. "Don't get me wrong. Diego is damn near perfect. I just don't want to get too into him." "Oh, you scared you gone and up liking him." She said. "Exactly. In fact, I like him now. You're my girl, so I don't mind telling you what I'm about to say. But he's got a daughter out there somewhere. And I don't want to come across shallow, but I don't want a ready-made family. You know what I mean?" My life was plenty stressful as it stood. The last thing I needed was baby mama drama and other miscellaneous bullshit to top it off. "Yeah, I hear you." "Things start getting complicated really fast when you start liking some-body." I said. "Allison, you're right about everything you said. But don't put too much thought into this. Just let that man scratch your itch, give you some good loving, and be done." Well, booty call it is. Besides, who the hell died and left me in charge of being mother Theresa? "You're my 'girl, and I love you and everything, but you need to learn to chill the fuck out and have a little fun from time to time. Of all the girls I kick it with, you the only one who got your shit together. You're a very responsible person, and you have a good career. If you kicked back and never did another thing in your life, you could retire on your current accolades." She was right. But that wasn't the point. The point is, I'm a big enough girl to know when someone is into me. And even though I just met Diego, he's not a dog. I liked what I saw and felt last night, and so did he. All I'm saying is, I need to proceed with caution. That way, nobody gets hurt. "Thanks." I said. "I mean that. I give credit where it's due. Out of all of us, you're the only one who is financially set. I understand you're a climber, so I know you ain't gone stop hustlin. But I will trade shoes with you in a New York minute." Yes, I needed to hear that. Sometimes you're so busy reaching for what you want, until you don't take time to enjoy what you've got.

"On a separate note, where the hell did you get those little ass condoms?" She asked. "Well, the box said they were large." I said as we both laughed. I kept a few different sizes on me. From large all the way to magnums. You never knew what size a man needed. But I was sure of two things when it came to condoms. Number one, I was going to be the one to put it on him. And two, you wasn't gettin between me without one. "Aaron tried to act like he didn't have any left. When I tried to put that little ass thing on him, it looked like it was cutting off his circulation. He finally reached into his wallet and said, oh, I think I got one left." She said as we both started laughing. "You know how men are. They'll pretend not to have one because they don't like wearing them." I said. "Yeah, because they know they're not the ones who have to worry about getting pregnant or walking away with a disease." She said. "But I should have a few different sizes in there." I said. "Yeah, you probably do. I just didn't see them."

"Where did you put the rest of that Hennessy?" I asked. "It's on the table, right there in the kitchen." "Do we have any Coke left?" "A whole bottle in the refrigerator. Did you guys even open it?" "Yeah, I used a little." As I open the refrigerator, "He apparently didn't put any in his." "Aaron and Diego are southern boys. They can drink theirs right out of the bottle." She said.

We started shooting ideas around about her up and coming record label. Before we knew it, it was 5 o'clock. The guys should be pulling up any minute now. "I need to handle something. Be right back." She said. I sat there taking it all in. The music label. Fine ass Diego. The fact that I got high for the first time. All in all, not too bad. Leak came back downstairs. "They're pulling up now." "Oh good." We walked out to the front patio to meet them. "Took you guys long enough." Said Leak. I sure didn't think so. "This fool wanted to stop and buy a deep fryer. I told him to throw that shit in a frying pan and be done. But he didn't hear me." Said Aaron as he and Leak embraced. "Hi Allison. Did we keep you girls waiting?" Said Diego as we embraced. "Not at all." I said. Damn, I don't think I'm ever going to get used to looking at this man. I'm more nervous now than I was last night.

We took everything they bought to cook from the car. Leak and Aaron made their way to the kitchen. "You guys need any help?" Asked Diego. "No, we got it" Said Aaron. "What did you guys end up buying?" Asked Leak. "Some of everything. We got some soul, snapper, and shrimp. Oh yeah and some onion rings." Said Aaron. "Oh cool. You guys must have gone to Lou's Fish market down in the IE." Said Leak. "Ding ding ding. You got it." Said Aaron. "Well then, you guys should have let them fry it." "I'm not letting those Asians fry a damn thing. Lou be back there trippin. Dropping peoples' food all over the floor. Talkin fast with spit flying everywhere." Said Aaron as we all laughed. "We're good. We could bring it home, wash it, and fry it our damn selves." Said Aaron. "So you guys got this, right?" Asked Diego. "Nigga, we got this." Said Aaron. "Yeah, we got it." Said Leak.

Diego gently took me by the hand, as we walked out of the kitchen. We went back into the living room. Leak closed the kitchen door. Diego and I gave each other a gentle kiss on the lips. "We got some unfinished business to handle. But I'm not gone pressure you with that right now." He said. We sat on the couch, and he put his arm around my shoulders. "What do you know about music equipment?" He asked. "Just enough to know, I don't know enough." We both laughed. "What about publishing?" He asked. "Not trying to be sarcastic. But I know enough about publishing to know I don't want to do it." I answered. "I figured you would be a good person to talk to. Not that we've known each other long. It's just that I feel you're trustworthy." He said. "The honest and short answer to anything to do with Music is take your money and run now! Most artist are lazy as hell, and don't want to work. Most executives are looking for the next hit, which always takes them back to the last hit. Overall, it's a giant pain in the ass. How's that for trustworthy?" I said. "Sounds like everybody's on a treadmill so to speak. Moving and exercising, but not getting anywhere." He said. "You got it. You're a fast learner. And unfortunately, in this industry, it won't be fast enough. Because just when you think you've got it figured out, it changes again." I said.

"You must be wondering if it's that complicated, why are we bothering?" I said. "Yes. That's exactly my next question." I took a little time to explain to him, how it takes time to put a good team together. "You have to get different people offering a variety of talent, and willing to work for free. Most of us work for a living. So, you are going to have to deal with your share of starving artist. Who unfortunately are not the most reliable people to deal with. The goal is to make money; but until you do it's a hobby. I've been in a high school marching band. Which isn't saying a lot. But it did teach me how up to 30 different instruments are supposed to sound. Listening to a variety of instruments day in and day out, year in and year out does something to the ears." I said. And it did. Listening to kids play treble and bass clef scales, up and down the music scale, both in and out of tune. Do that for a few years, and you'll start dreaming in music, the way I do. "I've never learned to play any one instrument good enough to make a living. But I can tell you when any instrument, no matter what, is in or out of tune." I said. Our band director was a perfectionist. But I came to appreciate him for every bit of it. "Everyone on our team has something to offer. Even with that, we can only hope things go in our favor." "Wow. Thanks. At least I know more of what I'm getting myself into. How the hell did you get to be so wise?" He asked. "You're just trying to get on my good side." "From where I'm sitting, all you've got is a good side." He said as we started kissing.

"You still got your CD book in here?" He asked. "Yeah. It's over on the mantle." We could hear talking and giggling coming from the kitchen. He took out my Prince greatest hits CD, Luther Vandross, and I couldn't see anything else he put into the CD player. Adore by Prince started playing. Leak came out of the kitchen. "No you guys didn't go there. I haven't heard this song in ages." She said. "Stop lying girl. This song hasn't been out long enough for you to have not heard it in ages." Said Aaron, as we all started to laugh. "How are you guys coming along with the fish?" Asked Diego. "Oh, it's done man." Said Aaron. Diego gently pulled my hand. "Let's go eat." He said. We both went into the kitchen. "Can I make you a plate?" He asked. "Yes. Please do. Thanks." "What do you want?" "Just one of everything. If it ain't right, I'm gone hop my ass in the car, and drive to Burger King." I said as we laughed. The food was good. It was perfectly seasoned.

"Let's go outside for a minute; I need to talk to you about something." Said Diego. Again, gently pulling my hand. "I got a room for tonight. I'm not sleeping on that floor again. I'm a grown ass man, and I need my rest. I would love for you to join me." He said as he started to squat below my eye level. "I won't do anything to you that you don't want me to do. But I would definitely appreciate your company." When the hell did he book a room? Arrowhead is a very popular vacation spot. Rooms up here are expensive. Even during this time of year. It's like Sam said, a man will do anything for you, when he's got some pussy to get. "Wouldn't you like to sleep in a comfortable bed tonight? Instead of riding that sofa again?" He said. Sleeping on her sofa never bothered me. Hell, I'm a firefighter. I could sleep practically anywhere. There's times we had to sleep on the damn engine for crying out loud. "Sure, that's fine. How much do I owe you?" As he looked up to the sky and started laughing. "Girl, you're killing me." After all, I didn't want to feel as though I owed him. I wanted to at least offer to pay my share. "It's on me. It's already paid for. So you don't have to feel as if you owe me. I was going to get the room rather you were on board or not. I'm glad as hell you are on board by the way." He said.

"But about this music thing. You're saying hands-down, there's more money in publishing." He said. "Exactly. Publishers get paid a lifetime. Artist are fortunate to get paid per album, maybe per gig. Sometimes they don't get paid at all. A lot of them fail to negotiate the terms of their own contracts. And even if they are smart enough to hire an attorney, they often times hire the wrong attorneys. We seldom see an artist show up with his or her own entertainment attorney at the time of signing a contract. Which is why they are so easily taken advantage of." "This is interesting." "And not that they're dumb. Most of them are some of the smartest people you'll ever meet. It's just that they're smart in different ways." I said. "You got that right. Most of them are street smart, and business savvy. Especially the average rapper. It's just that sometimes, you don't know what it is you don't know." He said.

A lot of blacks are still feeling the side effects of slavery and oppression. We are on the bottom side of education, because of oppression. And because we usually don't have the means, we're not afforded certain opportunities. And even after all of that. If we manage to somehow crawl our ways out of the ghettos. We're simply not welcome. No matter how educated, no matter how much money we've got. We're simply not welcome. And that's called, down wrong racism.

It was getting late. We could hear killing me softly by Al B sure playing as we walked back into the house. Leak and Aaron was nowhere to be found. I wrote Leak a note telling her that we had gotten a room at the Tavern. And that I would see her tomorrow after noon.

The Tavern was a very nice place. It blended nicely with the local cabins. It had all the modern conveniences of a 5-star hotel, while managing to keep that historical, rustic log cabin feel. "This is nice." I said. "I knew it would be. By it being the end of April, I knew I wasn't going to have to compete with a bunch of skiers for pricing." That's true. Starting in the month of November, clean through the middle of March, you can't get within 100 miles of this place. Some of these places are booked as far as two years out for ski season. That's the good thing about California. Where else can you go skiing and surfing all in the same day. "It's cold as hell in here." I said. Couldn't help but notice that there was no central air and heating. "Yeah, this place is at least 30 to 40 years old. I didn't expect there to be any air or heating. Which is why I bought plenty of logs for the fireplace." He said. Spoken exactly like someone who understands construction.

As he got a fire going, I headed over to the CD player hanging on the wall. Damn, I left my CD book back at Leaks place. Well, so much for music, so I thought. "What are we going to do about music? I forgot my CD book." "Relax girl. You're not the only person around here with CDs." He said as we laughed. "Come here." He pulled me towards him and we started kissing. "I'm about to go outside and get my CDs. I don't have as many as you, but I've got enough to get us through the night."

As he headed out to his truck, I thought about how I also forgot my condoms. If I decided to get busy with this dude, I didn't have any protection. Wait a minute, that's right. Leak put mines back in my bag. Oh shit! The reason she put them back is because they were too small. And if they were too small for Aaron, I know damn well they're going to be too small for Diego. Well he damn sure better have his own condoms, or we ain't doing a damn thing. As Diego came back into the room, "I think I saw a bear. I won't swear to it. But I think that's what I saw." "You probably did. They are coming out of hibernation." He had a bundle of wood on his shoulder and a small CD book in the pit of his arm. "Bet I won't be taking my black ass back out there tonight." He said. "You mind if I look through your CDs?" "Knock yourself out." Couldn't help but notice, he has just as big a variety of music as I do. Norman Connors, the average White band, Chicago, Earth wind and fire, Kenny Rogers, Johnny Cash, Bob Marley, and on and on.

"You got artists I wouldn't think of listening to." Laughter. "What do you mean?" He asked. "Bob Marley, Johnny Cash, Howling Wolf. Nothing wrong. Just that I thought I was eccentric when it came to music. But I don't listen to many blues or any reggae." "You know how it is. We were 70's kids. We grew up with our parents partying over our heads. They just popped in a red light and did their thing. Didn't matter if we were there or not." My story in a nutshell. "What do you want to listen to?" He asked. "Believe it or not, I would like to hear Kenny Rogers." "Greatest hits, or love songs?" Pretty much anything by Kenny Rogers is a love song. With the exception of the gambler. I'm sure the gambler was on his greatest hits. So I handed him Kenny Rogers love songs. This way, for sure the gambler wasn't going to come on in the middle of our making out.

The first song that played was lady. He went over to his duffel bag, and pulled out a fresh bottle of Hennessy, a bottle of Remy Martin, and a bottle of wine. "I didn't know what you were in the mood for, so I bought a little of everything." He said. "What, no glasses?" I said. "Got them right here." He said as we laughed. He took out two small drinking glasses. "So what will it be?" He asked. I've always wondered about Remy. Never had it before. My girlfriends all referred to it as love potion. "Remy, I've never tried it, so I'll have some tonight." I said. He made us both a drink, then he turned the lights off. The fire was going good. "Got a question for you? You from the hood and all." Uh oh. "Other than orange juice. What's the best chaser for Gin?" He asked. "Other than orange juice? If I didn't have any orange juice to chase it with, for me it's seven-up." "For us it is too. It must be a hood thing." "You guys are trying to figure out if it's a hood thing, or if it's a Southern thing? What if it's a black thing?" I said. "Could be." He replied. And if you don't have either, you better pour that shit on ice and stick an umbrella in it.

"Allison. Thank you for keeping me company tonight. You're different. Which makes you intriguingly unique. I'm glad those two knuckleheads decided to introduce us." She believes in me by Kenny Rogers came on. Oh, I love this song.

We started making out with even more passion than before. At this point, we were like two trains headed for a collision. There was nothing we could do to stop. This is going to happen. He put his hand down my pants. He very gently and slowly put his hand between my legs. One finger, now two fingers...damn, I'm as good as through! He took his fingers out of me and started licking them as if he was licking barbecue sauce off of them. He pulled my pants and panties down my legs and straddled my thighs. He took off his shirt and stared at me for a while. Then he slowly started to smell me. Finally, he put his head between my thighs and gave me the best oral sex of my 24-year-old life! I thought Alton was good. But this man just took the prize.

As I laid there in complete ecstasy, he reached into his pocket and pulled out a condom. It was a magnum. Black pack, gold writing. When he took off his pants, he was wearing a pair of boxer briefs. I could see his dick print through his underwear. What the hell am I gone do with all of that? The most man I've had up until this point was 8 inches long. This dude had to be at least 10 inches. He finally took off his underwear. And oh my goodness. There he was, standing there buck naked. All I could think was, you in trouble now bitch! He got back on the bed, straddled my thighs, partially opened the condom, and whispered, "Here, put it on." I took the condom out of the pack, pinched the tip of it, and then slowly rolled it up his penis. It's official; this dude is definitely 10 inches long and thick as hell! He put one arm under the arch of my back and used his other arm to balance himself. Just then he whispered, "Let me know how deep to go. Stop me if I start hurting you." "OK." I said in a very nervous voice. He slowly pushed himself inside of me. "There, right there." "You OK?" "Yes."

He was as gentle as any man could be in that situation. He wasn't all the way inside of me; he was obviously too big. Thank goodness he wasn't selfish. With his size and strength, I could have easily been overpowered. But he was too much of a gentleman to be domineering. He felt so damn good; with just a little of what I would call pleasurable pain. He could tell I was about to have an orgasm. He started humping me harder. At this point, both his hands were around my waist. I started moaning louder and louder, then suddenly, I came. "Hang in there, please, just hang in there a minute." He said. It was good while it lasted. But by this time, pleasure had left, and I was in complete pain. "It's starting to hurt, please get up." "All right, I'm sorry baby." Not that I wanted to stop him. But this was one big ass dude! If I let him keep going, I would be in pain for days to come. Not only that, I was not about to let this man wreck my shit.

"Are you OK?" "Yeah, I'm OK." I said as I started to doze off. I had that tired, satisfied, and relieved feeling you get after having good sex. Hell, this was great sex.

When I rolled over to go to the bathroom. It's morning already? Yesterday came and went so fast. Whoever said time flies when you're having fun, obviously had plenty of fun in her day. When I came out of the bathroom, Diego was lying on his side staring at me. "Good morning." "Good morning." When I got over to the bed, he put his arms around my waist and straddled me between his legs. We started kissing. He laid me back on the bed. "Ready for round two?" He asked. Damn. I'm still recovering from round one. "Of course." I said. He got another condom off the nightstand. He partially opened it, then gave it to me to put on him. Here we go again. Very heated, controlled, but passionate sex. He's a very confident and careful lover. And His stamina is off the damn charts! "You gone let me come this time?" "Yeah." At least I hope so. "Just lay still and relax. Breathe through your mouth." "OK." I did exactly what he said. He had more experience than I did, and he seemed to know what he was doing. After all, he obviously didn't have an orgasm last Night. So the least I could do was help him get satisfied now. Not to mention, I was loving every minute of it. About 20 minutes into it, "are you OK?" "Yes, I'm all right." And I was. We were in 7th heaven if there ever was one.

Finally, he started humping me harder and harder. This was where I jumped in. Not to help him, but to save my damn self! I started moaning louder and louder. Normally, I'm very quiet when it comes to sex. But this man had a way of bringing out the best in me. He went deeper and started hugging my waist tighter. Then finally, we both came at the same time. Talk about fireworks! We both were obviously tired. So, we went back to sleep.

"Room service." We both looked at each other and smiled. "What time is it?" I asked as he reached for his watch on the nightstand. "Oh, it's 11:30." "What time is checkout?" "12 noon. But I paid for late checkout, which is at 2 PM." "Good, let me get a quick shower." "Can I get in with you?" "Absolutely not." As we laughed. I fully intended to wash my ass. If I let him get in, we'd only end up fuckin again.

As I was getting out of the shower, I could hear Diego talking to someone at the front door. When I walked into the room, I could see an older white gentleman standing at the door. Once Diego close the door, "who was that?" "That was the hotel manager. He was telling me about a landslide further down the road. Somewhere near the high school." "Oh no." "Yeah, he said they're working on it though. It should be cleared up by tonight." The good thing was, at least we could get back to Leaks place. And the part of the road we needed to move about to function, was from the high school and up. Translation, we should be all right until things were moving again.

As we pulled up to Leaks, she and Aaron was outside on her front patio. I could tell from a distance they were in a serious conversation. "Well, let me give Aaron the good news about the road closure." "From here, it looks as if they've already gotten that news." We parked next to my SUV. Figured I would grab my duffel bag and all my things and put them in my car, since I was standing there. Aaron started with Diego. "Well look who's back." "Top of the day to you, Madame." Said Diego, as we laughed. "Don't know if you guys heard anything yet," as Aaron cut him off. "Yeah, we know, the road is closed. Leaks little brother just left with that news. They were on their way down to the IE and got turned around." "Oh well. Then I guess I need to holler at you about logistics." Said Diego. Diego and I were standing there holding hands when Leak said, "I need to talk with you about logistics to Allison." "Bet you do." I said as we all laughed. "Right this way please. Thank you." She said. Before I left. Diego kissed me on the cheek and said, "Don't go far." "I won't." As we gave each other a soft peck on the lips.

We went into the kitchen and close the door behind us. "You boned him; I know you did. You walked up the patio stairs more tired than you did Friday night. I know you guys boned." Dammit you. Calm your ass down. "Yes, we did." "I knew it. How was it?" "You know I don't kiss and tell." "You do today bitch!" "It was good. But we'll talk about it later." As we walked back to the living room, "What time is it?" I asked. "Think it's about 3 o'clock maybe 3:30." She said. "Thank you. Now can you please go check?" I asked. "I'm only letting you boss me around because I know you still drained from last night." "And this morning." "My girl! No wonder your ass is so tired."

At least I wasn't tired from my job for once. Lifting a bunch of heavy people, and heavy equipment all day. Leak sat really close to me on the couch. And in a near whispering voice said, "Girl you ain't gone believe this. Aaron wants us to be in a full time one on one." "What the hell?" Not that she shouldn't or couldn't be in a more committed relationship. Especially with a nice guy like Aaron. But I knew damn well she wasn't ready for that. "He does understand you're not looking for a commitment, correct?" "Well, it's complicated. I didn't want to get into a serious conversation about the way I'm feeling right now. So I just left it loose." Now, this is where I get mad! Both Aaron and Diego were good brothas. The last thing we wanted to do, is start playing with their hearts. Don't get me wrong. I know I do my share of messing around. But I'm always honest about where I am in the process. That way, nobody gets hurt. I know Leak. And I also knew her feelings for Aaron wasn't real. Not saying that they couldn't get real. Just that I knew they weren't in that moment. And it was only fair that he be the first one to know where she was coming from. Not the last. "Complicated my ass! This man is trying to take things to the next level with you. And you know damn well he ain't shit to you but a booty call! You betta straighten this shit out! Complicated!" As the guys were walking back into the house, "You're right. We'll talk about it later."

Just then Aaron yelled, "I'm hungry. Other than grizzly bears, and rattlesnakes. What do you guys have to eat in these mountains?" "You guys cooked for us last night. I feel it's only fair that we return the favor." I said. Diego chimed in and said, "Sounds good to me." Then Leak said, "No, I think it's time we start reserving our energy. We could have a long night ahead of us. No telling what time the road is going to re-open." From the sound of her voice, she was upset. So I said, "Burger King it is."

I got up and walked toward the front door. "Diego, I need to talk to you right quick. Leak, tell Aaron what you want from Burger King." "I'm not hungry." She said as Diego, and I walked outside. "Is everything OK?" He asked. "Yeah, everything's all right. We need to hang back and talk. Why don't you and Aaron go get our food." I gave him my order, told him what to get for Leak, then reached into my pocket and gave him $30. "Let me buy our dinner tonight, I'll cook for you some other time." "I'll let you pay for dinner, only if you promise that you'll cook for me soon." He said. "Pinky swear." We kissed, then they drove off to buy dinner.

I went back in to the house, sat on the couch, and said, "All right, spit." "I don't really want to talk about it right now." "But you in a soggy mood and takin it out on everybody else. I'm used to your funky ass attitude. But these guys don't know you like that." "So what. I don't owe them shit!" "But you could have a little more consideration, being that they are your guest!" She sat there speechless. "Look, I know things are hard for you right now. But you got to be honest with yourself and with Aaron. Hell. Right guy, wrong time. I know you didn't mean to mislead him. But it looks to me like he's someplace in the relationship you're not ready to go." "Yeah. I don't want to hurt his feelings. He's a good man. He's handsome and got a decent job." She got quiet again. "Look. I'm not saying you should say anything to him tonight. But tell him sooner rather than later about how you really feel. Take a few days to think about it. But be honest." Women always complain about how big of dogs men are. The only thing separating them from us, is the fact that most of us, at least try to be honest. "You're going to have to woman up and keep it 100 with Aaron." I said. "Alli, you crazy. But your crazy always counterbalances my crazy." As we laughed and gave each other a hug. "And that is why were friends." She said.

"Where is my CD book?" "Put on something fast. I don't want to hear any slow music right now." She said. The Doobie Brothers greatest hits it is. "What did you tell the guys to get me?" She asked. "You said you wasn't hungry, remember." "Stop playing; I know you told them to get me something." She said. "A whopper with cheese, no lettuce, extra pickles and onions, large fries, and a strawberry shake. How does that sound?" "It sounds like you are one kick-ass girlfriend." She said. "I know, I know, I deserve an award." "It's in the mail bitch, it's in the mail." As we laughed.

The guys made their way back from Burger King. "Is everything OK?" Asked Diego. "Everything is fine." I said. Leak and Aaron took their food and sat at the kitchen table. Diego and I ate our food out on the patio. "You know the damn road won't be open until midnight?" He said. "Wow. What time is it now?" "It's only about 5:30. If I would've known this, I would've kept that room another night." Yeah. We can't win them all.

We finished our food. Talked for a little while. Then went back into the house. He told Aaron that they would get up tomorrow morning and head out at about seven. The four of us sat there talking and listening to music until about 11 o'clock that night. Diego and I both slept on the couch. "This weekend was one for the books." I said as he kissed me on the neck. I meant that. If I ever wrote a book, this weekend would definitely be mentioned.

Chapter 17

BACK TO BUSINESS

Business as usual

Several months had gone by since I was in the mountains or seen Diego. We talked over the phone many times, for hours at a time. I even invited him for dinner a couple of times. He declined, because both times, it was at a restaurant. And as he said, "I wasn't the one doing the cooking, so it was cheating in a way."

In short, Diego was a smart guy. He figured out rather quickly that I didn't want anything serious with him. He didn't even pressure me for sex. If he simply wanted to get more of the goods, as they say, he would have gladly taken me up on one of those restaurant offers. Hoping that the invitation would lead back to my apartment. And thank goodness he didn't. Because I didn't plan to have sex with him again. The truth of the matter was, I didn't plan to have sex with him the first time. Women can obviously be as curious about what's going on in a man's pants, as much as men are curious about women. Diego was a piece of caramel covered in the perfect amount of chocolate. And of course, I had to have some.

We were also on summer break from the college I was attending. I had made and was sticking to my goal of two fire-related classes a semester, along with one music class. Things were moving along just fine. Things were also moving along surprisingly fast. It was just as the Councilwoman said, "You're going to breeze right through those classes." Just wish they were as interesting as my music classes. Don't get me wrong. Those classes had their moments. But the average student in my fire science and captains classes, a bunch of firefighters, were downright boring when you stood them next to the average student from one of my music classes. There was no comparison. They were obviously from two completely different worlds. One Group had more discipline and structure, which was obviously the firefighters. While the other group was much more relaxed; easy-going. Which served me quite well. It taught me that everything had a time and place. And that different people had different strengths and weaknesses. Having the opportunity to work with both groups also showed me how to be balanced. When I was around firefighters, politicians or the like, I had structure and discipline without being uptight or stiff. When I was in the music circles, I could let my hair down without being irresponsible.

As usual, I was being pulled in several different directions. Of course, there was my career and all the expectations that came with it. But we had also started working on putting a music lab together. We were still in the discovery phase, pricing different equipment, figuring out who was going to fill different positions, on and on.

It was also the height of campaign season. This was an election year. And everybody and their pet seemed to be up for election or re-election. The Councilwoman made it very clear to me she expected my help in several areas of her campaign. She took me down to her campaign headquarters to meet some of her staff. When she was done introducing me around, she excused herself and went into a separate office somewhere in the back for a meeting. "Hi, I'm Kamala." Said a lady who walked up and gently put her left hand on my shoulder while extending her right hand to introduce herself. "Hi, I'm Allison." "Oh I know who you are, and believe me, I'm a fan. Thank you for your service, and for being such a great example to your peers in the community. It's nice to finally meet you." She said. "It's nice to meet you too." "Have you worked on a campaign before?" She asked. No. Nor did I plan to start now. "No, not really." "Would you like to learn what it is we do at campaign headquarters?" She asked. "Sure, why not." I responded. She proceeded to walk me to various stations, in to and out of different cubicles, explaining every person's job. They did everything there from putting campaign signs together, to making phone calls to raise money. There were campaign signs, bumper stickers, buttons, pens, pencils, T-shirts, hats, coffee mugs, and every trinket imaginable with the council woman's name on them. "Do you have any family residing in the city of Compton?" She asked. "Yes. I still have lots of family and friends living here." I answered. "Well go ahead and take whatever you want, T-shirts, hats, whatever and give them to your family and friends." She said. "No. I'm good." I said. "Really. The more memorabilia we can get distributed with her name on it, the more people will remember her name at the ballot box. All the stuff you're looking at might appear to be a bunch of trinkets and junk. But it translates to votes. Which translates to victory." She said.

The family I was referring to who still lived in the city was my two grand-mothers, and one of my uncles. My maternal grandmother was a Jehovah's Witness, and wouldn't get involved with politics if her life depended on it. My paternal grandmother plain didn't give a damn! And my uncle was too crazy to care. The old expression, you can't give it away, rang true when it came to the council woman's memorabilia. "Thanks, but chances are I won't find anyone interested enough to use any of the memorabilia. But I will take a couple of signs. I think I have the perfect spot for those." "Be careful. Signs are tricky. You can't just place them anywhere. You have to know the person and ask their permission to place them on their property." She explained. To know someone in the city of Compton came easier to me than finding a big red nose on a clown. After all, I grew up here. And was now serving as a firefighter here.

I put one sign on the corner of Stockwell and Paulson. A bustling inter-section with a four-way stop sign. There were literally hundreds of cars passing through that intersection daily. The other sign was placed on the corner of Stockwell and Wilmington, where there was a four-way traffic light. There was triple, if not quadruple the traffic coming through that intersection as the first. As it turned out, the placement of those two signs were perfect. Although I knew very little about politics, I knew a lot about entertainment. And just like in entertainment, in politics, name recogni-tion was everything.

When I got home that evening, I had several messages on my answering machine. One of the messages was from Leak. She was ready to move for-ward with her new record company, so I immediately returned her call. "What up Leak?" "What's up Miss Firefighter, a.k.a. Superms." She said. "I told you guys I wanted to be in the soldier girl video. Not superms." "Well Buddha thought you would make a much better superms, being that you're a firefighter and all." She said. "Whatever. What's going on with the label? Sounds like you're ready to move forward." I said. "Yes, we are. I need you to come get me this Friday. I'm going to be at D's in the IE." She said. "Sure. How is D by the way?" I asked. "She's doing OK. Just ready to get to work like everyone else." Good. Hopefully, by the time I see you guys, you'll still be ready to work. "When was the last time you talked with Diego?" She asked. "About three maybe four weeks ago. What about you? How are things going so far between you and Aaron?" I asked. "Pretty good. Things are just fine between us. No complaints so far." As it turns out, Leak and Aaron are officially a couple. Oh, believe me, their relationship came with more than enough strings attached. He gets to see her once a week for a quickie. Then he gets to spend every other weekend with her at her place. Sounds like what they had before becoming a couple to me, but he agreed to those terms. If he continues to do shit her way, they'll continue to be a couple. We agreed to catch up on things this coming weekend. But until then, I was getting sleepy, so I had to get off the phone. After all, I had to work the next three days straight.

When I got to D's place to pick up Leak, D was nowhere to be found. Leak was sitting there with some elderly woman. "This is my grandmother. Everyone calls her Nana." She said as she introduced us. "Nana this is Allison." "Nice to meet you, baby. I've heard so much about you." She said with a nice warm fuzzy smile. "Nice to meet you too." I said. We proceeded to walk outside and get in the car, once I helped Leak's grandma in. "Sidebar. I need to chop it up with you for a quick sec." I said as I looked at Leak. We stepped to the front of the car. With the car running and the AC blasting, I was hoping Leak's grandmother couldn't hear our conversation. "Where the hell is D? And I know damn well you don't plan on taking your grandmother to the studio with us." I said. "D is going to meet us at the studio. And yes, I was planning on taking Nana to the studio with us." She said. "Have you lost your rabid ass mind? What the fuck is wrong with you? You know better than me a recording studio is no place for somebody's grandmother to be hanging out." I said. "Well, we already promised her she could come. So, she's coming now. We are just going to have to be on our best behavior." She said. "We...we as in me am going to do what I normally do, which is work my ass off. We as in you guys, are going to do I'm sure what you normally do. Which is why Nana shouldn't be there." I said. "She's my grandmother, so let me worry about her." She said in a very firm voice. "Have it your way." I insisted.

We got in the car and continued on our way. It was a very quiet car ride since the two of us were not talking to each other. We decided to play one of my smooth jazz CDs so as not to offend Leak's grandma. "Hollywood is a long way away from here. It's even further with the two of you not saying anything." Said Nana. "Yes ma'am it is. If you don't mind my asking, where are you from?" I asked. "I'm from here in California. Just as you all." She said. "That's nice." "My parents came here from Richmond Virginia, way back in the 20s. I was the first child born here. There was eight of us total. Half of my siblings were born in Virginia, the other half of us were born right here in California." She said. "Wow, that's interesting. Are you retired? Or do you still work?" I asked. "I'm retired baby. I spent more than 40 years teaching. All grade levels too." She said. "What subjects? Or did you teach a little bit of everything?" I asked. "Well, I spent the first half of my career teaching K through six. Then I spent the last 23 years of my career teaching English and drama in high school." She said.

Sounded like a nice enough lady. She seems to be rather laid back. Kind of cool so far. But not cool enough for what we were headed to. "But that's enough about me, how are you? How's your love life in particular?" She asked. That's a rather peculiar question coming from her. "It could be better. I'm not seeing anyone now. Don't have a lot of time for a relationship right now." I said. "Yeah, well I heard you was with that fine Diego. And I hear that boy is quite a stud. It's too bad you couldn't make things work with him." When she said that, I completely blew a fuse! The car started swerving from side to side, as I speeded up to find the nearest off-ramp. As soon as I got off the freeway, I pulled into the first driveway I could find and put on my haz lights. Leak and I both jumped out of the car at the same time. "What the fuck is wrong with you? You're talking to your grandmother about my sex life! It would be bad enough if you were talking to her about your own sex life! But mines!" "First of all, she's not my grand-mother; she's D's grandmother. So apparently D was the one who told her about you and Diego, not me." She said. "At this point I don't give a damn whose grandmother she is! Have you guys ever heard of decorum? Shit! First you bring this old lady to the recording studio to watch you guys do drugs half the damn day! That was already enough! Now she's talking about my sex life!" "Bitch what sex life? You had a weekend rendezvous with Diego. End of discussion! And just like that, the shit was over! And as far as I'm concerned, this conversation is too."

We took a few minutes to cool off before we got back in the car. We didn't know what was going to happen. But Leak and I both knew something had to happen. Neither of us was dumb enough to let our emotions get in the way of us making this future money.

"She's got a niece in L.A. she hasn't seen in a while. I'll just ask her if she would like to visit with her for a few hours." Said Leak. "OK. Then that's where we're taking her." I said as we got back in the car. "Don't worry about nothing baby, ain't nothing to be ashamed of. I had a couple of whoppers in my day too." Said Nana. "Nana. How would you like to go visit Elsie?" Asked Leak. "Elsie, my niece? I would love to go see Elsie." She said. "When was the last time you seen her?" Asked Leak. "Oh, it's been a while. I haven't seen her since last Thanksgiving." She said. "You know how it is. Folks get busy. And Elsie haven't been doing too good with her health." "Would she mind if we dropped in?" Asked Leak. "Sure wouldn't. She would love some company." Said Nana.

We took D's grandma over to her niece's house. Leak walked her to the front door. An older lady, not appearing to be much younger than Nana opened the door. They all went inside for a few minutes. Then finally, Leak reappeared by herself. As we got back on the freeway, "Yeah, you're right. I should've thought that one through a lot better." She said. "Not that I had anything against her. It's just, you know, the environment where in all day is not conducive for someone like her." I said. Hell, they had no business doing half the shit they did while in a recording session. Let alone bringing outsiders in to this chaos. Especially not someone's elderly grandmother.

When we got to the studio, it was business as usual. Drugs laying around everywhere. With absolutely no shame in it. It was as if they had fruit bowls all over the place instead. The weed and cigars, I was used to seeing. But powder cocaine. Who could that be for? We were working with a bunch of rap artist. And that's not their thing. They're more the weed and blunt crowds.

As the three backup singers were in a nice comfortable corner practicing, Leak and the guys were ready to do their thing. Just then, in walks the recording engineer. A white guy, approximately 6 feet tall, with shoulder length black hair. He was wearing all black and had black polish on his fingernails. He took a $20 bill out of his pocket, rolled it, put it in his nostril, and snorted one line up one side. Then he changed sides and snorted in the other line up his other nostril. When he was done, "You guys ready?" He asked as he looked around the room. "It's on you." Said Leak. When she said that, the sounds came on. There was a guitar rift, unlike anything I had ever heard. It was the intro to soldier girl. I had heard the song many times before. But not with the lead guitar separated from the rest of the intro. It was soul piercing to hear it being played that way. As he pushed up the various levels on the board, it got louder and louder. Then finally, he cued in the baseline along with the rest of the instruments. It was nice. It felt like we were sitting in the middle of a concert.

It took him about 20 minutes to get everything the way he wanted. Once he got the sounds to his liking, "Leak. You ready?" He asked. "Yeah." She said. Leak and I could disagree on just about any and everything until the cows came home. Most of our disagreements were about very poor choices, and lack of responsibilities in some important areas of Life. But the one thing we always agreed on was music. And this bitch had some serious talent. It took all of 10 minutes to lay the vocals to soldier girl. It took approximately another 30 minutes to do her ad Libs. She always took a little more time to do her ad libs. She liked to triple over the vocals to make them sound more exciting and professional. We had booked a 12-hour slot. From 12 noon, to 12 midnight. By 5:00 PM, she was done laying the vocals and ad libs to two completely different tracks.

While the engineer was working with the background vocalist, Leak and I decided to sneak out for a bite to eat. "You did good in there. I'm proud of you." "Thanks. I was so hungry I thought I was gone pass the fuck out." She said as we started laughing. "Do you think you've got another six hours in you. I mean, I wouldn't be terribly upset if you wanted to leave a little early." I said. "Damn! Look at you trying to take your foot off a Niggas neck a little bit!" She said as we started laughing. "I'm just saying. You never cease to amaze me in these sessions. You always seem to get right down to business when it comes to music. You're usually determined and focused which is why we get so much done in such a short time." "Thanks." She said. She was a lot more quiet than usual. Not that anything was wrong. I could tell she was OK. Just too damn quiet for me. "Penny for your thoughts." I said. "Just thinking about my future. What if this music thing doesn't pan out the way I want it to. What next?" "Don't worry about it. You'll be OK. No matter what happens, with or without music you'll be fine." I said. "We've been around each other too long. You're starting to sound like me." She said. She was right. Not that I was nonchalant about the situation. But I wasn't as uptight as I usually had the tendency to be.

We got back to the studio at about 6:30. When we walked in, the engineer had the three background singers in the recording booth. "Good. You girls are back. I wanted you to listen to a few things. I need your decision before I do any more editing." He said. "You got this Allison. I need to make a couple of calls right quick." Said Leak as she walked in to the game room. I sat there listening to different arrangements. It took what seemed to be hours to get the background vocals exactly the way we wanted them.

At about 9 PM, just as Leak had started to work on her third track, in walks Aaron and Diego. She ran over to Aaron and gave him a big hug and kiss. She also hugged Diego. "So you don't know nobody." Said Diego, as he looked at me. "Hi guys. I'm just surprised to see the two of you." I said as I gave them both a hug. Leak looked at me with a big ass grin. She had kind of a gotcha look on her face. Now I can assume that one of those calls she made earlier was to the fellas. "Since we were ahead of schedule, I thought it would be a good idea to invite you guys to see a real artist in action." She said. "That's right, and we appreciate the invite." Said Aaron. We all took a few minutes to catch up on things. About 10 minutes into the visit, "You ready Leak?" Asked the engineer. "Yep. Wish me luck." As she kissed Aaron. "Of course, but I have a feeling you don't need it." Said Aaron.

Leak and the engineer agreed to go ahead and lay down the intro to the album. It was a remake of wade in the water. It had a very wicked baseline. "I love what they did with those arrangements." Said Diego. "Have you ever heard her rap?" I asked the guys. "No. At least not in person. I've only ever heard her demos." Said Aaron. "Me to." Said Diego. "Well then have a seat. Take it all in. This girl is phenomenal." I said as we sat down. Leak finally laid the first verse to the intro. The guys were mesmerized. "I didn't know she could flow like that. I mean, I've heard her demos. But damn. She's even better in person." Said Diego. "Shit, she's good! I mean, she's really fuckin good!" Said Aaron. What she was demonstrating in that recording booth, was exactly why I nicknamed her lady Pac. She had the ability to do an entire album in one night if she wanted to. But like anything good in life, you want to savor it. As she always said, "Why rush it." As fast as we were moving, this was what she called taking her time.

It took her about 20 minutes to lay the vocals to wade in the water. She decided to take a 30-minute break before doing ad-libs. "What did you guys think?" Asked Leak. "Are you kidding me! You were freaking amazing. I knew you had talent. But to watch you work. Damn girl!" Said Diego. "You are beyond words. I didn't know you had it like that. You know we've heard your music before. But it's something about seeing you do it in person that just adds power to it." Said Aaron. "He's right. It was something about watching you lay the vocals in person that gave it a new feel." Said Diego. She looked around in complete amazement. She looked over at me and started smiling. "You already know I'm a fan." I said as we all started laughing. We were all talking before we looked up and it was time for Leak to get back to work.

"Come here you." Said Diego looking over at me. "We need to talk." He said. "Do we? All right, let's step into my office." I said as we walked toward the game room. "What do you know about shooting pool?" He asked. "Enough to have fun." I answered. "Do I intimidate you?" He asked. "A little." I answered. He looked toward the ceiling and started grinning. "You. Miss big bad firefighter. I intimidate you." He said. After all. I am only human. When it came to handsome men. I turned into a 12-year-old girl. Everybody has their weakness. Even Superman. "Well, you're going to have to get past it. Because I like you, even though you appeared to be running. Now I know you are, because you just admitted it." Did I? "Tell me, how is it that I even remotely scare you?" He asked. "Not that you really scare me, it's just that, I didn't want to get seriously involved with you. I got a way of messing up relationships. At least from what I know about myself so far." I said. "Your plan is to never get back out there and try again? That doesn't make sense. And what's worse is, that doesn't even sound like you." He said. "Yeah I know. But I've got a lot of learning to do when it comes to relation-ships." "And I'm ready to be as patient as you need me to be. I'll teach you anything you want to know. As long as you're willing to stop running and try." Talk about being backed into a corner. My heart was racing at 1000 beats per minute. And I literally had nowhere to run. "OK." I said. "Come here. OK what?" He said as he gently pulled my hand. "We can try being in a relationship." I said. "Well, OK, since you asked so nicely. And if it doesn't work out, we can always break up." He said as we started laughing. He put his arms around my waist as we started kissing.

Chapter 18

TWO ON THE TOWN

Two on the town

It's official. Diego and I are finally a couple. It could have happened a lot sooner. But like he said, I was running. Not that I realized that's what I was doing. But when I look back, the evidence clearly suggested I was running. And with a career and hobbies like mines, it was very easy to hide.

We spent as much time as possible making love to each other. Every chance we got, we made out. It was clear to me I was the last woman he was with sexually. And I knew damn well he was the last man I was with. We were both obviously sexually deprived. Even though, he was still his careful and patient self. My rule about no sex a day before work went right out the window. I started showing up for work late and tired. Not that I was technically late, but I was late for me. I usually got to work at about 7:30. Now I was showing up at about 7:55, sometimes at 8 AM on the nose, and sluggish as hell. Oh, I didn't let it get in the way of my performance as a firefighter. But believe me when I say my ass was being handed to me in every other area of my life.

One shift, after responding to a call, when we got back to the station, for some reason, we didn't have enough room to back the engine all the way into the station. "Stop. Just stop right there." As I gave the engineer the universal stop signal. "For some reason, we are not going to be able to get the engine back in." I said. "Didn't we just move the damn thing from this same exact spot." Said my captain, as he got off the engine to see what was going on. "Yes, we did. But for some reason, as you can see, there's about 5 feet worth of engine still hanging out the bay door, with only 2 feet worth of space to back it in." I said. "We should be able to get this thing back. I say let's go for it." He insisted. "Even if we completely kiss the front bumper of this vehicle with the engine bumper, we would still have approximately 3 feet worth of engine hanging out of the door." "Well we got the engine from this spot, so it has to fit back into this same spot." Said the captain as he motioned the engineer to continue backing. At this point, the engineer got out of the engine and took a look for himself. "What's going on?" He asked. "Go ahead and get this thing back in the station." Said the captain. I didn't bother uttering another word. To me, the evidence was clear and spoke for itself. There was not enough room to get this puppy all the way in, and that was that. "Well, what do you think Brooks?" Asked the engineer. "I don't know what happened between now and our last call, but there is no way we are going to get this apparatus back into this spot. We clearly only have about 2 feet to work with, and about 5 feet worth of engine to back in." I said. "And I say go for it. We just moved the damn thing from this same spot." Said the captain. "Well, we did just move it from here." Said the engineer as he got back on the engine.

And of course, in all his wisdom, the engineer gunned that engine back. He backed it dead smack and center into the vehicle behind it. That thing hit so damn hard it shook the entire station. It sounded like an explosion. Staff came running from everywhere to see what was happening.

There was about six different staff members standing there when the assistant Fire Chief looked over at me and said, "Let me guess. You backed the engineer right into the van parked behind him." "Bullshit! You got the engineer and the captain to thank for this debacle. It should have been my job to back the engineer. But when I told the engineer to stop, because we clearly didn't have enough room to get the Engine back in to the station, my captain jumped out of the engine and Monday morning quarterbacked everything I said." Everyone looked at the two vehicles in disbelief. The Engine not only damaged the vehicle parked immediately behind it. The impact was so powerful it pushed that vehicle into the one behind it as well. After explaining myself, I took my happy ass upstairs and ate my lunch. Yes, I had been showing up for work tired all right. But I wasn't delusional. I had enough wherewithal to know there wasn't enough room to get the engine back in to the station.

Loretta came into the kitchen about 30 minutes after me. "We need to talk." She said as she headed toward the female dormitory with me following closely behind her. "All right. Who's the guy?" "Wait a minute. Those two fuck ups have the biggest in-station accident in the department's history, and you're questioning me!" I exclaimed. "No. Those two fuck ups had the biggest in-house accident in the department's history, and the Fire Chief is now having the two of them submit their reports, but not you, even though you were the backing firefighter, and I'm questioning you." She said. "Look, I don't give a shit. It takes too much energy to care around here." I said. And it truly did. I had decided a long time ago, that I would simply come to work, do my job, and go home. Just like everyone else who didn't give a shit around here. Morale was obviously low, diplomacy was long gone, and the Fire Chief himself was the main culprit behind it all. This man is hardly a leader; he's a dictator. Not to excuse his behavior, but he's not alone. Most of corporate America was now heading in that same direction, dictatorships instead of partnerships. When you don't care about your guys, they learn not to care about you and eventually the Job. People will come to work and do a half-assed job until the company finally goes bankrupt.

"There's a way to not give a damn without letting it show. And right about now, your slip is hanging. So again, who's the guy? And let's try not to forget about that big ass hickey on your neck before you start lying." She said. Damn! Oh well, I had never lied to Loretta before. But I was definitely about to try my hand and see what came up. "Look, it's OK to have a boyfriend. Just remember, there are no three men worth what you got going. So try not to be so reckless. Pull your shit together." She said. "I'm good. I'm not the one around here running into shit." I said in a very nasty flip it tone. "Yeah, that might be true. But you have been showing up later than usual with only half of your ass on hand." "And the half that I show up with is still worth more than most of these guys entire asses." I said. "Again, no arguments here. You're good at what you do. I'm just warning you, be careful. Try not to let your personal life spill over into your career. We obviously have plenty of that going around. Just don't let it be you." She said.

She was right as usual. And I was struggling to keep everything together. Work wasn't the only place I was struggling. My grades started to suffer as well, in both my fire and music classes. I had a 4.0 GPA; it was now 2.8 at best. And my family. What family? I haven't seen most of them in months.

For the first time in my life, my personal life was going in the right direction. But everything else was going to hell! And Diego was right there to hold me and listen to me complain about it all.

By the way. The reason we couldn't get the engine back onto the engine room floor, was because the mechanic had pulled the van up about 10 feet to make room for the pickup truck. No one had noticed anything different because the van was always parked behind the engine, it was just much closer than before. We never even noticed the pickup truck behind the van. Nor should we have had to. It was common sense. If we didn't have enough space to completely put the engine back into its original spot. Then you have to figure something out. Crashing into the vehicle behind it didn't fix a damn thing.

As far as what those guys wrote in their reports. They could have written UFO's from another planet came from out of space and hit those vehicles for all I cared. They were in the business of covering each other, which included the habit of lying. As long as they didn't find a way to pin that shit on me, I wouldn't give a rat's ass about what was said!

Out of touch

My life was in full swing. Well, more like overdrive. Things were jumping off in all different directions. Believe it or not, Diego and I lasted six months before I started messing up.

The construction industry had taken off like a brushfire thanks to the housing boom. Diego and Aaron both worked in California, Arizona, New Mexico and Texas making plenty of money doing construction. Leaving the two of us girls at home to do plenty of playing and partying. And play I did! Not only was I hitting and missing Diego. Alton was flying to California several times a year, to visit with his mother and other family, so I would hook up with him when he was in town. Not to mention, I was back in touch with Darren. There it was, a complete love triangle. With my ass stuck dead smack in the middle. Not only was I fuckin all three of them off and on in the same timeline. I had a couple of other dudes I was talking to and playing with from time to time as well. When it came to men, I went from having none, to having more than I could handle.

The music thing had finally taken off too. We were doing so much with so many different artists, half the time I would forget who I was supposed to be working with and when. We had R&B singers and rappers we recorded with frequently. There were times men would show up ready to record, and I would swear they were rappers. Then there were other times women would show up, and I would swear they were R&B singers. Most of the time, it was the other way around. And there I was again, right in the middle, dropping shit. Appointments that should've been booked weren't. Recording sections that should have been canceled, were booked. And even though I had a team around me, I couldn't blame anyone but myself. After all, I went in knowing it was going to be predominately my job to keep everything together. To keep my eyes on everyone else, to make sure things were running smoothly. Not only was I not doing what I was supposed to do. As it turned out, I was the biggest fuck up there. It was equivalent to being the head clown of a circus.

"Hello." "Hey girl, what's up with you?" "Who is this?" "Wow, I know I'm not around a lot. But you should definitely know my voice by now." It was Alton. "I do. It's just that I've been so busy. How are you? What have you been up to?" I said. "I'm flying to L.A. this weekend and was hoping we could spend Valentines' Day together." What? Valentine's Day. When the hell is that. Damn time be flyin. "Sure. When is it?" I asked. "You're kidding, right?" "Actually I'm very serious. When is valentines' day?" I asked. "The same day it's always on, February 14, this Saturday. I was hoping we could go out for dinner and a movie." "We sure can." I said. We made arrangements to meet up at my place Saturday at 4 o'clock, which was only four days away.

Meanwhile back at work, all the guys continued to ask questions about the accident. "So there was an entire 10 to 12 feet of engine still hanging out the door after he hit the van behind him." Said one of the engineers as the rest of us laughed. Every time someone tells that story, it gets more colorful, with more and more engine hanging out of the door than before.

"Oh. The van was inside the station. Someone told me he hit the van parked outside of the station, then backed into the pickup truck inside of the station." Said another firefighter as we all laughed again. One thing these guys had in common was, they loved a good laugh at the other guy's expense. Which is why it was so hard to get past any mistakes around here. They would never let each other live it down.

"Call for firefighter Brooks on line 3. Phone call for Brooks on line three." "Compton fire department station three, Brooks speaking." "Hey babe, it's me Darren." "I know who you are." Actually I didn't. "Just calling to see if you had any plans for tomorrow." He said. "Should I have plans for tomorrow? I don't believe I do. Why, what did you have in mind?" I asked. "Tomorrow is Valentines' Day, and I was wondering if we could spend a quiet evening over at your place." That sounds nice. I hate going out on crowded holidays. Everybody and their mother is usually out. "Sure. That sounds good. But you're going to cook." I said "Of course. I'll cook dinner. But dessert is on you." He said in a suggestive voice. "Don't get fresh with me on this phone. See you tomorrow." We made arrangements to meet up at my place on Saturday at 2 o'clock.

The next day was Saturday, February 14, a.k.a., Valentine's Day. Not that I celebrated the day or any other holidays for that fact. But everyone else sure did, and it was in full bloom. There were flowers, balloons, and teddy bears being sold on every street corner.

At 2 o'clock, right on schedule, there was a knock at my door. It was Darren. He had a dozen of roses in his hand. We started kissing as he closed the door behind him. "Where's this food you're supposed to be cooking." "It's in the car. I'm about to go get the bags now." He said. "Do you need any help?" I asked. "No, I got it." When he came back inside, he had four bags with him. "What are you cooking?" I asked. "Seafood. I got lobster tails, shrimp, wild rice, and vegetables." He said. "I never realized you cooked like this." I said. "I do a little somethin somethin." We were talking, laughing, and having a good time while the music was playing in the background. Suddenly, there was a knock at the door. Wonder who this could be. When I opened the door, "Hi Allison. How is my favorite girl?" Damn, damn, damn! It was Alton. In all my running around, and dropping shit, I completely forgot he was flying in from St. Louis this weekend.

He was standing there with a dozen of roses and a big beautiful teddy bear. Shit! This will never work! When the hell did I get so clumsy? "You look like a deer stuck in headlights. What's wrong?" He said as I closed the door behind me. "Listen. I made a terrible mistake. I completely forgot you were going to be in town today. I'm sorry. We're going to have to take a reign check." As he stood there looking very disappointed, Darren opened the front door to see what was going on. "Oh, I didn't realize you had company." Said Alton, as both men were standing there. "Well, I bought these for you, so here you go." He gave me the roses and teddy bear then walked away. As he walked away, I went back inside. "Who was that?" "Someone really special to me." I answered. "Listen. We're going to have to do this another day. I'm not feeling very well." I said. "What's wrong?" Asked Darren. "I Wish I knew." We immediately packed up all the food he cooked, and he left.

When Darren left, I cried my eyes out. How could I have been so reckless? Alton was a perfectly good man, of whom I cared a great deal about. And even though we weren't in a relationship, he didn't fly all the way to California to see me with another man.

At about 6 o'clock that night, there was yet another knock at my door. When I looked out the peephole, it was Diego. He was standing there with a giant heart filled with chocolate, and of course, a dozen of roses. "What are you doing here? I thought you were in Texas this week." "I was. But I wanted to surprise you." He said. If you had gotten here a little earlier, you would've been the one surprised. "What's wrong? You look sick." He said. "I'm not feeling good." I sat him down and explained what happened earlier. "Allison, we're a couple now. And that should be the case if I'm in town or not. Are you saying that I can't trust you? Because it sure the hell sounds that way to me." "No, I'm not saying I shouldn't be trusted. Look, I don't know what the hell to say. But I'll start with I'm sorry." I said. "A relationship is about two people who are committed to each other. Physically, mentally, and emotionally. No matter where the hell on the planet the other one should end up. Unless you both decide otherwise." He said. He thanked me for being open and honest with him. Then we gave each other a hug. "I'm going back to the I.E. I need to clear my head for a few days." He said as he left my apartment.

It takes a fool to end up with three dozen roses, a box of chocolate, a teddy bear, and no date on valentines' day. The truth of the matter was, I wasn't relationship material. Not that I was a player. But I was damn sure hitting all the right notes. What I wanted, versus what was actually happening in my life, were two completely different things. So I decided to remain single for a while. I truly needed to take a break from men for a while, at least long enough to get my head right.

That Wednesday, after Valentine's Day, I had to call in to work sick. "Yeah, the flu has been going around. A lot of our guys have been calling in sick." Said the station captain. "I'll see you when I get better." I said as I hung up the phone. I spent the following week at home taking a bunch of over-the-counter medicines. No matter what I took, I felt terrible. Finally, about five days in to my being sick, I gave up trying to nurse myself and went to the doctor. "It's flu season. So you're going to have to be patient and ride it out. But just to be on the safe side, I will have my nurse run your labs." She said. "Thanks. Can I also get a slip to return to work?" I asked. "Absolutely not!" She responded. "Please...I'm tired of sitting at home. Why can't I go to work and be sick with everyone else." I said as she started laughing. "Because I'm not everyone else's doctor. I'm your doctor. So you get to go home until your better. Your job is dangerous enough without trying to perform while you're sick." She said. With that, she sent my ass right back home, cabin fever and all.

About eight days in to my having the flu, every puzzle I owned was completely put together and taken apart three times over. I even redid the body to one of my remote control cars; which was a very meticulous and time consuming endeavor. But as it was, I was stuck in the house. So I might as well have.

By day 10, I felt I was regaining my strength. So I decided to go grocery shopping. When I got home, there was a message on my machine from my doctor's office. "Allison, this is Dr. Ginsberg. I need you to get to my office as soon as you can." She said. Hopefully she's come to her senses and is going to allow me to return to work.

When I got to my doctor's office the next day, she and her nurse looked as if something was terribly wrong. "Well kiddo, I got your labs back yesterday, and you don't have the flu. You're pregnant... I'm sure you're still on the birth control pills I prescribed. But the only way to be sure not to get pregnant, is abstinence." Just then, the sky turned black, and thunder clashed. What the fuck! When the hell did this happen! And by who!